EXPERIENCING joy

Experiencing Joy
© 2007 by Allyson Tomkins

All rights reserved. Printed in the United States of America. No part of this book may be used or reproduced in any manner whatsoever without prior written consent of the author, except as provided by the United States of America copyright law.

Advantage is an imprint of Advantage Media Group.
Advantage, its Logos and Marks are trademarks of Advantage Media Group, Inc.

Published by:
Advantage Media Group
P.O. Box 272
Charleston, SC 29402
amglive.com

ISBN: 978-1-59932-032-8

Scriptures taken from the *Holy Bible, New International Version.* Copyright 1973, 1978, 1984 by International Bible Society. Used by permission of Zondervan. All rights reserved.

Most Advantage Media Group titles are available at special quantity discounts for bulk purchases for sales promotions, premiums, fundraising, and educational use. Special versions or book excerpts can also be created to fit specific needs.

For more information, please write: Special Markets, Advantage Media Group, P.O. Box 272, Charleston, SC 29401 or call 1.866.775.1696.

EXPERIENCING

ALLYSON J TOMKINS

This book is dedicated to my children -

Kelsey and James.

They are a joy!

I have no greater joy than to hear that my children are walking in the truth.
3 John 1:4

Acknowledgements

I want to give thanks to God, my Gardener, for planting the seeds and caring for the garden that produced this workbook. I pray it will produce much fruit for His enjoyment.

I want to thank all my friends and family who encouraged and supported me for so many years to be a finisher. I especially give thanks to Alice Richard who remained steadfast in her caring dedication to type and retype every page. I thank Vicki Terry for having the love to jump in to an unformed creation and help it to take shape. Thank you to Karlyn Ball for the tree illustration. Thanks also to Margaret deLawreal for the final edit and buckets of encouragement.

Without Pat Lyle and her spiritual direction and prayers, I would have given up a long time ago. Friday Morning Group, for fourteen years you have been Jesus to me. I love you, my sisters. Thank you for who you are.

Finally, to my family. God could not have blessed anyone more. I've been surrounded by your love and know my Lord because of you.

Jim, Kelsey and James—you are my joy and my crown. Thank you for your sacrifice that allows me to obey God's call on my life.

Thank you Jesus—you are my Tree of Life.

Preface

This book was written in thousands of ten minute intervals. Between diapers and phone calls and all the pulls and tugs of my life, I tried to be obedient to share what I've learned about the healing power of true joy.

As it is not a book that was written quickly, it is not a book to be read quickly. No two readers will experience the pages of this book in the same way for it will become a very personal recording of your journey to find true joy in the orchard of the Heart of God.

Whether you go through this workbook alone or in a group, take care to invite someone to pray with you when you feel God's healing touch is needed. He loves to heal His children.

If you faithfully complete all twelve units, I can promise that you will know what Jesus meant when He said, "I have told you this so that my joy may be in you and that your joy may be complete." -John 15:11

How to Use This Workbook

1. Allow yourself some quiet time to read each unit. It is recommended you do the units in order and try not to skip around.
2. Write out your answer to each exercise or prayer.
3. Follow the suggested amount of work for <u>each day.</u>
4. Allow time for the exercises and prayers to "soak in."
5. Look up each scripture under "Seeds of Faith." Have your Bible ready.
6. Discuss with a small group or spiritual director your progress or areas where you feel stuck.

Table of Contents

Entering the Orchard of Your Heart..11

Unit 1   The Joy of Eternal Salvation:
Freedom from Spiritual Death.. 31

Unit 2   The Joy of Eternal Acceptance:
Freedom from Self Hatred, Pride and False Images..................................49

Unit 3   The Joy of Eternal Truth:
Freedom from Lies, False Beliefs and Myths..91

Unit 4   The Joy of Eternal Security:
Freedom from Unholy Fear... 117

Unit 5   The Joy of Eternal Well-being:
Freedom in Sorrow, Loss, Pain, Suffering, or Distress............................145

Unit 6   The Joy of Eternal Righteousness:
Freedom from Sin and Disobedience..175

Unit 7   The Joy of Eternal Completion:
Freedom from Dissatisfaction and Self-pity...197

Unit 8   The Joy of Eternal Intimacy:
Freedom from Broken Relationships...229

Unit 9   The Joy of Eternal Health:
Freedom from the Disease of the Soul..257

Unit 10   The Joy of Creation...287

Unit 11   The Joy of Eternal Union with God:
Freedom from Alienation..331

Unit 12   The Joy of Eternal Victory:
The Celebration of a Life with Christ..367

References..395

ENTERING THE ORCHARD OF YOUR HEART

  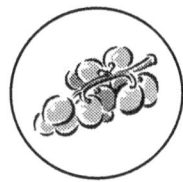   

*This is to my Father's glory, that you bear much fruit,
showing yourselves to be my disciples.....
I have told you this so that my joy may be in you
and that your joy may be complete.*

John 15: 8,11

Don't Let Anyone Steal Your Joy

When I was eight months pregnant with our first child, Kelsey, I began to have my first clues that I needed to know more about joy. One morning, as I sat with my husband at our local bank, the branch manager pointed to an elderly man walking through the bank lobby. The man, in his sixties, walked with a very severe limp and was dressed in the uniform of a Post Office employee. "Do you see that gentleman?" she asked. I asked him one time why he is always smiling, always looking so happy. Do you know what he said? I don't let anyone steal my joy!"

What an epiphany! I began to examine the times that I let someone steal my joy. A look, a comment, a forgotten promise . . . can ruin my day! At first, I get mad or hurt because I believe that person has no right to do that. But time and time again, I come back to the truth:

It is my responsibility to take care of my joy as best I can and make sure that I don't let someone or something "steal it."

What Is Joy?

I began to understand why the author C. S. Lewis titled his autobiography, **Surprised by Joy**. A lifelong atheist, Lewis shares that his quest for joy in life had exhausted all of the usual sources including books and fantasy, women, work, friendships, etc. Nothing had succeeded in satisfying his desire for true joy.

When Lewis accepted Jesus as his Lord and Savior, he saw joy for what it really is. Lewis asks us to throw away any preconceived notions of what we think joy is. We have to start from scratch.

Fifteen years ago, when I began this quest to understand joy, I followed Lewis' advice and have only scratched the surface - the tip of the iceberg.

The following chart contains some of the definitions I have used to capture joy in words. As you go through this book, you will add your own.

A woman giving birth to a child has pain because her time has come; but when her baby is born she forgets the anguish because of her joy that a child is born into the world. So with you. Now is your time of grief, but I will see you again and you will rejoice, and no one will take away your joy.

John 16:21-22

JOY IS:

- A Vital (life-giving) Relationship with Jesus
- Doing God's Will
- Faith in Action
- The Radiance of the Holy Spirit within
- A Fruit of the Holy Spirit
- The Desire which leads to a need to seek and find God
- A Destination - "enter into the Joy of all the saints"
- A Gift for God
- A Gift From God to Accept
- A Gift to Share With Others
- A Command to Rejoice
- A Filling Substance, a completion to my incompleteness
- A Comfort in times of sorrow - a promise of the future; a transformation of grief or pain
- Strength in Jesus through times of trials and problems
- The Presence of God through my pain

JOY IN THE BIBLE

My search led me to the Word of God. The Hebrews had many words to describe the different aspects of joy in the Old Testament. Since joy and its derivatives are mentioned some four hundred times in the Bible, I dare say that it is important enough to be studied. But that is not why we are here. Yes, we will discuss what Scripture says about joy, but not just to fill our heads with data.

For every human desire there must be a source. C.S. Lewis concluded in his book *Surprised by Joy*, there was no other source for true, eternal joy other than God himself. Therefore, joy is proof that there is a God! Think about that. Joy gave a hardened atheist enough conviction to turn his heart and become a true believer. His environment of academia did not encourage or foster this belief. Nevertheless, he stuck to his guns. As a result, his Christian books have turned many a skeptic into a believer as well. Praise God!

We are all on a Journey to Joy. As the *Book of Common Prayer* says, "May we come to share in the joy of all the saints." I guess I'm too impatient to wait until I'm dead. I want it now, don't you?

But let me give warning:

Just as a beautiful poem loses something if we rip apart each verse and examine its meaning, just as looking at a living cell under the microscope can't possibly explain life, we mustn't examine God's Joy and all its parts so closely that it loses its radiance.

We want to move from POSSESSION TO EXPRESSION. As soon as you possess God's gift of joy, you immediately need to express it, share it with others, and give it away. The idea is never to hold on to it for your sake only, but to pass it along.

Joy and Pain

As a Christian Counselor, I work with people in pain, and I make every attempt to help them heal from that pain. Years ago, I began to feel the need to go beyond the traditional psychotherapeutic process. Most therapy stops when the symptoms stop. I see a crucial and missing step for many people: learning how to accept joy and invite more of it into their lives. The absence of pain does not ensure a joyful life. A joyful life does not ensure a life without pain. All of us want to choose joy, but we may not know how. It is not enough to assume that once a hurt is healed or a problem is solved that joy will necessarily follow.

C.S. Lewis says about joy,
> " . . . it is that of an unsatisfied desire which is itself more desirable than any other satisfaction. I call it Joy, which is here a technical term and must be sharply distinguished both from Happiness and from Pleasure. Joy (in my sense) has indeed one characteristic, and one only, in common with them; the fact that anyone who has experienced it will want it again. . . . I doubt whether anyone who has tasted it would ever, if both were in his power, exchange it for all the pleasures in the world. But then Joy is never in our power and pleasure often is."
>
> - *Surprised by Joy*, C.S. Lewis

Joy is not the absence of pain, but the presence of God through pain. Joy can help to heal pain by transforming it. Joy is the balm that soothes us when we are down, tired, unhappy or broken.

The Source of Joy

It is necessary to learn how to be open to the experience of joy from the inside and not rely solely on outside sources to be joyful. One must discover the true source of all joy, which is God Himself.

I have seen people whose lives have been shattered by a single rejection. They seem unable to reestablish, for themselves, any joy in their lives once a person or job or house or lifestyle is gone. They cannot bridge the gap between sorrow and joy.

It is natural not to "feel" joy if you are grieving a loss, but we must learn new skills for finding and accepting joy without necessarily needing that joy to come from some person, place or thing. Tragic stories abound of men, women and teens who have committed suicide because they were unable to cope with an event such as the death of someone, the loss of a job or a home, a broken relationship, or being abused.

We must get back to the basics of where joy comes from in the first place and learn how we can receive it, even in the toughest of times. This workbook will help you do just that.

What Makes Joyful People Joyful?

Have you ever watched or listened to a joyful person? I used to find them too exuberant for my taste and their enthusiasm bothered me. And yet, I wanted to be like them. Why? Because it sure beats walking around sad, worried, unhappy, or frustrated. So, why not just "be happy" as the song says? As I began this study I realized something was blocking my own joy. There were times in my life when as hard as I tried, I could not get a hold on joy. It was as if I lacked a certain skill or knowledge that others had, and I had somehow missed out. That frustrated me! In observing others I tried to understand why some people seem to be more JOYFUL (full of joy) than others. So, I have become a student of JOY. This book will share my observations of what makes joyful people joy-filled.

What Blocks Joy?

I see in people the need for more joy in their lives, and yet some seem incapable of obtaining it when they need it the most. I've seen people go from one relationship to another, in the naïve pursuit of the person who will finally bring more joy into their lives.

When my first marriage, which had become physically and emotionally abusive, ended I fell "head over heels in love" with a man who brought such a "joy" into my life I thought I would "die" from the love I felt. I felt intoxicated just to be around him. When we left each other for the first time, I actually fainted from the withdrawal. I had never felt this way about anyone, and I misinterpreted the feeling as the purest form of joy imaginable. The feelings this man gave me were "to die for" and ironically, later the relationship did almost kill me. As the days of crazy fun turned into four years of Hell, I became less and less joyful. I was hooked on getting back the initial feelings of joy. I was a joy addict. In truth, I had no idea what joy really was.

What are Joy Reserves?

The relationship ended when I had completely bankrupted what I call my JOY RESERVES. My bank account of joy had been depleted, and my life was a mess. I remember wanting to end my life one day as I drove down a winding mountain road. Thank God I had my dog in the car. She was too great a source of joy in my life for me to harm her, too. At that moment, she was my lifeline. How many people might have chosen life if they had had with them a source of joy that was powerful enough to overcome all obstacles?

Imagine, if you will, that you don't have the money to pay your bills. At the same time imagine that you have a safety deposit box filled to the brim with valuables. Unfortunately, you don't have the key! The same may be true of your joy. You may have all the joy you would ever need right at your finger tips but do not know how to get to it. How frustrating!

This book will give you the keys to unlock those reserves so that you may never lack joy in your life again. All you need are a few simple skills and the willingness to let go of some old beliefs and behaviors which are blocking your own joy.

Exercise 1

On a scale of 1 - 10, how would you rate the following areas of your life?
1 = no joy   5 = OK, some ups and downs   10 = full and complete joy

_____ Social Life   _____ School or Education Life
_____ Emotional Health   _____ Practical or Day to Day Life
_____ Physical Health   _____ Spiritual Life
_____ Family Life   _____ Recreation/Leisure/Fun Life
_____ Work or Career Life

_____TOTAL

0 - 16 = Your joy reserves are dangerously low. Keep reading.
17-50 = There are some major life areas needing more joy. Keep reading.
51-75 = You have joy in your life, but your joy is blocked in some areas. Keep reading.
75-100 = Congratulations! You don't need this book but keep reading and then share it with someone else!

Is Your Joy in Danger?

Your Joy is precious. You must protect and cherish it. You must help it to grow in your life and in the lives of others. The world is sorely lacking in joy, especially in times of war, famine, strife, crime, violence and financial difficulties. It is my belief that you have the capacity to increase the joy you experience in your life. Once you become more JOY-FILLED, you can learn to protect it and share it when others need it most. You need never feel "joyless" again. You will learn ways in which you can take an active part in keeping your own joy safe once you've accepted it.

Your Journey To Joy

No matter what experiences you have had in the past, you have the capacity to be joyful NOW! The path to finding your own joy may be a hard one, but the journey is well worth the pain, trouble or time. You only have this one earthly life. Why not let it be the most joyful one that it can be?

Joy Defined: By The World

Joy is often experienced in a fleeting moment, a "stab", as C.S. Lewis calls it in *Surprised by Joy*, a human longing. It's slippery and can be hard to pin down and even harder to maintain over an extended period of time. Joy is a precious commodity. When you have it, you want it to last.

Happy moments are to be appreciated, never taken for granted. That is why you take pictures of your fun times. You want those memories preserved because, in some way, you know that you may not experience this feeling for long or possibly ever again. Parents who take pictures of their children's every sneeze are trying to capture on film seconds of pure joy that are so quickly over and gone.

> **The *Random House Dictionary* defines joy in the following way:**
>
> *The emotion of great delight or happiness caused by something exceptionally good or satisfying; keen pleasure; elation.*
> *A source or cause of keen pleasure or delight; something or someone greatly valued or appreciated.*
> *The expression or display of glad feeling; festive gaiety.*
> *A state of happiness or felicity.*
> *To feel joy; be glad; rejoice; to gladden, etc.*

Newspaper ads, TV, radio commercials, toys, cars, etc., entice you to enjoy life just a little more with this product or that trip. Next time you open the newspaper, especially around the Christmas holidays, count how many advertisements mention "JOY". And why not? The Public Relations companies know that that is what people crave, and if their product promises a little of it, you may not be able to resist. It's a safe marketing tool. You can't measure how long joy lasts or if it's real or not. It can't be quantified.

I remember the excitement of my first toy SLINKY. Watching those little metal rings magically follow each other down the stairs was so thrilling. Five minutes after I opened the box, the slinky was bent and would no longer slink. Needless to say, I no longer felt joy over this gift. My spirit crushed, I went on to another present. Oh, well! The point is everyone wants joy, and the advertisers know it.

You know that joy doesn't necessarily come in a box, or with cleaner clothes or a faster car. You need other ways of having joy that do not depend on purchasing anything, or having something or being with someone.

Exercise 2:

The Language of Joy: What words do you use for joy?

- ☐ Love
- ☐ Happiness
- ☐ Elation
- ☐ Gladness
- ☐ Delighted
- ☐ Cheerful
- ☐ Overjoyed
- ☐ Passionate
- ☐ Celebrate
- ☐ Jazzed
- ☐ Inspiration
- ☐ Excitement
- ☐ High
- ☐ Merry
- ☐ Happy
- ☐ Mirth
- ☐ Pleasure
- ☐ Jubilant
- ☐ Fulfilled
- ☐ Complete
- ☐ Radiance
- ☐ Enjoyment
- ☐ Exuberance
- ☐ Bliss
- ☐ Pleased
- ☐ Ecstasy
- ☐ Festive
- ☐ Rapture
- ☐ Glory
- ☐ Other:_____

Exercise 3

How do you define joy in your own words? What words best describe this feeling for you? Use as many words from the list above as you want.

When I feel joy, I feel...
What I am missing most in my life is feeling more...
Feeling this way makes me feel uncomfortable...
I'm scared of feeling too much...
I wish I was more...
I want to be the kind of person who is_____ or has _____
_____.

What stops me from feeling _____ is...

Exercise 4

What does the search for joy feel like? I feel...

- ☐ Frustrated
- ☐ Empty
- ☐ Hopeless
- ☐ Dissatisfied
- ☐ Depressed
- ☐ Thirsty
- ☐ Deprived
- ☐ Hungry
- ☐ Desperate
- ☐ An ache
- ☐ Other: _____

This workbook will show you different sources of joy that are always available and are absolutely free!!

Joy Connections

As the source of all true joy, God provides four types of connections which can bring you joy. These Joy Connections are:

1. A Connection to your true self
2. A Connection to others
3. A Connection to God's Creation
4. A Connection to Jesus and His Holy Spirit

Connections are the essence of human existence. From the moment of conception, perhaps even before, you are thrown into a whirlwind of connections (physically, emotionally, and spiritually) which define in the end who you will become. Your connections to parents, a special toy, a pet or a friend are reflective of your ONENESS with God or with your broken nature. It is through your connections that you learn. Therefore, what you learn and how you learn are all conditional on the types of connections you experience in your life. Some connections are out of choice: who you associate with, which groups you belong to, etc. Some are out of your control altogether: who your parents are, where you were born. But all in all, connections are your sources of joy. Ultimately, God is the source of all true joy.

When I am connected, I am as close as I can be to being ONE with that thing or being. Having a balance in the four categories of joy connections increases my chances of experiencing joy. I am talking about the type of connections that are based on your true self having a bond, not just strictly the number of people in your life, or the number of years you know someone, or the type of relationship you are in, i.e., that it's your Mother or wife. Unfortunately, not all marriages or families experience healthy Joy Connections and sometimes, there is little true joy.

Exercise 5

Where does your joy come from? Examples are: my children, work, therapy, teaching, loving others, giving.

Exercise 6

What do you believe would bring you joy in your future?

QUICK JOY?

For a "get rich quick," "instant gratification" society, waiting until we die and go to heaven to experience God's joy is asking the impossible. We can pick up the phone and have pizza in 30 minutes, or talk to someone on the other side of the globe. We can walk into a tanning booth or microwave our meal or push a button and E-mail a letter. Who can wait? We become anxious if we must wait. We've become a society that can't wait for anything, much less joy.

Connections are now big business. Seminars, self-help books, even TV shows like Sesame Street help us, from birth to death, to make the most out of every relationship. Our global connections make us feel somehow responsible or affected by events that happen in places most of us will never visit -- Ground Zero, Chernobyl, Valdez, Waco, Columbine, to name a few. Billions are spent on advertising, trying to get us to make connections to products and services to enhance our minds, bodies and spirits.

Think about it. If you made every phone call the TV implores you to make, if you maintained contact with every person you met, if you connected with every piece of mail you receive, you would certainly be too busy to do anything else! Our world is bombarded with possible connections and yet loneliness, apathy, fear and depression abound.

So the answer certainly can't be:

 **Increase the number of connections in your life and you'll be guaranteed Joy.**

On the contrary, simplifying and fine tuning your connections are crucial if you are to make room in your life for true Joy!

So, is there a formula? Can we boil down the nugget of truth in this book into an equation where "1+1=2?" Let's get started and find out.

I am coming to you now, but I say these things while I am still in the world, so that they may have the full measure of my joy within them...

John 17:13

Ezekiel 1:22-28

And the One who sat there had the appearance of jasper and carnelian. A rainbow, resembling an emerald, encircled the throne...Also before the throne there was what looked like a sea of glass, clear as crystal.
 Revelation 4:3, 6

There is a river whose streams make glad the city of God...
Psalm 46:4

Isaiah 55:1

The streams of God are filled with water...
Psalm 65:9

The River of Life: Water for the Thirsty

In my dream, I am standing on a beach. The sky is brilliant blue and above the sea is the brightest rainbow imaginable. It stretches from one end of the Earth to the next. The center of the rainbow opens like a scroll and out of it cascades the most magnificent water I can imagine. It is crystal clear, translucent, and aquamarine in color. It is also a substance I have never seen -- liquid yet solid. It is alive somehow. It is thick, pure, and three-dimensional. It flows freely like a river and pours down to the waiting Earth from Heaven, like a fabulous waterfall! My excitement, awe, and fear are increased when to my left I notice a lone man standing on the beach. He does not speak, but as I awaken I can't help but feel I was in the presence of someone holy.

I was eager to find references in the Bible to the symbols in my dream. This search led me to a passage from Revelation.

> And he showed me a river of the <u>water of life</u>, clear as crystal, coming from the throne of God and of the Lamb, in the middle of its street. And on either side of the river was <u>the tree of life</u>, bearing twelve kinds of fruit, yielding its fruit every month; and the leaves of the tree were for the <u>healing</u> of the nations. (Revelation 22:1-2, *New American Standard*)

I feel sure that this river flowing from the rainbow was "the water of life" or living water.

Two other scriptures talk of this special water. "He said to me: 'It is done. I am the Alpha and the Omega, the Beginning and the End. To him who is <u>thirsty</u> I will give to drink without cost from the spring of the water of life." (Revelation 21:6) "The Spirit and the bride say, 'Come!' And let him who hears say, 'Come!' Whoever is <u>thirsty</u>, let him come; and whoever wishes, let him take the free gift of the water of life." (Revelation 22:17) These passages assure me that when I am thirsty, this water is a free gift, mine for the taking. If my need is great enough, I will search for a source to satisfy it.

Are you really thirsty? Are you seeking more to life? Are you ready for those deep places within you to be satisfied? Then come to the River of the Water of Life. In this workbook you will drink freely of this river and learn how to thirst no more.

The Tree of Life: Food for the Hungry

Are you also hungry? Revelation 22:2 also makes reference to an interesting tree that grows by the side of the River of Life. Oddly enough, this strange tree has twelve different kinds of fruit on it. It is called the Tree of Life.

Where have you heard of this tree before? Look in Genesis 2:9 where you see God's newly created world starting to bloom: *And the Lord God made all kinds of trees grow out of the ground-trees that were pleasing to the eye and good for food. In the middle of the garden were the tree of life and the tree of the knowledge of good and evil.* In Revelation 22:1-2, you learn that this tree of life is actually a fruit tree. Why would God have a fruit tree at the beginning and the end of time? What are some of the spiritual truths you might draw from a fruit tree?

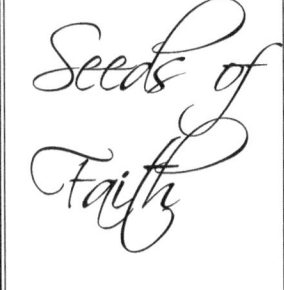

Fruit Trees	Spiritual Truth
Fruit trees flourish in good soil that is prepared.	You must prepare yourself for spiritual growth by the hand of the Gardener.
The fruit must be picked or harvested.	You must make a choice, reach out and take the gift of the tree. You must move to action and obedience to help harvest.
The fruit must be eaten to be enjoyed.	You must be hungry to seek God's gifts.
Fruit trees flourish near water if they have healthy roots.	You must drink from the river of life with healthy "roots" of your own.
The tree is a thing of beauty.	You must open the eyes of your spirit to see God's creation.
The fruit identifies the tree.	You must accept the eternal blessings offered by God. It's His orchard.
The leaves provide shade, rest from the hot sun, and a cool quiet place.	You must stop, rest, and meet your Maker.
The fruit grows in season and provides an abundant crop.	You must put aside worry that there will not be enough. God is provision.
The fruit is plentiful.	You must learn to share your good fruit with others.
Fruit trees produce seeds. A seed contains all it needs to grow a new tree.	You must spread the seeds, the Word of God, throughout God's orchard.

You will be like a well-watered garden, like a spring whose waters never fail.
Isaiah 58:11

Galatians 3:16

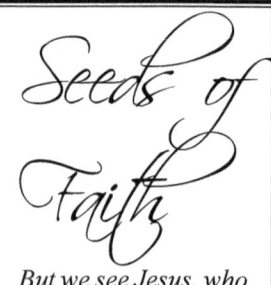

But we see Jesus, who was made a little lower than the angels, now crowned with glory and honor because he suffered death, so that by the grace of God he might taste death for everyone. In bringing many sons to glory, it was fitting that God, for whom and through whom everything exists, should make the author of their salvation perfect through suffering. Both the one who makes men holy and those who are made holy are of the same family. So Jesus is not ashamed to call them brothers. He says, "I will declare your name to my brothers; in the presence of the congregation I will sing your praises." And again, "I will put my trust in him." And again he says, "Here am I, and the children God has given me." Since the children have flesh and blood, he too shared in their humanity so that by his death he might destroy him who holds the power of death-that is, the devil-and free those who all their lives were held in slavery by their fear of death.

Hebrews 2:9-15

This fantastic tree, described in the first and last books of the Bible, is not only in Eden, but in the City of God, the New Jerusalem. It is the perfect symbol of the blessings and fullness of life God provides. God, the Great Provider, took care of all your needs before He created Man, and again He provides for all your needs until the end of time.

ACCESS TO THE TREE OF LIFE

Adam and Eve's bodies were not made to die. Adam and Eve were made in God's image and were not supposed to have to worry about death. Eating the forbidden fruit caused God to take away the Tree of Life from them and their disobedient descendants. Now we have death and separation from God as the consequence.

Then, when Jesus died in our place, He removed the consequence of death for those who believe in Him!

Therefore, could it be that we once again have access to the Tree of Life? Is that what eternal life means? Is that the joy of salvation?

A precious child of God died of cancer at age forty-two. Her grieving mother told me of a three year struggle where she watched her vibrant, beautiful daughter slowly deteriorate.

Her daughter clutched her Bible the entire time. Moments before her passing, the young woman called out, "Let everything that has breath praise the Lord! Let everything that has breath praise the Lord!"

Then, she pointed toward the hospital wall and said that she saw a tree by a river. Then she "fell asleep in Jesus."

What do you think? Could she have seen the City of God? I think so. Was she already living with Jesus before her physical life ended? Absolutely. Are you?

Joy Fruit is Good Fruit!

The Bible is filled with references to fruit. In the City of God, fruit will be available twelve months of the year. (Revelation 22:2) I have taken the liberty of naming these fruits to represent the twelve aspects of true joy. Perhaps you can think of other fruit which God will provide for all eternity. They will be the deepest and holiest desires of your soul and spirit.

Exercise 7: TWELVE ASPECTS OF JOY

Seeds of Faith

Directions: What kind of joy fruit are you hungry for? Put a check in the box next to those types of fruit you crave.

- ☐ Salvation
- ☐ Acceptance
- ☐ Truth
- ☐ Security
- ☐ Well-Being
- ☐ Righteousness
- ☐ Completion
- ☐ Intimacy
- ☐ Health
- ☐ Creation of Jesus in My heart
- ☐ Union with God
- ☐ Victory

Fruit trees of all kinds will grow on both banks of the river. Their leaves will not wither, nor will their fruit fail. Every month they will bear, because the water from the sanctuary flows to them. Their fruit will serve for food and their leaves for healing.
Ezekiel 47:12

God's desire is that you produce much good fruit. Seeds produce fruit. Jesus is called "the Seed of the woman"(Genesis 3:15), "the Seed of Abraham"(Galatians 3:16), and "the Seed of David"(2 Timothy 2:8). A seed must be buried and die to bear new fruit. The seed holds all the inner knowledge of new life for new fruit. Jesus as the "Seed" also holds all that is to be born in you from His death. In other words, any and all spiritual fruit in a Christian's life comes through the sacrificial death of "the Seed," Jesus. In the parable of the sower and the seed, God is the sower and His Word is the seed. Jesus is the Word made flesh.

Isaiah 55:10-13

The Seed Stealer

For you have been born again, not of perishable seed, but of imperishable, through the living and enduring word of God.
1 Peter 1:23

As he was scattering the seed, some fell along the path, and the birds came and ate it up.
Mark 4:4

The farmer sows the word. Some people are like seed along the path, where the word is sown. As soon as they hear it, Satan comes and takes away the word that was sown in them.
Mark 4:14-15

Ephesians 6:10-17

Jesus begins this parable (a short story with a powerful lesson) to explain what happens to some people when they hear God's Word. Sometimes, He says, Satan jumps right in and steals the Word. You can begin right now to disappoint Satan by refusing to let him steal your joy and steal the precious words that will grow good fruit in your life.

The Bible calls Satan the evil one, the slanderer, the tempter, the accuser of the brethren, and he is known as the liar, the deceiver, our adversary or enemy. Do you want him to have the victory? No, of course not. In fact, if you look at this as warfare, and you are protecting precious territory (your body, soul, and spirit), then you have to get tough and "stand firm" as it says in the 6th chapter of Ephesians.

God desires you to know His Son. He protects you from Satan's lies and deceits that try to keep you from Jesus. Paul describes in Ephesians exactly how God does this. Like a Roman soldier suited up for battle, God gives you a full set of armor that is better than any armored tank. From head to toe, you are prepared for anything that Satan may devise.

Here are the various pieces of that Holy armor of God for you to put on when you are doing this workbook:

1. The Helmet of Salvation
2. The Breastplate of Righteousness
3. The Belt of Truth
4. The Shield of Faith
5. The Sandals of Peace
6. The Sword of His Word

Preparing the Soil of the Soul: Do I have thorny soil?

Later in this workbook you will be exploring the "thorns" in your life. These, as Jesus explains in the Sower and Seed parable, are some of the things which can steal your joy simply because you are focused on them:

1. The worries of the world.
2. The deceitfulness of riches.
3. The desires for things other than the Good News of Jesus.

The very nature of a thorn bush is to choke and cut the life off of anything it touches. If I truly desire to know Him, Jesus is saying, I must first examine the desires of my heart which may be choking the seeds He is planting in me. Nothing can grow, especially the healing He desires for me, until I free His hand to touch my garden.

This passage (Mark 4:18-19) warns that the Word of God (the seed) becomes unfruitful if these things are allowed to choke the very life out of it. In this workbook you will look at all the fruit God wants to offer His children. This parable reminds you that your soul is the soil. His Word can grow in you and that is His desire, but you have some preparation to do first.

Exercise 8

Are you willing to remove the thorns and clear away anything which chokes God's purpose for your life? Or, are you saying that you want things to change and yet deep down are you unwilling to let go of something? Please comment.

You may have tried to rid your life of many of the thorn bushes but to no avail. Ask any gardener. A vine can take over a flower bed almost overnight. He must be diligent to pull the thorny weed out by its roots. Ouch! Remember God is the Gardener. He'll do the dirty work. All you have to be is willing soil. Then stand back and watch your garden grow!

Seeds of Faith

Still others, like seed sown among thorns, hear the word; but the worries of this life, the deceitfulness of wealth and the desires for other things come in and choke the word, making it unfruitful.
Mark 4:18-19

Units One through Twelve will take you on a step by step process to clear the soil, trim some dead branches and pull out some unhealthy roots. Be patient with yourself. It took a long time to get this way and with the help of the Holy Spirit, we will clear the soil together.

BACK TO THE JOY FRUIT

Growing the twelve aspects of joy described in this workbook (page 25) is the same as developing the wholeness of Christ, or developing His Character. As you do this workbook, you will be growing good fruit and pruning bad fruit in order to be more and more like Jesus.

Remember, you need not focus on the fruit or the healing needed to grow good fruit. Focus on God - the joy and its fruit will follow.

This book is designed as a workbook. As you read the exercises, you will begin to see your own personal JOURNEY TO JOY unfold. Don't be surprised if some of the exercises tap into painful experiences from your life.

1. **Make sure that when you do the work, you have the <u>time</u> to concentrate and the <u>privacy</u> to feel the feelings. Find a safe place to do your work and to store this book when you are not using it.**

2. **Find someone to pray with you about the feelings, questions, or memories that come up for you. And remember, the entire purpose of this book is to help you have more JOY! So don't stop half-way through the book. Be a finisher!**

Dear Lord God,

I love You and praise You. I worship You and glorify Your Holy Name. I thank You for all the blessings in my life. I thank you that You are a God that wants to heal my life and make it whole.

I pray that as I read this book, I will receive a full measure of your Divine Joy. I pray that you will cover me while I am reading these pages and remove all obstacles to the healing You desire for me. I pray your protection by the Blood of the Lamb that no harm may come and that your full armor will protect me from all evil. I pray You will open my eyes and ears as You guide me to a deeper understanding of Your will.

In Jesus' name I pray.

Amen.

I will bless them and the places surrounding my hill. I will send down showers in season; there will be showers of blessing. The trees of the field will yield their fruit and the ground will yield its crops; the people will be secure in their land. They will know that I am the Lord, when I break the bars of their yoke and rescue them from the hands of those who enslaved them.
Ezekiel 34:26-27

Unit One

The *Joy* of Eternal Salvation:
Freedom from Spiritual Death

  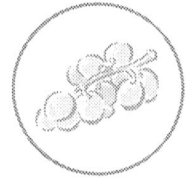   

Joy Choice # 1

**Joy is choosing to have a personal relationship with
Jesus Christ as my Lord and Savior.
Joy is choosing to live with Jesus for all eternity.**

*Come, let us sing for joy to the LORD;
let us shout aloud to the Rock of our salvation.*
Psalm 95:1

"Never allow anything that divides or destroys the oneness of your life with Christ to remain in your life without facing it. Beware of allowing the influence of your friends or your circumstances to divide your life. This only serves to sap your strength and slow your spiritual growth. Beware of anything that can split your oneness with Him, causing you to see yourself as separate from Him. Nothing is as important as staying right spiritually. And the only solution is a very simple one - Come to Me . . . "

My Utmost For His Highest, Oswald Chambers, August 19

"He then brought them out and asked, 'Sirs, what must I do to be saved?'

They replied, 'Believe in the Lord Jesus, and you will be saved-you and your household.' Then they spoke the word of the Lord to him and to all the others in his house. At that hour of the night the jailer took them and washed their wounds; then immediately he and all his family were baptized. The jailer brought them into his house and set a meal before them; he was filled with joy because he had come to believe in God-he and his whole family."

Acts 16:30-34

Day One

Imagine you are standing in a beautiful orchard. Weaving in and out of the fruit trees is a magnificent river with crystal clear water, teeming with life. The fruit on the trees is a little out of reach and much too glorious to touch. You decide to relax under a tree whose branches stretch far and wide, like a huge umbrella covering you from the bright sunlight. A beautiful dove lands on a branch without a sound. A gentle wind rustles the leaves on the trees.

As you sit there, Jesus joins you. He reaches for a piece of fruit and hands it to you. You gladly receive it and take your first bite. Immediately there is a sensation of such incredible joy that no words can describe. Jesus has given you His greatest gift, a life for all Eternity with Him. As you eat, He begins to share with you about the fruit you are eating and His desire for you. It is the fruit of Eternal Salvation which can only come if He gives it to you.

"My desire is that you know me," He says. "I have many names, and I will reveal all of Myself to you in time. Let Me tell you who I am."

I am *Jesus of Nazareth*.
I am *the Sent of the Father*.
I am *the Messiah, which is called Christ*.
I am *the Son of Man*.
I am *the Savior of the World*.
I am *the Savior of the Body*.
I am *the Deliverer*.
I am *the Seed of Abraham*.
I am *the Seed of David*.
I am *the Captain of your salvation*.

I am *the Rock of your salvation*.
I am *the Lamb of God*.
I am *Eternal Life*.
I am *the Door*.
I am *the Way*.
I am *your Lord and Savior*.
I am *the Life*.
I am *Christ the Firstfruits*.
I am *your Redeemer*.
I am *your Salvation*.

"I want you to receive me as your Savior. Then you and I will get to spend eternity together. This would give Me great joy! Then you can say, 'I am alive together with Christ. I have been born again, not of perishable seed, but of imperishable, through the living and enduring Word of God.' There is nothing you must do but believe in Me. Come to Me."

Spend some quiet moments in His Presence and hear what Jesus has to say to you.

NOTE: If you have a hard time with visualization exercises, you might try keeping your eyes open, looking outside at a real tree and imagining Jesus coming to talk to you. You also may try reading this page out loud. Read on and by the end of this book, these meditations will be real for you.

Let us fix our eyes on Jesus, ... who for the joy set before him endured the cross ... and sat down at the right hand of the throne of God.
Hebrews 12:2

The promises were spoken to Abraham and to his seed. The Scripture does not say "and to seeds," meaning many people, but "and to your seed," meaning one person, who is Christ...
Galatians 3:16

Galatians 3:26-29

GETTING TO KNOW JESUS

In order to grow good fruit, you must know who Jesus is. He has revealed Himself under the tree of life (His life in you). Revealed means to let you see Him for who He really is.

When you enter into a relationship with Jesus, He gradually lets you know more about Him every day.

Exercise 1

Repeated below are some of the names of Jesus. Have you already seen or heard these names? Check all that you are familiar with:

"I know that Jesus is"

- ☐ Jesus of Nazareth
- ☐ the Sent of the Father
- ☐ my Messiah, which is called the Christ
- ☐ the Son of Man
- ☐ my Redeemer
- ☐ the Captain of my salvation
- ☐ my Savior of the World
- ☐ my Savior of the Body
- ☐ my Deliverer
- ☐ my Eternal Life
- ☐ my Christ the Firstfruits
- ☐ my Seed of Abraham
- ☐ my Seed of David
- ☐ the Rock of my salvation
- ☐ my Lamb of God
- ☐ my Door
- ☐ my Way
- ☐ my Lord and Savior
- ☐ my Life
- ☐ my Salvation

Exercise 2

What do these names tell you about Jesus? What aspects of His nature do they reveal?

GETTING TO KNOW GOD

The following names or titles for God reveal how He is seen throughout scripture as producing the good fruit of Eternal Salvation.

"My Name Is"	"I Am..."	"I Create..."
Heleyou	Emancipation	S
Yahweh	Freedom	A
Adonai	Redemption	L
Lord	Mercy	V
Rock of his salvation	The anointing	A
the Tower of salvation	The atonement	T
Savior		I
Lord God of My salvation		O
Savior King		N
Redeemer		
Vinedresser		
Gardener		

GETTING TO KNOW THE HOLY SPIRIT

The Holy Spirit is the River of Life. You must come to the River every day. The Holy Spirit is the agent of your new birth as mentioned in John 3:5-8. He comes as the Wind and is gentle as a Dove. The Holy Spirit lives in you when you ask Jesus to be your Savior. As a believer you are given the gift of the Holy Spirit. Meditate for a time on this wonderful gift!

"Swarms of living creatures will live wherever the river flows. There will be large numbers of fish, because this water flows there and makes the salt water fresh; so where the river flows everything will live." Ezekiel 47:9

Day Two

GOOD FRUIT: THE JOY OF SALVATION

You have just met the man called Jesus in one of His revealed identities in the Bible: the Savior. Each chapter will introduce you to a unique facet of this One that you seek to know.

By the end of the book you will have been introduced in a new way to Him who has been called both the Man of Joy and the Man of Sorrows.

Seeds of Faith

Psalm 68:19-20

"Whoever believes in me, as the Scripture has said, streams of living water will flow from within him." By this he meant the Spirit whom those who believed in him were later to receive. Up to that time the Spirit had not been given, since Jesus had not yet been glorified. John 7:38-39

Thus, by their fruit you will recognize them.
Matthew 7:20

They feast on the abundance of your house; you give them drink from your river of delights. For with you is the fountain of life...
Psalm 36:8-9

The first fruit you are given from the Tree of Life is Eternal Life, or Salvation. Wow! What a gift! To spend eternity with God. This is true joy, and I know no greater desire in any human being than to be secure in the future when this life as we know it ends.

What joy: to partake of the fruit on the Tree of Life and drink from the River of Life forever! God must love you beyond measure to have given you this assurance as a free gift. To be allowed to enter by the gates into the city of Heaven is your highest honor. Read on and let's see how this fruit becomes yours.

Good Fruit: The Joy of Salvation

Exercise 3

Directions

Put an X next to the fruit that you still need to grow.

- ☐ Eternal Life
- ☐ A Changed Life
- ☐ Rest
- ☐ A Renewed spirit
- ☐ The Gift of the Holy Spirit

God's Salvage Company
The writer of Ecclesiastes writes in Chapter 3, verse 11, ... *He has also set eternity in the hearts of men . . .* God has blessed you with a desire, an inkling, that time is immeasurable and that you can look beyond the confines of your physical life to something which does not end.

This desire to live forever is part of God's plan to draw you closer to Him, the One who exists outside of time and knows no limits to His own existence. Eternal life is not all about time. It is a condition as well as a quantity of life. It cannot be measured in years.

The desire to have eternal existence cannot be separated from a desire to know and love God. Yet many have done just that, looking elsewhere for the "fountain of youth."

God's Plan
God's plan for you to be with Him in all eternity comes complete with the instructions and guidebook (the Bible) on how He achieves His plan.

Step One:	God loves you and yearns to be near you.
Step Two:	God knows you and why you are separated from Him.
Step Three:	God provided Jesus to bring you back to oneness with Him again. In His blood is life.
Step Four:	God chose you to accept His Son as Savior and Lord of your life.
Step Five:	Jesus gives you salvation, eternal life with Him in a personal relationship.
Step Six:	You accept by faith steps one through five and ask Jesus to be in a relationship with you as your Lord and Savior. (Acts 13:48)

GOOD FRUIT: ETERNAL LIFE

The words save and salvation mean:

1. to make free
2. to deliver
3. to aid
4. to live
5. to revive
6. to rescue
7. to defend
8. to cure
9. to preserve
10. liberty
11. deliverance
12. prosperity
13. to heal
14. to make whole
15. to complete
16. to fulfill

Savior means deliverer, one who makes safe or free. To say that Jesus is your Savior is to claim that He gives you the freedom you need from sin and spiritual death so that you can have spiritual life forever.

How are you saved: Choose or Refuse?
You are saved by God when you accept His Son, Jesus, and believe that His sacrificial death on the Cross was for you. There is no other way to be saved and given eternal life. Jesus says, *I am the Way . . .* (Luke 14:6) This is what He meant.

God demands a payment or a price in the marketplace of sin. There is a consequence to sin: a debt to be paid. The Jews were required by God to bring animal sacrifices to the tabernacle as a payment for their sin. There must be a life for a life. Jesus laid down His sinless life so that you wouldn't have to-Amazing!

Jesus, God's son, became the Lamb of God "once for all," one time on the Cross and for all people. Therefore, the price is paid in full, the debt is cancelled, the prisoner (you) is set free from slavery to sin and a new Master is your owner.

Seeds of Faith

"For God so loved the world that he gave his one and only Son, that whoever believes in him shall not perish but have eternal life..." John 3:16

...because through Christ Jesus the law of the Spirit of life set me free from the law of sin and death. Romans 8:2

Salvation is found in no one else, for there is no other name under heaven given to men by which we must be saved. Acts 4:12

God made him who had no sin to be sin for us, so that in him we might become the righteousness of God. 2 Corinthians 5:21

". . . just as the Son of Man did not come to be served, but to serve, and to give his life as a ransom for many." Matthew 20:28

God presented him as a sacrifice of atonement, through faith in his blood. He did this to demonstrate his justice, because in his forbearance he had left the sins committed beforehand unpunished... Romans 3:25

Restore to me the joy of your salvation and grant me a willing spirit, to sustain me. Psalm 51:12

Isaiah 53-all verses. (Please read this aloud.)

The Power is in the Blood

God hates sin, but Jesus' death satisfies God and is the only way to please God again. You share in this acceptance by God only because Jesus is acceptable to God.

The blood of Jesus has cleansing power. It makes you white as snow and purified to return to a relationship with God, the Father, who can't accept anything unclean. Jesus' gift is to restore your state of alienation to a state of reconciliation. You are no longer lost, you are found. And of course, as the song reminds, it is **all** because of God's *Amazing Grace*!

There are entire books dedicated to this aspect of joy. All of them would be empty words if the reader had not done one thing: Accept Jesus and what He did on the Cross.

Have you done this one thing? If not, then read the prayer below out loud and then tell someone.

You only need to pray this prayer once. There is no need to strive or continually rededicate yourself over and over. Jesus did everything necessary on the cross so you would not have to pay the wages of sin.

Note: You may have said this prayer a long time ago. That is great. But take a closer look. Do you experience the joy in your salvation or have you taken it for granted? Ask the Lord if there is something fresh and new for you to receive in this unit.

Prayer to Accept Jesus

Lord Jesus,

I come before you, just as I am. I am sorry for my sins. I repent of my sins. Please forgive me. In Your Name, I forgive all others for what they have done against me. I renounce Satan, the evil spirits and all their works.

I give You my entire self. Lord Jesus, now and forever, I invite You into my life. Jesus, I accept You as my Lord, God, and Savior. Heal me, change me, strengthen me in body, soul, and spirit.

Come, Lord Jesus, cover me with Your precious blood, and fill me with Your Holy Spirit. I love You, Lord Jesus. I praise You, Jesus. I thank You, Jesus. I shall follow You every day of my life.

Amen

Day Three

GOOD FRUIT: A CHANGED LIFE

Receiving Jesus and the salvation He gives results in a changed life. All of the fruit given to you under the Tree of Life in this workbook are the ways in which your life can change in Christ.

These changes happen quickly in some, slowly in others. "He has made everything beautiful in its time" it says in Ecclesiastes 3:11.

These changes occur when you accept not only the salvation your Lord gives, but His Lordship over your life as well. Others have described this as asking Jesus to be in the driver's seat; to be the pilot of the plane, boat, or train; to let Jesus sit on the throne of your life, etc.

When you ask Him into your life as Savior, He joins you as Lord of a surrendered life. To ask Him to be Savior without being Lord will not allow good fruit to grow.

GOOD FRUIT: REST FOR THE SOUL AND SPIRIT

When someone dies, you say "May he rest in Peace." You want rest from problems, troubles, sorrows, and exhaustion. This is just one reason you need God's salvation plan - you just can't do it alone. Jesus says, "Come to me... and I will give you rest." Matthew 11:28

When you try to survive life on your soul's own strength, choices, beliefs, knowledge, etc., you will come to a place where you are insufficient.

Jesus is totally sufficient. Matthew 16:24-27 tells that He is ready to help those who are ready to lose their life for Him. It is then that He can produce this Fruit of Salvation in you and call you into a new life. Then, even though you are physically alive, you can rest in peace that you are His forever. But, first you have to "come."

Coming and Going
The Gospels (Matthew, Mark, Luke and John) tell of Jesus' life on Earth. As you read about His journeys, you see Him coming to places, coming to people, and coming to serve His Father. He claims His purpose in coming is to "preach good news to the poor . . . to proclaim freedom for the prisoners and recovery of sight for the blind, to release the oppressed . . ." (Luke 4:18).

Seeds of Faith

Romans 6:1-10

Galatians 6:2

2 Corinthians 3:7-11

...that God was reconciling the world to himself in Christ, not counting men's sins against them. And he has committed to us the message of reconciliation. 2 Corinthians 5:19

Hebrews 4:9-10

He will be a joy and delight to you, and many will rejoice because of his birth...
Luke 1:14

"Here I am! I stand at the door and knock. If anyone hears my voice and opens the door, I will come in and eat with him, and he with me."
Revelation 3:20

With joy you will drink deeply from the fountain of salvation!
Isaiah 12:3 NLT

Exalted to the right hand of God, he has received from the Father the promised Holy Spirit and has poured out what you now see and hear.
Acts 2:33

Luke 1:41-44

You are all of the above: "the poor, the prisoner, the blind, the oppressed." He knows when, where, how and why He comes. He comes bringing salvation (redemption and cleansing). Why? So He can then tell you where He wants you to "go". But you won't hear Him until something miraculous happens.

You may have to have a "tune-up" or you may need a <u>new</u> spirit. The spirit in you is like the receiver in a radio. Sometimes it gets tuned to the wrong station. Receiving the "Jesus" station on the dial of your spirit is critical to growing the good fruit of a saved life in Christ.

When your "receiver" or spirit is damaged, wounded or turned to the wrong station, you will find it harder to receive Jesus. If your radio is broken you could (1) stop playing it (2) buy a new one or (3) take it to be fixed by an expert.

Many choose to stop using their spiritual receiver, some choose to search for a new source, and still others search for the manufacturer. The maker of the radio has all the parts, wrote the manual, and has the technical skill to fix what's broken.

How is your receiver? Spiritually are you numb, weak, or even worse, feeling dead? This is only an illusion because as long as you are living, you have a spirit receiver that can be made just like new. How? By going to the Maker and asking to be regenerated, born again, made a new creation. The human spirit needs to be remade to properly receive (tune into) God's plan for salvation, His message, and the calling on your life.

So, you ask Jesus to <u>come</u> into your own spirit (or heart.) You <u>receive</u> him with a renewed spirit.

Then, you can hear Him tell you where to <u>go</u> next.

Good Fruit:
The Gift of the Holy Spirit

The wonderful good fruit of a saved life includes another treat - the gift of the Holy Spirit who helps along the way and makes your sin nature ineffective. He gives you the Law of Christ and frees you to live a life pleasing to God.

The stories of Jesus tell not only of His comings, but of His goings. He was tuned into His Father's will through His receiver, His Spirit. Your spiritual health allows you to do the same. You have the Holy Spirit dwelling in you when you receive Jesus. Then, your receiver (spirit) is given all it needs to operate perfectly! Then, like Jesus, you come and go in the Father's will.

Is your receiver working? This workbook will offer suggestions for fine tuning your spirit, but first you must take it back to the Manufacturer for full replacement. Don't worry, your life came with a full warranty - Jesus sealed the contract with His blood just for you. You have a full replacement for your spirit waiting for you.

> *Come Holy Spirit,*
>
> *I gladly offer you my life. Renew my spirit today and everyday and restore in me the joy of salvation!*
> *Amen*

Day Four

BAD FRUIT

If your life is a "fruit tree," you probably have some good fruit and some bad fruit. The idea is to identify any bad fruit and then uncover the "root" cause of that bad fruit.

The following section will discuss two bad fruits which may grieve God the most.

Now let us look at the things which can block the joy of salvation from growing in your life. I call these <u>Bad Fruit.</u> In this workbook you will help God tend your tree by looking carefully for the bad fruit that needs to be plucked off the branches so that healthy fruit can grow.

Exercise 4
I have been experiencing...
- ☐ Despair
- ☐ Disconnection from God

BAD FRUIT: DISCONNECTION FROM GOD

What does it mean to be lost? If the good fruit Jesus is offering you is a life spent with Him, then a life apart from Him must be the bad fruit. Jesus says His is *the Life*. (Luke 14:6) The only life that matters is a life with Him. The opposite of life is death. Therefore, this bad fruit is about trying to live a life apart from the source of life itself. It is a life that is meaningless, empty, and frighteningly alone.

Seeds of Faith

" Likewise every good tree bears good fruit, but a bad tree bears bad fruit."
Matthew 7:17

John 11:25-26

"...For the Son of Man came to seek and save what was lost."
Luke 19:10

You were bought at a price. Therefore honor God with your body. 1 Corinthians 6:20

Therefore, get rid of all moral filth and the evil that is so prevalent and humbly accept the word planted in you, which can save you. James 1:21

To be separated from God for all eternity is beyond your comprehension. To be separated from God <u>right now</u> is a life of pain, emptiness, isolation, fear, and desperation. When your human spirit is disconnected from God, your soul begins to shrivel, weaken, die. What separates you? Your sin and your reaction to the sin of others.

BAD FRUIT: DESPAIR

In its disconnected state, your soul's tuning mechanism begins to register tones of despair. Despair is dangerous to the human spirit and soul and <u>must</u> be addressed quickly. Despair is an alarm sounding in your being that your grounding wire is frayed.

Despair is the feeling of being "without spirit." It is a lie for the believer. Despair is bad fruit and signals that spiritual death is possible. For unbelievers, this signal is especially dangerous because it rings true. Without Jesus, spiritual death is a certainty.

With Jesus, despair is a temporary reminder that being separated from God is to be avoided at all costs. After all, Jesus counted the cost, paid the price and assured you that your relationship with God was restored forever.

Feel despair? Then reconnect with God. How? Hook up with Jesus.

GROWING GOOD FRUIT: PARTICIPATING WITH THE GARDENER

Jesus said in John 15:1 that God is the Vinedresser or Gardener. Let's look at the Life Skills needed to participate in God's plan of salvation, His Gardening Plan.

Day Five

The growth of this good fruit in your own life depends on the following skills which are your gardening tools.

Exercise 5: CHOOSING GARDENING TOOLS - LIFE SKILLS

"In order to the grow good fruit, I need to become more..."
(Check all that apply.)

- ☐ Willing to accept Jesus as my personal Savior
- ☐ Open in my faith (not boxed in by old beliefs and patterns)
- ☐ Accepting that I need saving
- ☐ Accepting of God's saving help
- ☐ Child-like in my faith
- ☐ Open to believing in Jesus
- ☐ Open to the Holy Spirit
- ☐ Open to surrendering my life and my will to God
- ☐ Open to placing on God's Altar what bothers me
- ☐ Dependent on God, His strength and guidance
- ☐ Trusting that Jesus died for me
- ☐ Knowledgeable about Jesus
- ☐ Willing to let go and let Him be Lord
- ☐ Open to seeing God's hand in my life
- ☐ Other_____

Exercise 6

The <u>three</u> life skills which would help me most to claim the joy of God's salvation in my life are:
(from the list above)

_____

_____

_____

Seeds of Faith

"I am the true vine, and my Father is the gardener..."
John 15:1

"I tell you the truth, he who believes has everlasting life..."
John 6:47

Hebrews 5:9

Hebrews 7:25

Exercise 7

How would your life be different if you had these life skills?
(the three chosen on page 43)

Exercise 8:   PULLING UP WEEDS

Without these three life skills you may have been compensating (making do or covering up) for not having this skill. Check all that apply

"Instead of these life skills, I have been . . ."	Frequently	Sometimes	Rarely
Stubborn - "I'll do it myself"			
Willful			
Stuck in old beliefs			
Full of pride			
Overly dependent on people, places or things			
Defensive			
Resistant to the truth			
Unable to depend on anyone but myself			
Afraid			
Unwilling to have anything to do with God or Jesus or the Holy Spirit			
Confused - no answers, no solutions			
Unable to surrender to another's authority			
Exhausting myself, depending on my own ability, strength & talents			
Defiant			
Other:			

Exercise 9

These weeds or characteristics are getting in the way of your full acceptance of Jesus Christ as Lord and Savior. Pick the three which are your biggest stumbling blocks.

1. _____
_____
2. _____
_____
3. _____
_____

Exercise 10

How is each one getting in the way of your growing this good fruit in your life (the joy of Salvation)? Please explain:

Day Six

PREPARING THE SOIL OF THE SOUL

Grafted in: Holy Roots
So God the Gardener wants to grow good fruit on your own tree. The special thing about this tree - it's a grafted tree. Grafting is a process for taking the roots of one tree and attaching the branches of another tree to it. This produces a new creation - a new type of fruit can grow on the tree.

Jesus is the root and the stump and you are the new branches. Now, grafted into Him, you don't resemble your old tree. Now His good fruit can thrive on your meager branches. His fruit becomes your fruit. What a miracle!

Seeds of Faith

This is to my Father's glory, that you bear much fruit, showing yourselves to be my disciples...
John 15:8

You will say then, "Branches were broken off so that I could be grafted in."
Romans 11:19

If the part of the dough offered as firstfruits is holy, then the whole batch is holy; if the root is holy, so are the branches.
Romans 11:16

Exercise 11: UPROOTING UNHOLY ROOTS

As God begins to pull out your unholy roots and replace them with the Holy Roots from Jesus, He also will clean up the soil around the roots. Whatever is blocking the joy in your life needs to be removed with the help of the Gardener.

This whole workbook is a gardening tool for this purpose. Every exercise, every prayer, every scripture and every teaching has been carefully chosen to unblock your joy.

Begin now by using this prayer to open the "eyes of your heart" to God's plan for your garden.

Write a prayer asking Jesus to help remove any stumbling blocks to your joy.

Dear Jesus,

You are my Savior. You are the Lamb of God who surrendered all. You are the Way to the Father who is in Heaven. You are my Redeemer and the Rock of my salvation.

I want the joy of Your salvation to grow in my life but I find at times these stumbling blocks (name them):

My prayer to you this day dear Lord, is:

Amen.

Day Seven

A CHANGE OF HEART

In each unit you will be asked to examine the changes happening in your spirit (your heart.) Your heart is now the "command center" of your life, not your soul. The joy of salvation can only grow in a believing, receiving heart that is yielded to Jesus.

Exercise 12

Check all the words below that describe the changes in your spirit:

My Old Heart Was:	My New Heart Is:
☐ Unbelieving	☐ Believing
☐ Closed	☐ Open
☐ Un-receiving	☐ Receiving
☐ Unyielding	☐ Yielding
☐ Lost	☐ Found
☐ Other:	☐ Other:
☐ Other:	☐ Other:
See to it, brothers, that none of you has a sinful, unbelieving heart that turns away from the living God. Hebrews 3:12	*But I trust in your unfailing love; my heart rejoices in your salvation.* Psalm 13:6

Baptism: the Sacrament of Belonging

If you have not already done so, you need to be baptized so that you, too, can join in the family of believers who have received Jesus as Lord and Savior. In baptism, you are sealed as Christ's own forever, and you belong to His family. Seek a church that will instruct you in the Sacrament of Baptism or ask your church how you can become baptized.

Soul Searching

Your soul is your mind, your will and your emotions. It is not a "bad" part of you. But over the years it is the soul that collects not only the good, but the bad memories, beliefs, attitudes and behaviors. It is the soul which must be restored and made holy. Remember, it is the Holy Spirit who can do this restoration. He is God's foreman of the gardening projects on earth.

As a result of the work I've done in this unit:

MIND
What new beliefs or thoughts do I have?

What old beliefs am I ready to put on God's altar?

WILL
What new choices have I made?

What old choices can I give to God?

EMOTIONS
My feelings have changed in the following way:

What feelings or emotions am I giving to the Lord?

Unit Two

The *Joy* of Eternal Acceptance:
Freedom from Self-Hatred, Pride, and False Images

  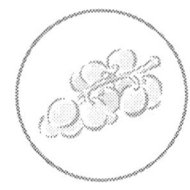  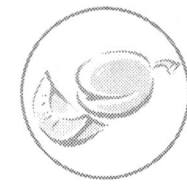 

Joy Choice # 2

Joy is knowing that I am acceptable to God through my belief in Jesus. It is choosing to be my true, authentic self called into life by Jesus, my Friend.

You did not choose me, but I chose you and appointed you to go and bear fruit—fruit that will last. Then the Father will give you whatever you ask in my name.
John 15:16

"I will accept you as fragrant incense."

Ezekial 20:41

"These two things are sweet before the Most High; and for the sake of His doing and His dying, His substitutionary sufferings and His vicarious obedience, the Lord our God accepts us. What a preciousness there must be in Him to overcome our lack of preciousness! What a sweet savor to put away our ill savor! What a purifying power in His blood to take away sin such as ours! And what glory in His righteousness to make such unacceptable creatures to be accepted in the Beloved! Note, believer, how sure and unchanging our acceptance must be, since it is in Him! Take care that you never doubt your acceptance in Jesus. You can't be accepted without Christ; but, when you have received His merit, you can't be unaccepted... You are always accepted in Christ, are always blessed and dear to the Father's heart."

Morning and Evening, Charles H. Spurgeon, March 28

"Do not work for food that spoils, but for food that endures to eternal life, which the Son of Man will give you. On him God the Father has placed his seal of approval."

John 6:27

"But now, this is what the LORD says — he who created you, O Jacob, he who formed you, O Israel: 'Fear not, for I have redeemed you; I have summoned you by name; you are mine.'"

Day One

This time as you approach the orchard, Jesus is already there, waiting for you. He is carving your name in a big heart on the trunk of the Tree of Life. He turns and smiles. Jesus reaches for another beautiful piece of fruit and says, "The second fruit is My Acceptance of you. I accept you even when you don't feel acceptable. I know the real you, the authentic person My Father intended you to be."

"You have heard of Me in ways that explain how I can accept you:"

I am *your Maker*.
I am *the Name Above All Names*.
I am *the Real Life*.
I am *who I Am*.
I am *the Lifter of your head*.
I am *the Son of God*.
I am *the Gift of God*.
I am *the Son of the Father*.
I am *the Son of the Blessed*.
I am *the Firstborn of the dead*.
I am *the Holy Child Jesus*.

I am *the Chosen of God*.
I am *the Sower of the Seeds*.
I am *the Beloved*.
I am *the Most Blessed Forever*.
I am *a Lamb Without Blemish and Without Spot*.
I am *Him that was Valued*.
I am *the Only Begotten*.
I am *His Unspeakable Gift*.
I am *the Seed of the Woman*.
I am *the last Adam*.
I am *Love*.

"You are acceptable to Me and in Me. Therefore, this piece of fruit I offer you now is My Acceptance of you. When you eat of it, you can truthfully say:

"I am a new creation."
"I am a child of God...born of God."
"I was predestined to be adopted as God's child."
"I am God's workmanship, created in Christ Jesus to do good works which God prepared in advance for me to do."
"I am a son (or daughter) of God."
"I delight in you. My Soul is well pleased with you. You are My friend. Please accept My acceptance of you. It would give Me great joy."

Spend a few moments tasting this fruit. Listen. Is there anything you feel is blocking you from believing that you are acceptable to Jesus?

Getting to Know Jesus

Accepting Jesus means to accept all that his Holy Name includes. His acceptance of you and ultimately your own acceptance of yourself in Him are what you will explore in this Unit.

Under the tree, Jesus told you more about Himself. The more you know Jesus and "hang out" with Him the more you will become like Him.

Repeated below are the names revealed just now. Read this list out loud. Which of these names did you already know, really know about Jesus?

Exercise 1

"I know that Jesus is…"

- ☐ my Maker
- ☐ the Name Above All Names
- ☐ the Real Life
- ☐ the I Am
- ☐ the Lifter of my head
- ☐ the Son of God
- ☐ my Gift of God
- ☐ the Firstborn of the dead
- ☐ the Holy Child Jesus
- ☐ the last Adam
- ☐ the Sower of the Seeds
- ☐ the Son of the Father
- ☐ the Son of the Blessed
- ☐ the Chosen of God
- ☐ my Beloved
- ☐ the Most Blessed Forever
- ☐ a Lamb Without Blemish and Without Spot
- ☐ Him that was Valued
- ☐ the Only Begotten
- ☐ His Unspeakable Gift
- ☐ the Seed of the Woman
- ☐ Love

Exercise 2

What do these names reveal about the true nature of Jesus?

In the same way you get to know Jesus through His revealed names, you get to know His Father by the scriptural names given by God Himself.

GETTING TO KNOW GOD

Jesus is the full revelation of His Father. The following names or titles for God reveal how He is seen throughout scripture as producing the good fruit of Eternal Acceptance.

"My Name Is…"	"I Am…"	"I Create…"
Elah, Eloah—the Adorable One	Affirmation	A
Jehovah is His Name	Blessing	C
Abba "Daddy"	The Name	C
I AM WHO I AM	The Self-Existing One	E
the Lord God of your fathers	He that always was, always is and always will be	P
the Rock who begot you	Covenant	T
A Father to the Fatherless	Everloving	A
	Constant	N
	Unchanging	C
	Absolute	E
	Unchangeable	
	Lovingkindness	

Exercise 3

The divine names listed above describe attributes of God which help make the joy fruit of Eternal Acceptance possible. Which one name or characteristic from this list "speaks" to you? Re-read them aloud.

"My God is _____."

GETTING TO KNOW THE HOLY SPIRIT

The Holy Spirit is called:

the Spirit of the Lord (Jehovah)
the Spirit of the Lord God
the Spirit of Jesus Christ
the Spirit of Adoption
the Spirit of His Son

He is God's special agent and is sent to you on His behalf. As The Spirit, He is a Person with full personality—Heart, mind, and will, not encased in any physical body except yours, the believer. He baptizes the believer, welcoming you into the family of God, the Church.

Seeds of Faith

We love because he first loved us.
1 John 4:19

Psalm 68:5

Colossians 1:26

Isaiah 43:1

…because those who are led by the Spirit of God are sons of God. For you did not receive a spirit that makes you a slave again to fear, but you received the Spirit of sonship. And by him we cry, "Abba, Father." The Spirit himself testifies with our spirit that we are God's children.
Romans 8:14-16

They will still bear fruit in old age, they will stay fresh and green...
Psalm 92:14

Everyone who believes that Jesus is the Christ is born of God, and everyone who loves the father loves his child as well. 1 John 5:1

Day Two

Good Fruit: The Joy of Acceptance

Exercise 4

Directions
Put a check by every fruit that you have already received from Jesus.
Put an X next to the fruit that you still need to grow.

- ☐ Acceptance of my body
- ☐ My true self
- ☐ Humility
- ☐ Acceptance of Myself
- ☐ A new name
- ☐ Affirmation and Blessing
- ☐ Acceptance of my spirit
- ☐ The Desire to Worship
- ☐ Positive Self Care
- ☐ Friendship with Jesus
- ☐ Knowing how to pray in His Name

The fruit on the Tree of Life for this chapter is Eternal Acceptance. The blessed acceptance of the One who made you, frees you from all forms of pride, including arrogance and self-hatred.

Any personal religion that is self centered will eventually dry up like an old prune. A belief in a living God that is God centered stays fresh and vital. The first 10 units of this workbook are written to help the reader move from a self focused spirituality to a God focused one.

This joy fruit leads to the Christian virtue of self-acceptance, which ultimately is based not on you at all, but in the One who made you.

Good fruit: Acceptance by a Friend

If you have given your life to Jesus, accepted Him as Lord and Savior, then you are a "new creation." Say this, "I am a new creation."

Who created this new creation? God, of course, the Creator, your Maker.

Why a new creation? Because He knows you and knows much has happened in your life to hide the person, change the person, wound the person He meant you to be. His Son's blood, shed for you on the Cross, changes the believer.

Under the Lordship of Jesus and by His Saving (health-giving, wholeness-making) grace you are not who you were before Christ. You are changed! Your sins are annihilated and your heart washed clean—no more guilt and the pollution sin causes. (More in Unit 6.)

In union, connection and relationship with your Friend Jesus, you are totally acceptable to the Creator because He (Jesus) has made you that way! And this acceptance is for all Eternity!

As you met Jesus under the Tree of Life this time, He handed you this good fruit, His acceptance of you. Did you take it? Have you already taken a bite?

Having more of this good fruit grow in your life will do many things.
Good Fruit helps:

1. Remove self-doubt
2. Erase self-pity
3. Increase your authenticity and integrity
4. Empower you to accept others and the Christ in them.

God Draws out the True Person
God wants to draw out the true person in you, out of slavery and bondage to the past, just as Moses helped draw his people out of Egypt and brought them to the Promised Land. Your Promised Land is your true self, in union with Jesus. He wants your authentic self to be in a relationship with Him forever, joined with all other believers.

> Not that I have already obtained all this, or have already been made perfect, but I press on to take hold of that for which Christ Jesus took hold of me. Brothers, I do not consider myself yet to have taken hold of it. But one thing I do: Forgetting what is behind and straining toward what is ahead, I press on toward the goal to win the prize for which God has called me heavenward in Christ Jesus. (Philippians 3:12-14)

The "prize" that Paul refers to is the "real" me in Christ — made whole (healed) by His wounds, and alive with Jesus forever.

Seeds of Faith

Therefore, if anyone is in Christ, he is a new creation; the old has gone, the new has come!
2 Corinthians 5:17

John 15:14

Good Fruit: Becoming Your True Self

Then Jesus said to her, "Your sins are forgiven." The other guests began to say among themselves, "Who is this who even forgives sins?" Jesus said to the woman, "Your faith has saved you; go in peace."
Luke 7:48-50

Jesus knows who you really are. The Bible says in Psalm 139:13-14 that God "knit me together in my mother's womb" and that "I am fearfully and wonderfully made." He created you and has therefore a knowing of who you are supposed to be.

There are several examples in the Gospels of Jesus calling out the true person. One of these is a beautiful story in the Gospel of Luke, chapter seven, verses 36-50. Open your Bible now and read this story about His true love for you, His child.

In this story, you find Jesus being invited to have dinner at a Pharisee's home. Pharisees were devout Jews who followed the Law of Moses to the letter. As the men are having dinner, reclining on the floor as was the custom, a bizarre event takes place. A woman, who was a sinner, bursts through the door and comes straight to Jesus!

As she weeps, her tears fall on His feet and she leans down to wipe His feet with her hair. Then she begins to kiss His feet. If that's not enough, she takes an alabaster jar of precious perfume and rubs it all over His tear-cleansed feet!

Needless to say, this shocked the Pharisee and brought new doubts to his mind about Jesus and the company He kept. If Jesus really was a holy man, would he associate Himself with a sinner and allow her to touch Him? Of course not!

Jesus uses this circumstance to teach a powerful lesson on the forgiveness of sins and the love someone who has been forgiven much has for God. He did not embrace her sin. He forgave her sins. There is a difference. *"Then Jesus said to her, 'Your sins are forgiven.'"* (Luke 7:48). The beauty of this story is His total acceptance of this woman who had sinned.

Jesus knew that underneath the sinner was the real woman: the compassionate, generous, sacrificing, caring, loyal, honorable and worthy person. In Jesus' presence she became this "new" person and her tears of sorrow turned to tears of joy. "Jesus said to the woman, 'Your faith has saved you; go in peace.'" (Luke 7:50). She walked in with a life of bad fruit and exchanged all for peace, well-being, and self-acceptance; new, good fruit.

To become your true self, you may need to let your tears wash the feet of Jesus.

Create in me a clean heart, O God, . . .
Psalm 51:10

GOOD FRUIT: THE DESIRE TO WORSHIP

Jesus accepted the true person in her and through her faith in Him she could begin to accept herself in a powerful new way. Her transformation brought her to her knees and without saying a word, God saw the brokenness in her spirit and created in her a clean heart (Psalm 51). She worshipped Him and adored Him not because of what it might get her, but because this new acceptance created a desire to worship. Nothing could have kept her away. She became bold, ignoring social taboos, not letting what others would say or think stop her from seeking Jesus.

Exercise 5

Do you come to seek Jesus in the same way? Do you have that boldness? If not, what is blocking you?

For the woman in this Gospel reading, it was her sin as well as the low opinion she must have had of herself that was blocking her relationship to God. You can only imagine from the depth of her reaction that is recorded here, that her shame ran deep like roots of a tree, and that her heart was full of pain. As she realized just how far she had gone down the path away from God, the fear must have been unbearable. You can imagine the emptiness in the pit of her soul: empty relationships and empty connections that would bring no lasting joy.

The story implies that she seemed driven to seek the Lord, coming into a stranger's house where she was unwelcome. She seemed to know on a deep level the healing power of Jesus.

Jesus does not seem shocked by this display of adoration. He does not push her away or shame her in front of others. He is <u>gentle</u>, <u>merciful</u>, <u>tender</u>, <u>loving</u>, and <u>accepting</u>. He accepts her offerings and sacrifices willingly. He quickly puts the false piety of his host in sharp comparison to her true piety.

Seeds of Faith

Therefore, I urge you, brothers, in view of God's mercy, to offer your bodies as living sacrifices, holy and pleasing to God—this is your spiritual act of worship.
Romans 12:1

Seeds of Faith

Love and faithfulness meet together; righteousness and peace kiss each other. Psalm 85:10

Read Psalm 51

But you are a shield around me, O Lord; you bestow glory on me and lift up my head. Psalm 3:3

Then my head will be exalted above the enemies who surround me; at his tabernacle will I sacrifice with shouts of joy; I will sing and make music to the LORD. Psalm 27:6

She washes His feet with her tears, her first sacrificial offering and then anoints his feet with precious perfume, her thanksgiving offering. In return, He forgives her sins, washes her soul clean and anoints her new life with righteousness and peace. How much more can He do? And with His death on the Cross and the sinless blood poured out there, He made this gift of eternal atonement available to all of us. Alleluia!

Exercise 6

Can you see yourself in this woman's place? What would you bring to His feet? What is your sacrificial offering? Your sin? Your tears? Write about this in the space provided.

If this woman had spoken to Jesus, I wonder if she would have said words similar to David's plea in Psalm 51 for God's mercy and restoration. You can almost see David, face down on the floor (as this woman was) bearing a heavy load of sin and shame, seeking relief from the misery.

Housecleaning

As in David's psalm, this woman may have asked Jesus to create in her a clean heart, and to come into her soul and sweep away the hurt, the pain, the anguish and the sorrow. Then, once cleaned out, fill her spirit with all He has to offer: His joy, His love, His acceptance of her. This renewal of her soul and spirit makes her "right" again, able to come before the Lord's presence erect, standing, chin held high. Jesus is the "lifter of your head". Your shame draws you down. Jesus despises shame (Hebrews 12:2) and took it to the Cross. He lifts your eyes and your whole countenance up, calling you to worship!

Each person comes with their own precious vial of perfume to give Him tribute. Each of us has been given much, and I dare say been <u>forgiven</u> much. We want the Master's hand as this woman did, to heal, to restore, and to accept us.

Exercise 7

What is in your alabaster jar? Is it your gift of prayer, your gift of hospitality, your love of God's children, your ability to share His Word? Is it your faith, your hope, your compassion?

Exercise 8

Are you ready, as this woman was, to empty your alabaster jar, to sacrifice all?
- ☐ Yes
- ☐ Not yet

What is stopping you?

Exercise 9

What does Jesus want to give you in return?
- ☐ Peace
- ☐ Love
- ☐ Joy
- ☐ Other:

Are you ready to not care what others think of you?
- ☐ Yes
- ☐ Not yet - What is stopping you?

Seeds of Faith

Enter his gates with thanksgiving and his courts with praise... Psalm 100:4

Do not conform any longer to the pattern of this world, but be transformed by the renewing of your mind. Then you will be able to test and approve what God's will is--his good, pleasing and perfect will. Romans 12:2

Jesus replied: "Love the Lord your God with all your heart and with all your soul and with all your mind." Matthew 22:37

for they loved praise from men more than praise from God. John 12:43

Seeds of Faith

Accept one another, then, just as Christ accepted you, in order to bring praise to God.
Romans 15:7

Colossians 1:13

For we were all baptized by one Spirit into one body--whether Jews or Greeks, slave or free--and we were all given the one Spirit to drink.
1 Corinthians 12:13

1 Peter 1:4

When Christ, who is your life, appears, then you also will appear with him in glory.
Colossians 3:4

Ephesians 2:6

God, who has called you into fellowship with his Son Jesus Christ our Lord, is faithful.
1 Corinthians 1:9

I pray that as you read this book you will prayerfully consider the gifts you bring to the Lord's feet. Your greatest gift is yourself. It is completely acceptable to Him.

From this Gospel reading you see that this woman does not speak to her Lord. Like this woman of the city that desperately sought out Jesus of Nazareth, I remember all too well a time when I couldn't speak to Him. But I knew I needed Him. He willingly restored to me the joy of His salvation. He freely created in my soul a clean slate with new words written on it! He renewed within me a spirit that never again wants to be "cast away from His presence."

Like King David, I can say "my sin is ever before me," but unlike David I can say, "but by the grace of God and through His Son, my soul no longer has to act out of that sin, because I have been forgiven and my sins forgotten."

It is only when you become an overcomer, walking by the power that is the Holy Spirit that you can also say,

> "Restore to me the joy of your salvation and grant me a willing spirit, to sustain me. Then I will teach transgressors your ways, and sinners will turn back to you. Save me from bloodguilt, O God, the God who saves me, and my tongue will sing of your righteousness. O Lord, open my lips, and my mouth will declare your praise." Psalm 51:12-15

The woman of the city who opened her life to the Lord's touch, walked in with nothing and walked out with everything. It is the same for you and me!

Good Fruit: Self-Acceptance from Conception to Birth

What does Self-Acceptance mean? Where does it begin?

Acceptance means to be wanted and received just as I am. Acceptance begins at the moment of conception. But many people grow up in environments where they are not accepted for who they really are.

If you have felt unacceptable to yourself, God, or others, you need healing. Healing means to take out lies and put in God's Truth. Healing was one of Jesus' favorite things to do, then and now. I believe He can heal you of even your deepest hurts and the doubts about yourself. So, let's start at your beginning.

Ask the Lord to come along side your own story and when you are ready, say this healing prayer.

Dear Lord Jesus,

I invite You to come into my birth experience. I allow Your Holy Spirit to heal my soul of any ways from conception to birth that I need.

Jesus, come into my conception. I know that you knew me before this moment in time. You created me Lord. I accept your healing touch. Holy Spirit, walk through each month in the womb and touch all places that need healing. Replace all lies with truth. Give me the assurance I need that I was and am still wanted, loved, worthy and adequate. Tell me of my purpose in God's eyes. (Stop and hear Him.)

You placed in me gifts and talents. You made me unique, different, special. You gave me life. Help me to always choose life and to live my life in You.

Come into my earliest moments dear Lord, and restore my sense of self. Increase in me an awareness of my "being-ness," my "I am-ness." Allow me to feel the safety and gentleness all babies deserve.

Amen

Now, see yourself cradled in the arms of Jesus and let Him rock you, all the while telling you who you really are.

Seeds of Faith

By faith in the name of Jesus, this man whom you see and know was made strong. It is Jesus' name and the faith that comes through him that has given this complete healing to him, as you can all see.
Acts 3:16

May the words of my mouth and the meditation of my heart be pleasing in your sight, O Lord, my Rock and my Redeemer.
Psalm 19:14

Day Three

What's in a Name?

Around the time of your birth you were given a name. By your name you are known. What is the story of your name? Has it changed in your life time (through adoption, divorce, marriage, etc.)?

Exercise 10

Write what you know about your own name.

As you know, in many cultures, a name has a meaning — such as Running Deer or White Cloud. The name Kennedy or Stalin or Mao brings an immediate picture to mind.

When someone calls out your name, you might say, "Here I am!" Your name is how you are called, identified, and known.

God called out to Moses from the burning bush, "Moses, Moses!" And Moses said, "Here I am." (Exodus 3:4) Moses became aware that God "knew" him.

In the scriptures, God Himself was named and in Genesis 4:26 it says, "At that time men began to call on the name of the Lord." The Hebrews had many names for their God, the most significant being YHWH (pronounced Yahweh). The name Yahweh is mentioned over six thousand times in the Old Testament alone.

God told Moses from the burning bush, "I AM WHO I AM." (Exodus 3:14). God created all mankind beginning with the first Adam. He breathed life into the nostrils of Adam and continues to give the breath of heaven. He gives you your "I-am-ness," the full expression of your true self in Christ.

The peoples of the Old Testament knew that to use the name of the Lord was to call upon Him and all His power, love, wisdom and understanding. When Jesus came, He talked a lot about His name and the name of His Father.

Seeds of Faith

For where two or three come together in my name, there am I with them. Matt 18:20

The watchman opens the gate for him, and the sheep listen to his voice. He calls his own sheep by name and leads them out. John 10:3

My sheep listen to my voice; I know them, and they follow me. I give them eternal life, and they shall never perish; no one can snatch them out of my hand. John 10:27-28

I am the good shepherd; I know my sheep and my sheep know me... John 10:14

Yet to all who received him, to those who believed in his name, he gave the right to become children of God... John 1:12

"I tell you the truth," Jesus answered, "before Abraham was born, I am!" (John 8:58) He has eternal existence and is Yahweh.

Jesus said, "I have come in My Father's name . . ." (John 5:43).

When you received Jesus, His gift of salvation and Lordship, you received His name to use. You can call yourself a Christian and it can become the beginning of your new "I am" statement. Say, "I am a Christian." "I am His friend."

He has given you the "power of attorney" to use His name in your life. This is because His name is how you know Him, really know him. His name is Jesus Christ. His name also includes all aspects and all attributes that have been revealed to you about Him.

Jesus says in John 14:13-14, "And I will do whatever you ask in my name, so that the Son may bring glory to the Father. You may ask Me for anything in My name, and I will do it."

His name represents all His "I AM" statements, all that He is and all that He does. In the same way, my name presents (in Christ) all that "I am" and all that "I do."

Mathematically this equation reads:

Jesus + "I am" + "I do" = THE TRUE ME (my true, real, authentic self in Christ)

When a client seems lacking in a firm grasp of who they are, or what their true nature is, I will often ask them to go home and write their "I am" statement. The truly wounded ones usually come back with a short list, mostly negative.

Exercise 11 - My "I AM" Statement

Try this exercise now. Without thinking too hard, list below the extended names you would give yourself (Example: I am a woman, I am a mother, I am a friend, I am artistic, etc.). If there are "negative" labels you attach to yourself, record them here too (eg. fat, ugly, unworthy, etc.).

"I am . . ."

1.
2.
3.
4.
5.
6.
7.
8.
9.
10.

If you have trouble, ask a close friend to tell you what he or she sees in you. The list can include adjectives (cute, loveable, driven), the roles you have (son, teacher, priest), the identities you claim (Mrs. Tomkins, Mommy, etc.), your virtues (loyal, truthful, trustworthy, etc.), as well as your self-doubts.

Therefore God exalted him to the highest place and gave him the name that is above every name, that at the name of Jesus every knee should bow, in heaven and on earth and under the earth...
Philippians 2:9-10

John 12:20-33

And everyone who calls on the name of the Lord will be saved.
Acts 2:21

...Everyone who calls on the name of the Lord will be saved.
Romans 10:13

Isaiah 62:2-4

Exercise 12

"In my own eyes I am . . ." (Check all that apply.)	Frequently	Sometimes	Rarely
Lovable			
Wanted			
Adequate			
Worthy			
Special			
Important			
Precious			
Unique			
Gifted			
Talented			
Cherished			
Wonderful			
Acceptable			
Courageous			
Honest			
Victorious			
Other			

GOOD FRUIT: A CHANGED NAME

Our Lord Jesus knew the power of one's name. The identity He sees in you is not always the one you see. He sees beyond the words that others have cast on you and sees only the words He has lovingly given.

The most famous example of this was with His friendship to Mary Magdalene. It has been said that she had a rather shady reputation when she met Jesus. In fact, seven demons had to be cast out of her! I wonder which seven: fear, loneliness, torment, shame, unworthiness, depression, or possibly suicide?

It is also known that Mary loved her Lord and put herself in harm's way for Him, even after His crucifixion. Identifying herself openly with Him, she went to His tomb, only to find it empty. (John 20:11-18)

When Jesus spoke to her, He called her by name, "Mary, Mary . . ." It wasn't the old Mary, the woman she used to be that he called. He did not see her old life in her. He loved her and called forth the true Mary, the loveable, precious woman of great worth, the faithful servant, the beloved friend, and the leader. He had changed her name. Her name was still Mary, but she was a different Mary forever. She was the person God intended her to be! He does the same for you.

Exercise 13

How has God changed your name? Imagine Jesus calling out your name. Can you hear Him? What do you hear when He says your name?

"My child, _____, you are so precious to Me. I know that you no longer will be called . . ."

"Your new name is…"

Love,

Jesus

Now look back over your lists in Exercises 11 and 12. Ask God to tell you which words He applies to you.

Did He add any new ones to your list? In the days ahead listen and hear if He adds to your list in any way.

Acts 9:15

I will show him how much he must suffer for my name.
Acts 9:16

Seeds of Faith

I have been crucified with Christ and I no longer live, but Christ lives in me. The life I live in the body, I live by faith in the Son of God, who loved me and gave himself for me.
Galatians 2:20

Numbers 6:24-26

But these are written that you may believe that Jesus is the Christ, the Son of God, and that by believing you may have life in his name. John 20:31

Luke 10:20

Yes, and I ask you, loyal yokefellow, help these women who have contended at my side in the cause of the gospel, along with Clement and the rest of my fellow workers, whose names are in the book of life.
Philippians 4:3

Exercise 14

"In God's eyes I am:" (check all that apply)

- ☐ Lovable
- ☐ Wanted
- ☐ Adequate
- ☐ Worthy
- ☐ Special
- ☐ Important
- ☐ Precious
- ☐ Unique
- ☐ Gifted
- ☐ Talented
- ☐ Cherished
- ☐ Wonderful
- ☐ Acceptable
- ☐ Courageous
- ☐ Honest
- ☐ Victorious
- ☐ Other:

Gently "till the soil" and behold, as you shine the light of God's truth, He shows you what has been hidden there all the time!

The Bible says, as a believer, your name is written in the Lamb's Book of Life, and therefore you have a place in the City of God for all Eternity.

Exercise 15

Have some fun and write out here how your name might read in the Lamb's Book of Life (Example: "Allyson, Precious, Loved, Cherished, Tomkins"):

"In the Book of Life my name reads..."

GOOD FRUIT: PRAYING IN THE NAME OF JESUS

As mentioned earlier, the scriptures tell us that the name Jesus is yours to use. It is the "Name above all names."

At the beginning of each unit are the names of Jesus as revealed in Scripture. A shortened list is presented below:

I am *the Resurrection*.
I am *the Christ*.
I am *the Rock of Salvation*.
I am *the Way, the Truth and the Life*.
I am *your Sure Defense*.
I am *the Bread of Life*.
I am *the Alpha and the Omega*.

I am *the Lion of Judah*.
I am *the High Tower*.
I am *Righteousness*.
I am *the Lawgiver and Judge*.
I am *the Root and Offspring of Jesse*.
and on and on.

NOTE: *For more names of Jesus, see the meditation at the start of each unit.*

Just reading this list slowly and out loud will give you a sense of your multi-dimensional Messiah who is both human and divine.

Now here's the best news of all. He gives you permission to name drop any time you want. In fact, you give Him great pleasure by doing so. "...ask in my name . . ." John 14:13 means "Use my various qualities, dimensions, and attributes and wear them like a cloak over your own identity." This is one benefit of the New Covenant: using His Name.

In His kingdom, doors will open at the sound of His name. In your prayers, the throne room is accessible by His name. In His name, others are healed when you pray over them. His name (and all that it implies) pours through the believer's faith into the world around. The power is in His name, because it is all that He is.

In His Kingdom, I can say, "I am the daughter or son of the King and in His name . . ." Not for my gain or pride, but to His glory. This is the kind of authority that scares some Christians, especially if they do not know all the aspects of Jesus' name, do not understand the power of His name and do not feel a present day part of His intimate circle of friends (disciples) who healed the sick and performed miracles after His death. Don't let the power of His name frighten you. Let it move you to reverential awe, holy fear, and obedience and then claim its authority. It will give you joy and please your Father, too!

And I will do whatever you ask in my name,
so that the Son may bring glory to the Father.

John 14:13

GOOD FRUIT: AFFIRMATION AND BLESSING

As adults we have the awesome power and responsibility of blessing and affirming the children of the world. When a child has the sense that an adult is calling forth the true person, the "real me", that child has a better chance of thriving, of discovering true potentials and capacities that might otherwise remain hidden. They are blessed.

Exercise 16

Blessings come from words of approval, encouragement, praise, guidance, and truth. Have there been people in your life who have affirmed you, accepted you, encouraged you? Remember how that felt? Name a few of those people and what they did to affirm you.

Every child deserves to feel that special kind of love where they know they don't have to pretend to be something that they're not. They can just bask in the warmth and comfort of pure acceptance.

The fruit in this unit is Acceptance. You are asked to accept Jesus in His full identity just as He accepts you in yours. Open up your eyes and ears to know Jesus from Genesis to Revelation. Then open up your eyes and ears to accept who Jesus is creating you to be: His special treasure, His possession, His joy!

How do we as parents, teachers, or caregivers express this kind of relationship to children? Here are a few ways that are powerful, yet simple:

1. Use a child's name when you speak to them (not just when you're scolding).
2. Speak kindly (at least five times for every one scold).
3. Look at a child directly when you speak, especially when disciplining.
4. Look at a child directly when he or she speaks to you.
5. Get down on their level (sit on the floor, kneel down, etc.).
6. Say something positive, encouraging, and uplifting.
7. Agree with them; praise their ideas, dreams and plans.
8. Forgive them when they've done wrong (your last words should never be "Go in time out") - remember education is the goal of discipline. Help them see you aren't keeping a list of every wrongdoing.
9. Make a point of remembering things about them and tell them stories about themselves.
10. Laugh, play, be silly—your humor tells a child life is not always serious, and that it's ok to have His joy!

Can you think of any other ways to let the children in your life find the true person God meant them to be?

If we see our children as blank slates and we have the chalk and eraser, we forget that a greater power than ourselves created us all. He's the Creator and we are his creatures He created. A more accurate picture would have children as shiny enamel boards. Words would periodically appear that accurately describe the child. The parents' responsibility is to bless and affirm those words as truth.

Any false labels would be lovingly erased so that by early adulthood, the enamel board is filled with the person's "I am" statement. Our job is to co-parent with God, to call forth the precious child of wonder He meant for us all to become.

Seek your affirmation from Jesus. Then watch the good fruit of self-acceptance grow in your life and feed others with this delicious fruit.

Good Fruit: Humility

Humility comes from mistakes, not perfection. Humility is often the fruit born out of humiliation—being humbled by the loss of all pride.

It seems that the longer Mother Theresa served in God's Kingdom, the more humble she became. The more humble she became, the more Christ-like she was. She exalted Christ and in Him, she became exalted by the good fruit she produced.

The good fruit of humility comes not in your perfection but in your imperfection, weaknesses and failures. But, it doesn't mean to hide or put aside your strengths, gifts and talents either. Humility blends with integrity to form that aspect of Jesus that allowed Him to wash the disciples feet, touch the lepers, speak to street people and hang on a Cross.

You, too, are capable of humility. It is good fruit. I thank my own father for showing me this fruit. Anyone who knows Nelson Jones knows his self-sacrificing nature, his true, genuine generosity that comes often at his own expense of time, treasure or talent.

Now, let's look at some of the Bad Fruit that blocks the joy of acceptance in Christ Jesus.

For you did not receive a spirit that makes you a slave again to fear, but you received the Spirit of sonship. And by him we cry, "Abba, Father." Romans 8:15

He has showed you, O man, what is good. And what does the Lord require of you? To act justly and to love mercy and to walk humbly with your God. Micah 6:8

Day Four

Bad Fruit:

"For when we were controlled by the sinful nature, the sinful passions aroused by the law were at work in our bodies, so that we bore fruit for death." Romans 7:5

Exercise 17

Directions: Read over the list of bad fruits and check any that you need to have pruned in your life in order to grow the joy of eternal acceptance:

- ☐ A broken connection to your True Self
- ☐ Receiving false names
- ☐ Believing the curse
- ☐ Self Hatred
- ☐ Not accepting your body and appearance
- ☐ Wanting to change the unchangeable
- ☐ Self-doubt
- ☐ Alienation from God

Bad Fruit:
A Broken Connection to your True Self

The joy connection within ourselves is often referred to today as the "inner child." This is the part of ourselves that can feel joy, love and excitement, trust, openness, and eagerness to learn. It is also the part of us that gets hurt by all of life's painful experiences. "Walls" are built around this child in order to feel protected and safe, but those very protections can also keep out the joy or block it from being expressed.

I agree there is an aspect of my adult self that is "like a child." Jesus Himself mentions this part of us in Matthew 18:1-4.

> At that time the disciples came to Jesus and asked, 'Who is the greatest in the kingdom of heaven?' He called a little child and had him stand among them. And he said: 'I tell you the truth, unless you change and become like little children, you will never enter the kingdom of heaven. Therefore, whoever humbles himself like this child is the greatest in the kingdom of heaven.'

For many years I used "Inner Child Therapy" as a therapeutic technique with my clients. Teddy Bear in hand, we would spend time "dialoguing" with the "wounded" or abandoned child or its "critical" parent. All in all, many found relief from symptoms and maybe even deep healing.

Seeds of Faith

The earth will become desolate because of its inhabitants, and the result of their deeds. Micah 7:13

"Not only so, but we ourselves, who have the firstfruits of the Spirit, groan inwardly as we wait eagerly for our adoption as sons, the redemption of our bodies." Romans 8:23

I no longer use this method unless the client can bring the "hidden part" to Jesus for answers and truth. Of course, this takes an openness to hearing from Jesus about the past and about the self.

Even people who know little about Jesus but are open to Him, "hear" from Him. They only need "ears to hear." (Mark 4:9)

Jan's Story
A married woman in her early 40's came to therapy hoping to get over her debilitating depression. Two years before, after two healthy children, she had aborted her third child. The anguish over this act had plagued her for two years. She had stopped laughing, could barely get out of bed in the morning and had difficulty connecting with her sons, her husband, herself or anyone else. Spiritually bankrupt, her relationship with God was stagnant and suicide was a constant option. She believed that physical death would end her emotional pain. That, of course, was a great lie.

As we began to painfully unravel the events leading up to the abortion, she began to see how completely disconnected she had been at the time of the abortion from her true self. It wasn't until she began to connect with her pain and guilt that true healing could begin. She began to feel again and was slowly open to receiving the joy that Christ had to offer her in a personal relationship with Himself.

The connection to the true self and the God who created you is crucial to experience joy. If you are disconnected, you are like a lamp that is not plugged into the wall socket. You can try to turn on the lamp, but until the electricity can flow, all attempts will be futile at creating light.

All the therapy in the world and the best self-help books can't bring you into a joyful connection with your true self.

The connection to self is never enough. Therapies and treatment modalities will always leave you feeling incomplete. Using the lamp analogy, if the lamp is hooked up to a battery the lamp will only shine for a limited time. Jesus is the source! So plug Him in.

BAD FRUIT: RECEIVING FALSE NAMES

One of the biggest lies of all is the one that goes: "Sticks and stones may break my bones but words will never hurt me." Words do hurt. Words have power. Words can bless and words can curse. If left unguarded, the heart is defenseless against the power of words of criticism, shame, cruelty, insult, blame, rage or mockery. From the time you were conceived, you received the words of others and therefore may need to filter out the lies from the truth. We'll talk more about this in Unit Three.

Seeds of Faith

Surely you desire truth in the inner parts; you teach me wisdom in the inmost place.
Psalm 51:6

The tongue that brings healing is a tree of life, but a deceitful tongue crushes the spirit.
Proverbs 15:4

John 18:30

Exercise 18

What are the nicknames, the insulting remarks, the critical comments you have received that have caused pain and self-doubt? Make a list of those words below:

1.

2.

3.

Other

Exercise 19

Now look over this list. Did you receive (accept) any of them to be true? Do you still "feel" that way sometimes? Briefly describe how these words changed your name (who you really are).

BAD FRUIT: BELIEVING THE CURSE

"Curse" words are offensive in any culture. But "four-letter" words are not the only way to curse. Words like, "You're no good!" "You'll never amount to anything!" "You'll never be happy!" are another way words can be used to curse. A curse can linger for generations. There is not enough room here to give a complete understanding of the power of the curse. The point here is to examine the bad fruit that may be in your life from a curse. If you are aware of any curse on your life from the unloving thoughts, words or deeds of others, you will have an opportunity to ask the Lord to remove the effects at the end of this unit.

HEALING FROM THE MEMORY OF A PAST HURT

Exercise 20

Pick one memory of a painful experience where someone tried to "change your name" (exercises 18-19.) Write what happened here.

Exercise 21

What feelings do you have about this incident or painful experience?

Exercise 22

Ask Christ to come into the memory. What would He do? What would He say to you? To the other person(s)? Listen and then record His words and actions here.

Exercise 23

Today, when you have these same feelings (as in Exercise 21), they may be cues that something similar is blocking your joy. You have different choices now. What are some of the things you can do now to unblock your joy?

Exercise 24

Write in the space below the Lies from this memory: (example: "I must be unloveable.")

Lies	Truths
example: "I must be unloveable."	example: "I am the beloved."

Exercise 25

Now offer up the Lies to God and wait to hear His Truth and record one for every lie in the chart above.

Bad Fruit: Self-Hatred Blocks Self-Acceptance

> We were therefore buried with him through baptism into death in order that, just as Christ was raised from the dead through the glory of the Father, we too may live a new life. If we have been united with him like this in his death, we will certainly also be united with him in his resurrection. For we know that our old self was crucified with him so that the body of sin might be done away with, that we should no longer be slaves to sin—because anyone who has died has been freed from sin. Now if we died with Christ, we believe that we will also live with him. For we know that since Christ was raised from the dead, he cannot die again; death no longer has mastery over him. The death he died, he died to sin once for all; but the life he lives, he lives to God. In the same way, count yourselves dead to sin but alive to God in Christ Jesus.
>
> Romans 6:4-11

Unit 6 will discuss in detail the part sin plays in blocking good fruit from growing in your life. But for now, look at how the sin of self-hatred may be blocking your ability to accept yourself.

When you refuse to accept yourself, the self God created, you are pridefully saying, "You made a mistake in me, God. There is nothing in me that can possibly be acceptable to you. Therefore, I hate this creature you have created and reject it."

Exercise 26

Write below the thoughts, words, and deeds that are blocking your own acceptance of yourself.

Exercise 27

Do you need forgiveness? Do you need to forgive yourself? Do you need to forgive another? Do you need to forgive God? In the space below, write a letter to Jesus asking for His forgiveness and telling Him what you will do differently about the prideful sin of self-hatred you wrote about above.

Dear Jesus,

Amen

Bad Fruit: Not Accepting Your Body and Appearance

For many, looking in the mirror is an unpleasant experience. No matter that others may complement your hair, nose, figure, etc., you can't accept the complement. They bounce off and are not received as truth into the soul. Furthermore, any hope of true inner healing is blocked when your outward appearance is the main aspect of self focus.

In other words, "My eyes won't accept the outside self I see in the mirror. How can I ever accept the me on the inside?"

What is happening? A form of self-hatred is being practiced daily, almost like a ritual. "Good morning, face. I wish you weren't so ugly, Nose. Hips, couldn't you get a little smaller? Stomach, what is wrong with you? I hate the way you poke out! You know I'm so mad at all of you for not getting things under control here! You make me sick!!" and on and on.

Practicing the presence of the hated self is almost a form of worship, "worth - ship." These rejected or unacceptable parts become worthy of at least two or three minutes a day of concentrated hateful attention. This doesn't even count the other rituals of exercise programs, diets, deprivations, products bought, and time spent preparing the body to go out into the world.

Annette's Story: Battle Scars

Annette was born with a cleft palate and a hair lip. To date she has suffered through 23 surgeries on her face and she is only 23 years old.

A beautiful and extremely talented woman, Annette admitted in our first session to her self - loathing. Able to compensate, she exuded confidence, and she talked of wanting to be "an exceptional woman."

Her deep emotional wounds from the teasing she received as a child, of her parents' divorce when she was five and numerous experiences of people staring at her with unforgiving glares, culminated in "scar tissue" in the soul more pronounced than any on her face. Loving and supportive care by her mother and grandparents left a rich deposit of truth there as well. So the tension between the two parts of self, the unacceptable vs. the acceptable raged like a war.

This truly lovely young woman sorely needed to learn to accept herself. At the end of our first session I asked her to go home and journal about one question, "How would self - acceptance look on you?"

A week later this is what she reported:

"I filled the bath tub and lit several candles. I poured bath oils and perfumes into the water and locked the door. As I closed my eyes, I asked God to forgive me for all that I had said or thought about my body that was cruel or negative. I then touched each part of my body gently and asked for forgiveness for all I had said or done in hatred. I felt cleansed from the inside out and can now accept my body and appearance the way God does."

Seeds of Faith

Who has believed our message and to whom has the arm of the LORD been revealed? He grew up before him like a tender shoot, and like a root out of dry ground. He had no beauty or majesty to attract us to him, nothing in his appearance that we should desire him. He was despised and rejected by men, a man of sorrows, and familiar with suffering. Like one from whom men hide their faces he was despised, and we esteemed him not. (Isaiah 53:1-3)

Annette could only accept the aspects of her physical, outer appearance by forgiving those parts of herself that had caused her pain.

As she **touched** each part of her body and **spoke** words of forgiveness, she experienced a release of the pent up pain. A burden began to be lifted.

Forgiveness allowed her to:
1. Release the anger at her body
2. Receive each part of herself into the whole instead of casting off the unloved parts with hatred and shame.
3. Increase the patience with herself so that she could begin changing old habits and attitudes.

True inner healing could begin because the gatekeeper, the eyes, would now be more willing to let her go inside with the help of the Holy Spirit.

Annette's father left when she was at a critical stage of development. At around age five a child becomes aware of the reaction of others (outside the family) to her appearance. Her father was not there to help shield her, affirm her, counteract others' words with the blessing of his own. But even if he had been, the stinging words of her classmates probably would have entered into her soul and planted seeds of doubts. Ultimately, like all of us, she needed to come to God the Father for true affirmation and healing. (Leanne Payne, *Restoring the Christian Soul*)

Exercise 28

What would self-acceptance look like on you?

1. Start with your appearance and body. Find a private place where you can do this exercise, your shower, bathtub, your room, a place where you can lock the door.

2. Quietly, tell each part of your body that you forgive it for any problems, hurts, disappointments it has caused. End each part by adding " ... and I accept you just the way you are."

3. Even if the words sound awkward or you do not yet believe them, say them anyway. As you do this be aware of the negative words and attitudes which come up.

4. Gently tell yourself that these criticisms are not of God and ask Him to tell you the truth, His Truth. Listen to God's affirming Word.

5. Now, go "inside" and repeat these exercises about the inner self.

Exercise 29

It might help to pray this affirmation prayer:

> *Dear Heavenly Father,*
>
> *You made me, You formed me in my mother's womb. I come before You to ask Your help. I have been critical, sometimes cruel to myself, especially about my outward appearance. I bring all of my body to You and ask You to affirm me.*
>
> *I know You don't judge me by my _____ (mouth, nose, hips, weight, height, skin color, hair, complexion, handicap). Help me to accept the body You gave me and to break the vicious cycle of self-loathing, critical remarks and angry reactions. I need Your help to break my inner-dialogue of put-downs and unrealistic expectations. I confess the prideful way I reject the body You created, always coveting another.*
>
> *Lord, I know that when I come into Your Presence, all You see is the Christ in me. Help me to see myself as You see me, wholly acceptable, no part discarded. I forgive my (body part named) for causing me hurt and I release all of my (anger, hurt, pain, disappointment, expectations) to You, Lord. In return, I receive Your image of me, and who I really am.*
>
> *I renounce any unhealthy practices that I now use or have used to reach my own idealized body image (fad diets, starvation, bingeing and purging, laxatives, plastic surgeries, etc.) I confess all ways I have used my body which were sinful. I confess all ways I have been prideful (even by hating myself), and I ask Your forgiveness, Lord.*
>
> *Fill me with Your acceptance of me so that I may share Your glory. In Jesus' name I pray.*
>
> *Amen.*

Seeds of Faith

This is the day the LORD has made; let us rejoice and be glad in it.
Psalm 118:24

Do not work for food that spoils, but for food that endures to eternal life, which the Son of Man will give you. On him God the Father has placed his seal of approval.
John 6:27

Psalm 149:4

Appearances of Beauty

God does not necessarily value the same things humans value. What is beautiful to man may have no attraction to God. "The true beauty of Jesus was His willingness to suffer, and the true majesty was in His humility. Let's concentrate on making ourselves beautiful — to God." (*The Bible Reader's Companion* by Lawrence O. Richards, pg. 438, Victor Books, © 1991)

Remember, appearances are just that: an appearance.

> *The Lord does not look at the things man looks at.*
> *Man looks at the outward appearance, but the Lord looks at the heart.*
>
> 1 Samuel 16:7b

Oh, The Blood of Jesus

The accepted one in the Lord is often the hated one in the world. Just as Jesus is the Accepted One, the Lamb of Atonement, the perfect sacrifice, when you are in Him, you become acceptable to the only one that matters: God.

Read the story of Cain and Abel in Genesis 4. You will see the sharp contrast between Abel and the behavior and heart attitude of Cain, who hates his brother.

Abel's blood was shed by his own brother who could not accept him. Jesus' blood was shed by those who could not accept Him. But it is by His blood that you have been made holy and therefore acceptable in God's sight. So the inability of those in Jesus' life to accept Him brought forth the sweet fruit of your own eternal acceptance.

Exercise 30

Could the ways you are not being accepted by others bring a sacrifice to the Lord and produce good fruit for Him?

Take a minute to describe below an example of this in your own life. (e.g.—persecution has deepened your faith.)

BAD FRUIT:
WANTING TO CHANGE THE UNCHANGEABLE

Exercise 31 - Things I can't change

I find it hard to accept myself because of something to do with: (please describe)

1. My birth order:

2. My family:

3. My age:

4. My race:

5. My gender (male or female):

6. My nationality:

7. My mental status:

8. My emotional status:

9. My physical status:

10. Other:

These aspects of your life that you have no control over will continue to block the joy of self-acceptance until you are willing to accept them. God accepts these parts of who you are and is willing to help you do the same.

There may even be some usefulness to Him in these areas. Pick one troublesome area from the list above and reflect on how it is of use in God's kingdom (Example: You've been able to help others in this same situation.).

BAD FRUIT: SELF-DOUBTS

The belief that you are unacceptable to yourself, others, or God may come in the form of self-doubts. These doubts (fears) usually boil down to these:

"If the truth were known, deep down I am really..."

A Unworthy   C. Inadequate
B Unlovable   D. Un-wantable (my word)

These doubts may be labeled with adjectives like "dumb" "stupid" or "fat" but they all point to some perceived flaw.

Seeds of Faith

Colossians 3:9-11

For you have been born again, not of perishable seed, but of imperishable, through the living and enduring word of God.
1 Peter 1:23

Luke 9:20

Colossians 1:19-22

Colossians 1:28

Here's the key: these self-doubts are usually based on lies or false beliefs that trap the doubt in your very soul. They have nothing to do with God's point of view and are very dangerous to your spiritual health.

Exercise 32

Check all that you think apply to you.

I feel I am…	Frequently	Sometimes	Rarely
Unlovable			
Unworthy			
Inadequate			
Un-wantable			

Now take some time to ask Jesus to show you His truth about how lovable, worthy, adequate and wanted you are to Him.

BAD FRUIT: ALIENATION FROM GOD

When you are alienated (cut off, isolated, estranged) from God, it is harder to accept yourself or the strange notion that He could accept you. You are not able to see yourself the way He sees you, knows you, and understands you. The way you see yourself is as a by-product of Adam and Eve's sin. They foolishly distanced themselves from God. Do you do the same?

He loves you perfectly. Not that you are perfect. His love is. You love imperfectly – especially yourself.

So knowing and believing that you are "of God" gives you inner worth and acceptance. In Unit 11 you will strengthen this union with God, the source of all joy and learn to practice His presence daily rather than practice the presence of the unaccepted self.

Joy TRUTH — **God loves, accepts and wants you. He wants you to become just like His Son.**

SELF-ACCEPTANCE AND JOY

A   **Affirmation** is how you first learned to accept yourself. Affirmation can come in the form of a spoken "Blessing." God is the Affirmer. Receive His blessing. (James 4:10; John 5:19-47)

C   You are **Called** into your true self when Christ calls you into His salvation and brings you to fullness and completion (the perfection we all crave) which is what Paul means when he says ". . . and you are complete in Him . . ." (Colossians 2:10 *New King James Version*). Jesus accepts you for who He calls you to be and He will see you through to your completion.

C   Creatures created by the Creator. "But now, O Lord, You are our Father; We are the clay, and You our potter; and all we are the work of Your hand." (Isaiah 64:8 *New King James Version*) To not accept the self God created is to sin against Him who created you, a sin of self-hatred and pride. Once healed of self-hatred, creativity and all its joy can flow. (Leanne Payne, *Restoring the Christian Soul*)

E   **Everyone** needs to hear the good news of acceptance spoken through Jesus, whether or not you received a healthy acceptance from your early life. You bring your self to the Lord, and in unity with Him and Him living inside, you can come alive.

P   **Parents** are called to bless and affirm their children, particularly the father. If authority is handled appropriately, the child will (usually) respect and obey as well as receive the affirming word from the parent. Christ Himself needed the affirming word from His Father-"You are My Beloved Son, in whom I am well pleased." (Mark 1:11 *New King James Version*) At that moment He was called into life by His Parent and you can be, too.

T   **Truth**. You may Trust your five senses and your feelings to find the Truth but Jesus says in John 14:6, "I am the way, the truth, and the life ..." (*New King James Version*) "Show me Your ways, O Lord; Teach me Your paths. Lead me in Your truth and teach me, for You are the God of my salvation...." (Psalm 25:4-5 *New King James Version*) Jesus is the Truth. Look to Him for answers.

A   **Acceptance** of the true self and acceptance of Christ as Lord and Savior go hand in hand. It's hard to have one without the other. Inviting Him into your heart as Savior opens the door for the outpouring of His acceptance of you and therefore your own acceptance of Him in you. (Colossians 1:21-22)

N   Your **New** self is received at the time of being saved (or called into being by Jesus). Continual renewing happens as the new self takes dominion over your life "...and have put on the new self, which is being renewed in knowledge in the image of its Creator." (Colossians 3:10) Welcome the new you!

C   **Connection** to our Lord brings the gift of true joy. He wants you to find joy in the connection to your true self that is made whole by His blood. "...by his wounds you have been healed." (1 Peter 2:24) Let Him affirm you. Your faith in Him will allow His healing touch to flow unimpeded and bring you joy "unspeakable."

E   **Eternity** is the greatest gift of our Lord. We all seek joy and acceptance. Seek Him first and joy and self-acceptance will follow! "But seek first the kingdom of God and His righteousness, and all these things shall be added to you." (Matthew 6:33 *New King James Version*)

Day Five

GROWING GOOD FRUIT

Exercise 33

"The life skills I need to develop are…" (Check all that apply.)

- ☐ To see God as my Maker
- ☐ To see Jesus as God (Divine, All-loving)
- ☐ To receive from God
- ☐ To see the Christ in me
- ☐ To accept myself for who I really am
- ☐ To let my old self "die"
- ☐ To accept my limitations
- ☐ To allow myself to be known (intimate) by God
- ☐ To know the power of Jesus' name
- ☐ To be humble
- ☐ To listen to people who affirm my true self
- ☐ To accept compliments
- ☐ Other _____

Exercise 34

The three which would help me most to develop this fruit in my life are: (from the list above)
1. _____
2. _____
3. _____

Exercise 35

How would you or your life be different if you had these life skills?

Exercise 36 - Pulling Up Weeds

"Instead of the Life Skills I've just checked, I find I am…"	Frequently	Sometimes	Rarely
Arrogant			
Prideful			
Critical of self or others			
Perfectionistic			
Immature			
Flirtatious			
Extravagant			
Promiscuous (using sex to gain attention or approval)			
Self-centered			
Seeking attention			
A hermit			
Hateful of myself			
Avoiding others			
Using false selves			
Needing an audience			
Hating attention			
Doubting myself			
Low in self esteem			
Seeking approval			
Low in self worth			
Accepting all criticism as truth			
Unable to receive compliments			
Obsessed with weight, hair, nails, clothes, etc.			
Overusing flattery			
Unable to give compliments			
Self pitying			
Comparing myself to others			
Underachieving			
Using status symbols			
Unable to look someone in the eye			
Having unrealistic expectations of others			
Exaggerating			
Other:			

Exercise 37

Which one item of Exercise 36 gives you the most trouble, or causes the most pain and blocks joy in your life?

Exercise 38

Why? Please Explain.

Exercise 39

Now write a short prayer asking Jesus to help you remove this obstacle to your joy and your ability to fully accept both Him and yourself.

Dear Jesus,

I know you are my Gift of God. You are God's Only Begotten, His Unspeakable Gift. You are the Most Blessed Forever, the Son of the Father, and the Name Above All Names. You are Him that was Valued.

I want so much to join in your relationship with the Father, but there is so much about me I find unacceptable (name what you don't accept about yourself here):

At this time Lord, I ask You to remove any curse and its effects on my life. Remove the effects of anyone's words or actions. I offer You any sin of my own that is blocking my acceptance of myself in You.

    My prayer dear Jesus is:

Amen

Day Six

PREPARING THE SOIL OF THE SOUL: UPROOTING UNHOLY ROOTS

"Others, like seed sown on rocky places, hear the word and at once receive it with joy. But since they have no root, they last only a short time. When trouble or persecution comes because of the word, they quickly fall away." (Mark 4:16-17)

If you are planting a garden and the soil is rocky, what must you do? Remove the rocks. The seeds may try to take root and even succeed in growing for awhile, but if the soil is rocky, eventually the roots won't be able to get to the nourishment the plant needs and the plant will die. So initially, it looks like there will be fruit, but sadly there is no success.

Jesus says that these are the people who hear His word and "receive it with joy." It is such good news that the person can't help but feel the joy temporarily. But what happens?

I am a terrible gardener, I admit. I should never go near a nursery in the Spring. Flowers seduce me with their beauty, and each year I am tempted to give my garden one more try. I rush in, pick what looks good, never ask any questions of a real gardener, pull a few weeds and plop my new plants in the ground. I'm excited and anticipate a bed of wonder straight out of the magazines.

The first few days I water, I pull any new weeds that may threaten my masterpiece, and I watch and wait. Oh, by the way, I need to mention that my husband usually comes behind me and waters when I forget and does what he can with my best efforts. He also usually teases me, because he knows I did nothing to prepare the soil and he fears the worst.

You see, my eagerness to get to the result gets in my way every time. I "know" what a garden looks like so I seek the quickest way. But God gently reminds me, "...my thoughts are not your thoughts, neither are your ways my ways..." (Isaiah 55:8) He appreciates my efforts but waits patiently for me to seek His way. What is His way? Jesus knows exactly what kind of soil I am and what "rocks" are in the way. He wants to prepare my soil.

In the parable He says the problem is that the person "has no firm root in themselves but are only temporary."

What are you rooted or anchored in? What beliefs about yourself and the world do you hold on to like a root holds on to the soil?

Jesus has described a problem that fills the self-help book shelves. He could be describing any number of modern conditions, such as co-dependency, addictions, depression, etc. He is describing the condition of not knowing your true self and having one or more false selves (which have no firm root).

Jesus says the things which steal the joy from the "rocky soil" folks are: 1) the afflictions they encounter, and 2) persecution because of the Word. Then He warns they will fall away immediately from following Him.

Afflictions can be physical, mental or spiritual and can be chronic (long term) or acute (sudden). Being attacked because of what you believe or your adherence to what God is telling you is a very difficult challenge to any believer. To stand firm in what you believe requires deep roots, like a tree in a hurricane wind. He wants the roots to grow and for the soil itself to be more permanent (not temporary) for the seeds (His Word). If He desires that to happen, He must certainly have a way to remove rocks, right? Read on. The best is yet to come.

Firm Roots Produce Good Fruit

Do you have a "firm root in yourself?" If no, then God's Word will <u>feel</u> good and bring you joy temporarily, but Jesus says as soon as any trouble comes along, faith will "fall away." What does it take to have a "firm root" in yourself?

You need a strong sense of self-acceptance, a belief that you are <u>truly</u> lovable, deserving and adequate in Christ. This allows you to develop a soil rich enough so the Word of God can take root in you.

Exercise 40

Meditate for a while on the condition of your soil. Are you "rocky soil", are you "thorny", or are you "good soil?" Close your eyes and imagine yourself as a fruit tree in good, prepared soil. See yourself growing deep, strong roots.

Each unit will have a section for keeping your soil (soul) prepared for the planting of good seeds. This is the only way to grow Good Fruit. The Holy Spirit uses your roots to send you everything you need to grow good fruit.

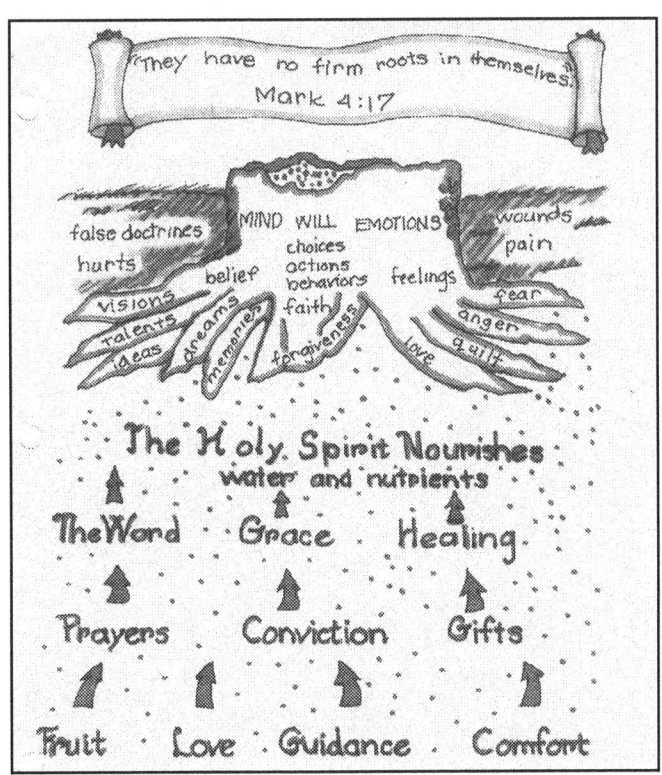

Day Seven

A Change of Heart

Exercise 41

Mark how your heart is changing. Check all that apply to you.

My Old Heart Was...	My New Heart Is...
Unaccepting	Accepting
Closed	Affirming
Un-affirming	Humble
Proud	Tender
Critical	God-fearing
Arrogant	Other
Other	Other
The Lord saw how great man's wickedness on the earth had become, and that every inclination of the thoughts of his heart was only evil all the time. Genesis 6:5	May the words of my mouth and the meditation of my heart be pleasing in your sight, O Lord, my rock and my Redeemer. Psalm 19:14

SOUL SEARCHING

As my soul is forever changed, it can begin to thrive in the fruit of self-acceptance in Christ.

As a result of the work I've done in this unit:

MIND
What new beliefs or thoughts do I have?

What old beliefs am I ready to put on God's altar?

WILL
What new choices have I made?

What old choices can I give to God?

EMOTIONS
My feelings have changed in the following way:

What feelings or emotions am I giving to the Lord?

Unit Three

The *Joy* of Eternal Truth:
Freedom from Lies, False Beliefs, Secrets, and Myths

    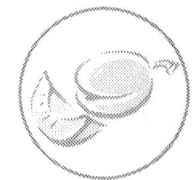 

Joy Choice # 3

Joy is choosing a life based on Jesus, the Truth, knowing I am being set free from the bondage of lies.

Jesus answered, 'I am the way and the truth and the life. No one comes to the Father except through me.'
John 14:6

"With a golden sash around his chest."

Revelation 1:13

"We need to bind the sash of truth more and more tightly around our loins. It is a golden sash, and so will be our richest ornament, and we greatly need it, for a heart that is not well braced up with the truth as it is in Jesus, and with fidelity which is wrought of the Spirit, will be easily entangled with the things of this life, and tripped by the snares of temptation. It is in vain that we possess the Scriptures unless we bind them around us like a sash, surrounding our entire nature, keeping each part of our character in order, and giving compactness to our whole person. If in heaven Jesus doesn't unbind the sash, much less may we upon earth. Stand, therefore, having your waist surrounded about with truth.!"

Morning and Evening, Charles H. Spurgeon, December 6

"To the Jews who had believed him, Jesus said, 'If you hold to my teaching, you are really my disciples.'"

John 8:31

Day One

You decide to go to the orchard near dusk as the sun is just about to set. Jesus has lit a small oil lamp and the warm glow from its fire draws you near.

Now that you have accepted Jesus and know that He accepts you, He reaches for another piece of fruit and says, "The third fruit on My tree is the fruit of Truth. So much of what blocks your joy now are the lies you hold onto and believe to be truths.

Again, let Me tell you who I am:

I am *the Light Of The World.*
I am *your Wisdom.*
I am *the Word of Life.*
I am *the True Witness.*
I am *a Man that has told you the Truth.*
I am *He who bears witness of Myself.*
I am *the Dayspring from on High.*
I am *your Everlasting Light.*
I am *a Light to lighten the Gentiles.*
I am *the Day Star.*
I am *the One who has the sharp two-edged sword.*

I am *the Light.*
I am *Faithful and True.*
I am *a Teacher From God.*
I am *the Light of Men.*
I am *the True Light.*
I am *a Great Light.*
I am *He that is True.*
I am *the Wisdom of God.*
I am *a Light Come into the World.*
I am *the Truth.*
I am *the Word of God.*

"If you eat of this fruit, you will come out of the darkness forever and into My light. I welcome you!"

"If you choose this fruit, you will truly be able to say, 'I am a child of light and not of darkness. I am the light of the world.'"

"Deep within you in your spirit is where I place my Truth. When you eat of this fruit, no lie can take hold there. Get to know Me, my child. I am the Truth."

Now you can say of yourself,

"I am a son of the light and son of the day. I do not belong to the night or to the darkness."

"I am qualified to share in the inheritance of the saints in the kingdom of light."

"I am rescued from the dominion of darkness and brought into the kingdom of the Son He loves…"

"Choose this day to live in the Truth."

Meditate for a few minutes on the words Jesus has spoken to you. Listen to whatever comes to mind that may be blocking you from receiving this fruit.

We know also that the Son of God has come and has given us understanding, so that we may know him who is true. And we are in him who is true-even in his Son Jesus Christ. He is the true God and eternal life.
1 John 5:20

Getting to Know Jesus

Exercise 1

Did Jesus reveal a new aspect of Himself to you under the tree? Reread the names revealed this time and ask yourself when and where you first knew Jesus in these ways. Check all names that you personally know.

"I know that Jesus is...."

- ☐ the Light Of The World
- ☐ my Wisdom
- ☐ the Word of Life
- ☐ the True Witness
- ☐ a Man that has told me the Truth
- ☐ He who bears witness of Himself
- ☐ the Dayspring from on High
- ☐ my Everlasting Light
- ☐ a Light to lighten the Gentiles
- ☐ the Day Star
- ☐ The One who has the sharp two-edged sword
- ☐ the Light
- ☐ The One who is Faithful and True
- ☐ a Teacher From God
- ☐ the Light of Men
- ☐ the True Light
- ☐ a Great Light
- ☐ He that is True
- ☐ the Wisdom of God
- ☐ A Light Come into the World
- ☐ the Truth
- ☐ the Word of God

When the Bible gives a revelation about Jesus, it is telling you about His very nature. These names separately and together teach you who Jesus is. They also tell you what He provides, and how you are to become more like Him.

He is saying He is the Truth and nothing but the Truth. Jesus wants you to have the joy of knowing the truth, as He is the Truth. (John 17:17)

Exercise 2

What do these names tell you about Jesus? Describe below what characteristics these names imply about Him:

GETTING TO KNOW GOD

The following names or titles for God reveal how He is seen throughout scripture as producing the good fruit of Eternal Truth.

"My Name Is..."	"I Am..."	"I Create..."
El Roi-the God who sees	Illumination	T
Lamp	Light	R
Father of Lights	Power	U
Sun	Authority	T
	Absolutes	H
	Wisdom	

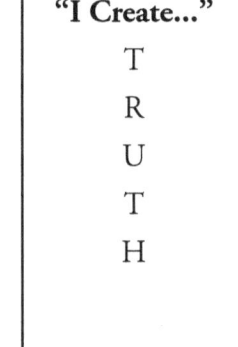

For who has known the mind of the Lord that he may instruct him? But we have the mind of Christ.
1 Corinthians 2:16

GETTING TO KNOW THE HOLY SPIRIT

The Holy Spirit is known as *the Spirit of Truth* who will teach all things. He lets you know who Jesus is. He lets you know the truth about yourself and others. The Holy Spirit wants to lead you to full awareness of your authentic, acceptable self.

He is the Spirit of wisdom and understanding. He is the Spirit of revelation and the Spirit of prophecy. He will instruct you and help you obey the truth.

The third fruit on the tree of life is Eternal Truth and its gift to you is freedom forever from all lies and false beliefs that have a stronghold over you. You have heard the scripture, "...the truth will set you free." (John 8:32). God loves you and wants you in the Light and so He sent the Light to you in the person of Jesus. The Bible says, "...in him there is no darkness at all." (1 John 1:5)

It is important that you meet this Christ of Light and Truth to have joy fully restored. You may have collected over the years a package of untruths which block out the Light and keep you in the dark. Let's take a closer look.

This is the one who came by water and blood-Jesus Christ. He did not come by water only, but by water and blood. And it is the Spirit who testifies, because the Spirit is the truth. For there are three that testify...
1 John 5:6-7

She is a tree of life to those who embrace her; those who lay hold of her will be blessed.
Proverbs 3:18

Genesis 3:22

Your word is a lamp to my feet and a light for my path.
Psalm 119:105

...a faith and knowledge resting on the hope of eternal life, which God, who does not lie, promised before the beginning of time... Titus 1:2

1 John 5:11-12

Day Two

GOOD FRUIT: THE JOY OF ETERNAL TRUTH

Exercise 3

Directions:
Put an X next to the fruit that you still need to grow.

Joy in Trials
- ☐ Protected Joy
- ☐ Abundant Joy
- ☐ Joy Received
- ☐ Comfortable with Joy
- ☐ Fearless Joy
- ☐ Open to Joy

A Lamp Unto My Feet
Jesus is the Truth. With the help of the sword of the Holy Spirit, this unit will cut truth from lie. First you will look at some common lies (false beliefs, myths) about joy itself. Then you will ask Him to help you discern any lies which are hidden in your soul that need to be brought into the light of truth.

Ancient and modern peoples have used the symbolic language of <u>light</u> for truth and <u>darkness</u> for lies. Christians believe that God's Word is a lamp and that Jesus Himself is the Light. Provided are the tools needed to walk the path of life. Join me in seeking God's truth. He wants you to grow this good fruit in the orchard of your heart.

"Send forth your light and your truth, let them guide me; let them bring me to your holy mountain, to the place where you dwell." (Psalm 43:3)

Absolute Truth
Our God is absolute and so it follows that His truths are absolute. Jesus is the "... way and the truth and the life." (John 14:6) As you walk into the Temple each day in your heart, you enter The Way and walk into The Truth in order to have The Life. As you approach the Holy of Holies, all falsehood must be burned as a sacrifice.

All lies must be left outside, as they will defile you. All myths, half-truths, jumbled truths, and false religions must be laid on the altar and burned away so you may enter into God's presence. His Holy Spirit along with His Great High Priest, Jesus, does everything to present you holy before your God.

The renewing of the mind (Romans 12:2) is necessary for the purification of the saints. You must allow your mind to be cleansed, a process that usually meets with great resistance. I'm not talking of other humans brainwashing you. It is the Holy Spirit, the River of Life, who gently and effectively "brain-washes" you of all un-truth. It is the Blood of Jesus, the Lamb, that cleanses and purifies all lies.

If you choose the joy of living in our Lord's Truth, then you must also allow Him to clean house. The best place to begin is by looking at common false beliefs about joy, and then allowing God's Truth to replace truth for lie.

Good Fruit: Joy in Trials

 **Joy is the same as happiness, and I don't have what it takes in my life right now to be happy. I don't feel happy so I don't have joy.**

Perhaps the most common misconception about joy is that it is dependent on circumstances and that it is a feeling somewhat equal to happiness.

Clearly the Bible contradicts this belief and in fact in the Kingdom of God on Earth, joy is in spite of circumstances or emotional status. Joy is not always related to happiness or good things happening to you.

Joy is what will carry you through horrific circumstances, trials and tribulations.

The definition of joy that explains this paradox is: Joy is the result of the vital union with Jesus Christ, a personal relationship with Him as my Lord and Savior. He is my all in all.

Therefore, if I am in joy, but am in a problem at the same time, because I am in Christ, I can therefore be free of anxiety, worry, or concern. Joy joins its cousins Peace and Hope and gives perfect freedom from any bondage.

The Joy Truth then is:

 **Joy is not the same as happiness or pleasure. I can be having tremendous trials in my life and still be full of joy. This can only happen in a vital relationship with Jesus.**

Seeds of Faith

John 16:13

Consider it pure joy, My brothers, whenever you face trials of many kinds...
James 1:2

For you know that it was not with perishable things such as silver or gold that you were redeemed from the empty way of life handed down to you from your forefathers, but with the precious blood of Christ, a lamb without blemish or defect.
1 Peter 1:18-19

Ephesians 6:14

Good Fruit: Protected Joy

 **Joy LIE** **Other people have the right to steal my joy from me, and to make me feel bad.**

Joy is a precious gift. A gift to be treasured, protected, and cherished. Your joy was bought with a great price, the sacrificial death of Jesus. You dare not take that for granted.

When, in your relationships with others, something happens which steals your happiness or any other good feeling, you get mad, hurt, scared, etc. But Jesus says no man steals your joy. He means no one steals your union with Him. You are one with Him and as a believer nothing can separate you from the love of Christ and God, His Father.

Emotions are not always based on the whole truth. They paint part of a picture, give it a tint or hue, but they are rarely the whole picture. In fact your emotions can outright lie! When you are controlled by your emotions you literally can not "see" the truth.

God will help you to see clearly and sort through your emotions if you let Him. Then the cloud or veil which temporarily concealed your joy is removed and you are restored.

Learn to protect your joy by managing your emotions, turning problems over to the Lord and stepping out of His way.

The Joy Truth looks something like this:

 **Joy TRUTH** **I am responsible for managing my emotions and not letting them control me. I have to protect my joy.**

Good Fruit: Abundant Joy

 **Joy LIE** **Too much joy in life is bad.**

I don't think I'll ever be able to comprehend all that Jesus is, all that He has to offer me and all that I mean to Him.

Jesus didn't almost die on the cross. He didn't sort of come to save me. He doesn't partially love me. He didn't half-heartedly send His Holy Spirit. He didn't kind of suffer for me. He did <u>all</u> of this <u>all</u> the way.

So why would He only partially, half-heartedly, or sort of give me joy?

No, He gives "full and complete" joy.

The problem isn't the giver or the gift...It's the receiver. If I am so busy trying to satisfy my own needs and desires, then I don't have time or space for the joy of Jesus (more in Unit Seven).

Now if this is a worthiness issue that is different. You see the crazy thing is you are <u>not</u> worthy and yet you get the joy as if you are! You get the gift meant for a King because you are His family and heir. To those born again, the joy is a family heirloom passed down for thousands of years.

The incompleteness you feel is part of God's plan to make you hunger and thirst for more, and not to be satisfied until you see Him face to face.

So the Joy Truth is:

True joy is what makes me full and complete. Jesus wants my joy to be complete. I can have His all.

Good Fruit: Receiving Joy

I am responsible for creating my own joy. I don't have any, therefore there must be something wrong with me.

This false belief says "I am able to take care of my needs. I'm self-reliant. I am the source of my own joy." In a pleasure seeking world it is easy to fall into the trap of thinking "I am god," the greatest lie of all.

The lie here is that I can make, buy, manipulate, build, develop, or control my life to such a degree that I don't need God or His Son to supply my joy.

With this mentality, a person will eventually run into a problem. What happens or who is responsible if there is no joy?

So this lie about joy eventually leads to an examination of life. Some will lead a fruitless search for the "What's wrong with me?" question, leading to even greater depression and despair.

Read the Gospel of John 15:1-17

Others will stumble on the Truth which is that true joy comes from accepting Jesus and accepting Him leads to an acceptance of yourself and that increases the joy that He has to offer.

Then He allows us to be co-creators of joy through participation in His Kingdom, giving to others, praising Him, thanking Him for His many blessings, etc.

The Joy Truth then is:

 **I don't create joy. Joy is a gift I choose to receive (accept). When I accept myself through Jesus Christ I can better receive (accept) His joy.**

Good Fruit: Comfortable Joy

 **When I feel joyful, I feel something bad is bound to happen, so I don't feel comfortable with joy.**

A common false belief is that the "other shoe will drop" or that "what goes up must come down." This thinking can spill into our beliefs about joy.

Some learn as children that they should never count on good things happening or happy endings. As adults, these folks carry that same belief into their attitude about life. The result: anxiety, cynicism, and negativity. Any hope is crushed for themselves and others as a way to fend off the hurt of disappointment. These are the folks who say, "Don't count on it." Their pessimism defends against future pain.

"Oh, I know I'll probably flunk that test." "I'm not going to get that job." "It will probably rain." They are the "Eyeores" of this world, the lovable character from Pooh Corner that waits for rejection and expects bad news. (*House at Pooh Corner*, by A.A. Milne)

Their discomfort with joy becomes a block to receiving the very thing they need the most. This all or nothing thinking can get in the way of their faith, their hope, and their joy.

So what is the Truth? That all of us go through seasons of joy and sorrow, bumpy roads and smooth paths, peaks and valleys. God gives to each a drink from the cup of sorrow and the cup of joy. No two people have the same journey or the same seasonal pattern. But we all share in the words of our Lord when He promised, "You too now have sorrow...but your sorrow will turn to joy."

 **The presence of joys and sorrows happens to everyone (even Christians)!**

Day Three

Good Fruit: Fearless Joy

 **I'm afraid, but I have no control over my own fears. Therefore I can't help it if my fears block my joy.**

All human beings experience human fear. It is one of our common bonds. Fear is mentioned throughout the Bible and one of God's persistent commands is to "fear not".

Many people suffer terribly with fear: fear of death; fear of intimacy; fear of failure; fear of rejection; fear of change; etc.

Fear is such a powerful emotional state that it can leak out of one's soul and affect the spirit. Paul reminds us: "For God did not give us a spirit of timidity, but a spirit of power, of love and of self-discipline." (2 Timothy 1:7)

Unit four will go into this in greater detail.

Remember, true joy is the result of your personal relationship with Jesus and is enabled to grow deeper as you go through the seasons of your life. When fear raises its ugly head you need to call on Him who conquered fear on your behalf. You need to choose which side you are on: Jesus or fear.

Then, when you get into the habit of choosing not to be afraid and putting your trust in Him, your joy will follow.

God is spirit, and his worshipers must worship in spirit and in truth.
John 4:24

The true light that gives light to every man was coming into the world.
John 1:9

So our Joy Truth statement reads:

I can choose not to be in fear at this moment and therefore not let my fears wipe away my joy. "...the joy of the Lord is your strength." Nehemiah 8:10

Good Fruit: Openness to Joy

Other people can feel joy, but not me. I feel destined to a life without joy.

These words were spoken to me by a woman named Carol. She had a very deprived childhood, one of the worst I have ever heard. There were no sources of joy offered to her. God had never been properly introduced to this chronically depressed person.

She had no "faith-story." She was so severely damaged in her soul that suicide was a constant thought.

She lived in constant fear and a state of "doom and gloom." She lived alone, had no friends and was cut off from her family.

Carol had so many "issues," but only one true need, the need to feel loved and accepted by the God who made her. Until her early woundedness could be healed by the Lord, she would not be able to experience true joy.

The "Catch-22" was that she had no openness to receiving the Good News. Her perceived undeservingness (unworthiness) blocked her at that time from entertaining such a message and therefore receiving the joy of the Lord.

If you are like Carol, I pray you will complete Unit 9. All of us have inner wounds and all of us need the healing touch of the Master's Hand.

The Joy Truth is:

Even I can be joyful. Jesus wants to heal those parts of me that can't accept His love. I am worth it!

Good Fruit: Anticipation of Joy

 **If I get too excited and anticipate the joy, then it won't happen the way I'd like it to and that will disappoint me. Disappointment hurts and I don't want to be hurt."**

The joy of anticipation is my childlike excitement of an upcoming event that allows my joy to build and allows me to feel it before it has even happened. Many Christians, for example, feel this way about the Second Coming of Christ. It hasn't happened yet, but it sure can bring joy!

One day, as we were walking along the beach, my husband shook his head and said, "Why do you always say, 'Oh, I can't wait until the whales come' or 'I can't wait until the baby's born.'" Suddenly, a young Gray whale jumped out of the water not more than twenty feet away from us! I thought my husband was going to jump in after him, he was so excited. The following year, I believe I heard him say, "Gee, I wonder when the whales are coming?"

You see, as a child he learned to hate surprises. He learned not to anticipate something positive, and then he wouldn't have to be let down. He learned it was best to just assume that nothing good was going to happen, and then he would never be disappointed. It was a great protection from feeling the pain of disappointment, but it also stopped him from feeling the joy of anticipation. Joy events actually became scary and something to be avoided. Christmas, birthdays, vacations, group gatherings of any kind, in fact, all events that might have a chance of bringing more joy were also risky, because it meant he might get hurt. Someone wouldn't come who said he would. The pain overrode the joy.

Too many children are being taught that exact same lesson today. "Don't get too excited." "Settle down." "Behave." "Don't wiggle." "Don't anticipate the positive." "Don't be optimistic." Instead, keep a steady, practical handle on your emotions and never let anyone know you are expecting to feel joy, especially in church!

 **Joy is not what hurts me. People can and will disappoint me. About true joy Jesus says, "... and no one will take away your joy." (John 16:22) No one can take Jesus away from me and He will not disappoint or hurt me ever!**

Seeds of Faith

3 John 1:4

For what is our hope, our joy, or the crown in which we will glory in the presence of our Lord Jesus when he comes? Is it not you? Indeed, you are our glory and joy.
1 Thessalonians 2:19-20

Go ahead, get a little excited about something . . . it can't hurt you.

Exercise 4

Can you remember a time when you anticipated something happening and felt joy, excitement, at just the thought?

Exercise 5

What happened?

Exercise 6

What did you learn from this experience?

The capacity to joyfully anticipate a coming event or the hope of a dream fulfilled signifies a person's ability to be connected to God's promises, and His ability to see you through. In other words, it is a reflection of your faith in Him. If you believe anything is possible through God, you can anticipate the gift of joy from Him. Even my dogs anticipate going for a walk, running in the surf, hiking in a field. They act differently as I grab the leash, the dog food bowl, or the flea spray! *"Everything is possible for him who believes."* (Mark 9:23)

Go ahead. Let joy happen!

Good Fruit: Discernment

 **I can't seem to tell who is lying to me and who is telling the truth. I'm destined to be trapped by evil people.**

Luke 10:21

Romans 16:19

The Holy Spirit is a generous giver of gifts. He knows what you need at the moment you need it. When you "walk" in the indwelling, infilling presence of the Holy Spirit, He directs you into the truth. He tells you in your spirit who and what is good or evil. This discernment is a gift and a fruit, as it grows in the life of a Christian. Call on Him for this gift and watch as it grows in the orchard of your heart.

Note on Spiritual Warfare
Satan is called the father of lies. In spiritual warfare, Christians must be prepared at all costs to pull out all lies, and combat them from returning. Some have such a tangled mat of lies that all light is blocked. The view is obscured. It is too dark and the person can't find their way out into the light alone.

The Holy Spirit brings the Light and the Truth of Jesus into the darkness and reveals the way out. Greater is He that is in us (Jesus) than he who is in the world (Satan.)

So, don't forget to invite the Holy Spirit every day into everything you do!!

---

1 John 5:7-8

You, dear children, are from God and have overcome them, because the one who is in you is greater than the one who is in the world.
1 John 4:4

 **The Holy Spirit tells us who and what is evil. By listening to Him, my joy is safe and so am I.**

Romans 16:20

John 8:44

You're Invited!

Holy Spirit, I invite you into my life today. Guide me throughout the day. Bring the Light and Truth of Jesus into my life and show me the way.

No good tree bears bad fruit, nor does a bad tree bear good fruit.
Luke 6:43

This is the verdict: Light has come into the world, but men loved darkness instead of light because their deeds were evil. Everyone who does evil hates the light, and will not come into the light for fear that his deeds will be exposed. But whoever lives by the truth comes into the light, so that it may be seen plainly that what he has done has been done through God."
John 3:19-21

Day Four

Bad Fruit

You belong to your father, the devil, and you want to carry out your father's desire. He was a murderer from the beginning, not holding to the truth, for there is no truth in him. When he lies, he speaks his native language, for he is a liar and the father of lies. (John 8:44)

Exercise 7

Directions: Read over the list of bad fruits and check any that you need to have pruned in your life in order to grow the joy of eternal truth:

☐ Secrets
☐ Obsessive Thoughts
☐ Confusion
☐ Deception and Lying

Bad Fruit: Secrets

 **I have a deep dark secret and I must never tell anyone, not even God. I must keep this secret even if it blocks my joy.**

A secret is a truth or a lie held inside, unspoken, like a seed in the dark soil. The seed germinates and something begins to grow, pushing up and out to the surface.

Stacy's Story
A young eleven year old girl is excited to board the Greyhound Bus. In five short hours she will be with her friend Stephanie at their cottage on a bay. Her parents wave good-bye, and she takes her seat.

The man takes the seat next to her and says nothing. The girl, in her anticipation of good things to come, dreamingly stares out the window. This is her first adventure away from her parents, alone.

Somewhere, in hour one, two, three, four or five the man begins to touch her. For an unremembered length of time his hands go where she knows they don't belong.

Her daydreams now become an escape, a place where he can't come. Somehow the place where her body is, is not the place where she has put her soul. By removing herself from the bus, this is not happening and therefore she has no feelings.

She leaves the bus . . . tells no one, not even her friend, Stephanie.

In that dreamy, distant place, an illusion of safety, a decision is made - "Tell no one." There is no discussion, or option. The secret is hers and hers alone. At least there is control over that.

Over the next twenty years the secret has pushed to the surface over and over. Unfortunately, not with the good fruit of relief and peace and healing, but with the bad fruit of shame, guilt and a twenty year history of promiscuous behavior and confusion in her sexuality and her relations with men.

The secret buried long ago has now spilled over into other areas of her life. When she gets back home, another five hour bus ride, her parents never notice that she has stopped talking to them. No one asks and she doesn't say a word. To say anything at all might open the trap door to the cellar which holds the secret and that must <u>never</u> happen.

By this time, one short week after the man touched her, she believes it is all her fault, her sin, her shame. The secret, which was the truth, that someone molested her had been colored by the lies; "it's my fault, I am bad, I am the one who did wrong."

In order to keep the secret in and others out of its hiding place, she must pretend all is well. So she becomes really good at pretending. She stops accepting herself, the true self God made her to be.

Her new "truth" is "I am unacceptable and I am bad." She can only relate to men who reflect this truth back to her and so it goes, on and on.

At 31, her therapist says, "You seem dead inside." She responds in anger, as if to scream, "No!", the real life in her (before the secret) comes to the surface, gasping for air. Supported by the trends in popular psychology, she goes on a search and rescue mission to recover that which seemed lost, her authentic self. Eventually, the healing process leads her back to the source of life itself and in her reconciliation with the Father, the secret is brought to the Light (Jesus) for <u>true</u> healing.

She finally allowed the secret to come out of hiding. Through the help of prayer counselors, she invited the Holy Spirit to shine His gentle light. The secret became the most precious possession she had to give to the Lord. Her dirty, ugly secret and the dirty ugly self that had grown out of it were washed clean and pure by the blood of Christ. He actually wanted her secret and gave her in return a "new self." Such a deal!

This is the message we have heard from him and declare to you: God is light; in him there is no darkness at all. If we claim to have fellowship with him yet walk in the darkness, we lie and do not live by the truth. But if we walk in the light, as he is in the light, we have fellowship with one another, and the blood of Jesus, his Son, purifies us from all sin.
1 John 1:5-7

Matthew 6:6

John 8:32

Surely you desire truth in the inner parts; you teach me wisdom in the inmost place. Psalm 51:6

Psalm 139:1

1 Thessalonians 5:4-5

Joy TRUTH

God knows our secrets and wants to heal us from the effects they have on us.

Not only that but all the "stuff" that was somehow connected to that secret. He took that too! The more He renewed her, the deeper her friendship with the Lord grew. The deeper her friendship grew, the greater her joy! The secret had almost destroyed her joy and her connection to the source of joy. Now joy was hers forever. What a trade-off!

Her willingness to allow the Holy Spirit to clean house grew as well. He alone knew the path for wholeness that her soul would take. Her surrender to Him meant that out of her could flow "rivers of water" to bring healing joy to others and living in the Truth and nothing but the Truth, so help her God!

"Whoever believes in me, as the Scripture has said, streams of living water will flow from within him." (John 7:38)

Healing of Secrets
What secret(s) lie hidden that you are aware of? Ask the Holy Spirit to shed the Light of Truth in those inner-most places where you have tucked a secret or two. As you invite Him into those hiding places, ask Him to reveal His truth and bring forth the lies to be discarded.

Exercise 8

Describe in the space below a secret:

Exercise 9

What lies grew out of this secret? Examples: "I am undeserving," "What I did is unforgivable."

Exercise 10

What truths does God give you to replace those lies? Examples: "I am worthy," "I am loveable," "I am forgiven."

Exercise 11

Write how this secret has affected the joy in your life.

Exercise 12

Are you willing to let this secret steal your joy again? Explain.

BAD FRUIT: OBSESSIVE THOUGHTS

Joy LIE: My thoughts have control over me and can steal my joy at random.

These thoughts so preoccupy your mind that very little if any joy can be felt. It is as if your joy were a young child that is trying to be seen, heard, or understood by an aloof or preoccupied parent. The child tries and tries and eventually gives up, goes away and sulks in a corner. That parent's mind is blocking out the power of the joy itself to rid you of any obsessions.

Seeds of Faith

Search me, O God, and know my heart; test me and know my anxious thoughts. See if there is any offensive way in me, and lead me in the way everlasting.
Psalm 139:23-24

2 Corinthians 10:5

2 Corinthians 10:5

Finally, brothers, whatever is true, whatever is noble, whatever is right, whatever is pure, whatever is lovely, whatever is admirable- if anything is excellent or praiseworthy-think about such things.
Philippians 4:8

Colossians 2:6-8

Colossians 3:9-10
Outside are the dogs, those who practice magic arts, the sexually immoral, the murderers, the idolaters and everyone who loves and practices falsehood.
Revelation 22:15

Ephesians 4:25

Proverbs 6:16-17

Revelation 21:27

It's another Catch-22. You need to stop obsessing to feel your joy's presence and let it grow. You need to feel joy sometimes just to stop the obsessions.

TRUTH — **Jesus can take every thought, even unwilling ones captive. He is the Master, not my thoughts. He can restore my joy, not me.**

BAD FRUIT: DECEPTION AND LYING

The bad fruit of lying and deception must be identified, whether in its subtle form of simple denial or in its most wicked form, pathological and purposeful. In early childhood, children begin to tell "fibs' or "white lies." The consequences teach them lying is just not worth it.

Once again in adolescence, lying and deception are used as the Will tries to assert itself. Again, hopefully, consequences put these tendencies in check.

As adults, there are no more excuses. The Holy Spirit will convict any lie in every attempt to keep us in the Truth. Probably more than any other bad fruit, this one must grieve the Holy Spirit and break our Father's heart.

Ask the Holy Spirit to shine the Light of Truth into areas of lying and deception. Then write below what He says:

Day Five

GROWING GOOD FRUIT

Exercise 14 - LIFESKILLS

"I need to become a person who is able..."

- ☐ To discern the truth
- ☐ To tell the truth (be a truth teller)
- ☐ To be accountable to another
- ☐ To be honest
- ☐ To seek advice
- ☐ To be straight with others
- ☐ To encourage others to be honest with you
- ☐ To have integrity
- ☐ To tell a dark secret when it is safe
- ☐ To accept the truth
- ☐ To ask for feedback

Exercise 15 - PULLING UP WEEDS

Without these life skills, you may have been compensating (making do or covering up) for not having this skill. Check all that apply.

"I sometimes use:"

- ☐ Lies
- ☐ Con artist tactics
- ☐ Distrust
- ☐ Deception
- ☐ Denial
- ☐ Manipulation
- ☐ Covert activities
- ☐ Cunning
- ☐ White lies
- ☐ Half truths
- ☐ Confusion
- ☐ Judgment
- ☐ Indecision
- ☐ Other: _____

Exercise 16

Pick three "Weeds" or characteristics from Exercise 15 which get in your way of living in the Truth.

_____
_____
_____

Exercise 17

"I would like to become more:"

- ☐ Discreet
- ☐ Accepting of the truth
- ☐ Able to receive feedback
- ☐ Honest with others
- ☐ Able to get rid of my secrets
- ☐ Trustworthy
- ☐ Persuasive with the truth
- ☐ Discerning good and evil
- ☐ Honest with myself
- ☐ Decisive
- ☐ Of a person who is strong in my convictions
- ☐ Other_____

Exercise 18

How would you honestly describe yourself?

"Others say I am:"

- ☐ Confused
- ☐ Judgmental
- ☐ Contentious
- ☐ Cunning
- ☐ Distrustful
- ☐ Deceitful
- ☐ Untrustworthy
- ☐ A liar
- ☐ Manipulative
- ☐ Indecisive
- ☐ Other: _____

Exercise 19

Which of these characteristics are you ready to ask the Holy Spirit to pluck out?

Day Six

PREPARING THE SOIL OF THE SOUL: UPROOTING UNHOLY ROOTS

As you have read in this unit, Jesus wants you to bear the good fruit of truth, His truth and your truth. Underneath most mental illness and psychopathology, most anxiety and depression are <u>lies</u>. Health means the lies have been uprooted from the soil of the soul and replaced with God's truth.

Exercise 20

Are there any "unholy roots" blocking the Truth in your life?

Examples might be:

- ☐ Lies of others
- ☐ Lies to yourself
- ☐ Lies about God
- ☐ False beliefs in any area
- ☐ Involvement in the occult (witchcraft, psychics, horoscopes, Ouiji boards, cults, sorcery, fortune telling, etc.)

Write about these unholy roots here:

So then, just as you received Christ Jesus as Lord, continue to live in him, rooted and built up in him, strengthened in the faith as you were taught, and overflowing with thankfulness.
Colossians 2:6-7

Seeds of Faith

He was assigned a grave with the wicked, and with the rich in his death, though he had done no violence, nor was any deceit in his mouth. Isaiah 53:9

Truthful lips endure forever, but a lying tongue lasts only a moment. Proverbs 12:19

The Lord detests lying lips, but he delights in men who are truthful. Proverbs 12:22

A false witness will not go unpunished, and he who pours out lies will not go free. Proverbs 19:5

What a man desires is unfailing love; better to be poor than a liar. Proverbs 19:22

Exercise 21

Offer to Jesus these unholy roots and help Him uproot them so that His seeds of Truth can flourish in your soul.

Dear Jesus,

You are the Light of the World. You are the Truth. You are my Wisdom and a Man who has told me the Truth.

I want to live each day in your truth and I reject the darkness. I need your help Lord.

There are lies, false beliefs and myths that shroud the eyes of my heart and prevent me from seeing your Truth: (name them)

My prayer dear Lord is:

Amen.

Day Seven

A CHANGE OF HEART

As we eat of the fruit of Truth and receive the joy of His Truth, Jesus continues to do a work in our spirit. He breaks us free of the bondage of lies and replaces those lies with the freedom of the Truth. Out with the old. In with the new.

Exercise 22

How is Jesus changing your heart? Mark the boxes that show your old and new heart.

My Old Heart Was	My New Heart Is
Deceitful	Wise
Confused	Discerning
Thieving	Truthful
Lying	Teachable
Deluded	Teaching
Slanderous	Honest
Wicked	Sincere
Other:	Other:
"...rebellion and treachery against the Lord, turning our backs on our God, fomenting oppression and revolt, uttering lies our hearts have conceived." Isaiah 59:13	"There is deceit in the hearts of those who plot evil, but joy for those who promote peace." Proverbs 12:20

Seeds of Faith

But the things that come out of the mouth come from the heart, and these make a man 'unclean.' For out of the heart come evil thoughts, murder, adultery, sexual immorality, theft, false testimony, slander. These are what make a man 'unclean'; but eating with unwashed hands does not make him 'unclean.'
Matthew 15:18-20

2 Corinthians 4:6

2 Corinthians 3:3

Soul Searching

As a result of the work I've done in this unit:

MIND
What new beliefs or thoughts do I have?

What old beliefs am I ready to put on God's altar?

WILL
What new choices have I made?

What old choices can I give to God?

EMOTIONS
My feelings have changed in the following way:

What feelings or emotions am I giving to the Lord?

Unit Four

  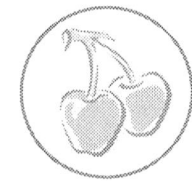   

The *Joy* of Eternal Security:
Freedom from Unholy Fear

  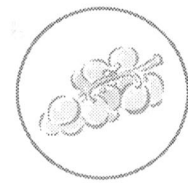   

Joy Choice # 4

Joy is choosing a life eternally secure, trusting in Jesus to cover and protect me.

The joy of the LORD is your strength.
Nehemiah 8:10

Be Not Afraid

"Trembling and bewildered, the women went out and fled from the tomb. They said nothing to anyone, because they were afraid."

Mark 16:8

When you forget your true identity as a beloved child of God, you lose your way in life. You become scared and start doing things, not freely, but because of fear. You find yourself preoccupied trying to please others and you lose your sense of yourself. You work hard to avoid rejection, or abandonment, or loneliness and you may cling to people and places more from fear than from freedom. Making compromises, you may please people but lose touch with your original blessing, the deep and everlasting love of God.

Jesus came to announce to you, "Do not be afraid. I have come that you may have life and have it more abundantly."

From Fear to Love, The Estate of Henri Nouwen, 1998

Day One

A cool breeze blows through the orchard and Jesus hands you His robe for a covering. As you relax, warmed in His presence, all the fears and worries of the day fade away.

Jesus reaches for another beautiful piece of fruit and says, "My fourth fruit is powerful and gentle at the same time. It is my gift of eternal Security and Protection. I promise that you will always be safe with Me. As you eat this fruit, I will reveal another part of Me:

I am *your Refuge from the Storm*.
I am *your Fortress*.
I am *your Sanctuary*.
I am *the Surety*.
I am *Jehovah, Mighty in Battle*.
I am *your Horn of Salvation*.
I am *the Power of God*.
I am *the Arm of the Lord*
I am *He who Opens and no one shuts,*
I am *He who Shuts and no one opens*

I am *the Strong Tower*.
I am *the Sure Foundation*.
I am *the Lion of the Tribe of Judah*.
I am *your Strong Rock*.
I am *your Deliverer*.
I am *your Shield*.
I am *the Rock Of All Ages*.
I am *the Chief Shepherd*."

"Eating of this fruit of Security, Safety and Protection, you will see Me as *the Chief Shepherd* and I will give you freedom from <u>all the fears in your life</u>. The enemy of your soul, who can never eat of this fruit, is jealous of you. But now you can forever say":

I am born of God and the evil one cannot touch me.
I am an enemy of the devil. and
I am now hidden with Christ in God.

"So, my child, do not fear for I am with you always!"

Sit for a minute in the safe embrace of the Lord and bask in the warmth of His protective, loving care.

Getting to Know Jesus

Jesus reveals Himself to each person in a unique way. What has He told you about Himself?

Exercise 1

Repeated below are the names Jesus revealed to you under the tree. Read them <u>aloud</u> and check those that are already familiar to you.

"I know that Jesus is…."
- ☐ my Refuge from the Storm.
- ☐ my Fortress.
- ☐ my Sanctuary.
- ☐ my Surety.
- ☐ Jehovah, Mighty in Battle.
- ☐ my Horn of Salvation.
- ☐ my Power of God.
- ☐ my Arm of the Lord.
- ☐ the One who opens and no one shuts.
- ☐ the One who shuts and no one opens.
- ☐ my Strong Tower.
- ☐ my Sure Foundation.
- ☐ my Lion of the Tribe of Judah.
- ☐ my Strong Rock.
- ☐ my Deliverer.
- ☐ my Shield.
- ☐ my Rock Of All Ages.
- ☐ my Chief Shepherd.

As you read this list, do you feel His strength? He is no wimp. Here is a man who is a strong protector. Here is Jesus as a hero, with might and power, standing on solid footing. He is the provider of safe, eternal security. So why be afraid?

Exercise 2

Describe below what these names tell you about Jesus. As you spend more time with Him, you will know Him in these ways. Pray that these aspects of His character will take root and grow good fruit in you, too.

GETTING TO KNOW GOD

The following names or titles for God reveal how He is seen throughout Scripture as producing the good fruit of Eternal Security.

"My Name Is…"	"I Am…:	"I Create…"
Jehovah-Rohi.	Strength	S
El.	Protection	E
Shepherd of Israel.	Stability	C
the Rock.	Permanent Shelter	U
a Sure Foundation.	A Hiding Place	R
Tower of the Flock.	Safety	I
the Shield of Help.	Asylum	T
Wall of Fire.	Promise	Y
the Lord Strength of Israel.	Deliverance	
Fortress.	Preservation	
Defense.	Faith	
Covert.	Assurance	
a Lion.	Impregnable	
Shield.	Indestructible Trust	
Deliverer.	A Secret Place	
High Tower.		
Refuge.		
Mighty One of Israel.		
Horn of my Salvation.		
the Mighty.		
the Great.		
Preserver of Men.		

GETTING TO KNOW THE HOLY SPIRIT

The Holy Spirit is the "free" Spirit. He is the Spirit of counsel and might. He makes you full of power and strengthens you from the inside out. He is the source of hope.

Let's take a look at the good fruit that Jesus wants you to have from the Tree of Life. It is through His might and power that you receive security.

He will be like a tree planted by the water that sends out its roots by the stream. It does not fear when heat comes; its leaves are always green. It has no worries in a year of drought and never fails to bear fruit.
Jeremiah 17:8

Day Two

Good Fruit: The Joy of Security

Exercise 3

Directions:
Put a check next to the good fruit you have already received from Jesus.
Put an X next to the fruit that you still need to grow.

- ☐ Protection
- ☐ Strength
- ☐ Refuge
- ☐ Freedom from Unholy Fear
- ☐ Safety
- ☐ Discernment
- ☐ Faith
- ☐ Trust
- ☐ Freedom from Anxiety/Worry

Good Fruit: Freedom From Unholy Fear

One of the greatest blocks to joy is fear. *God wants nothing to separate you from Him or His joy!* I repeat that God wants <u>nothing</u> to separate you from Him or His joy. Therefore, I contend that if you are ready to hand Him your fears, He will replace them with a special kind of joy which comes from His security.

One Hebrew word for fear, "yave" means "to revere," to have Holy Fear. You are called to have a holy, reverential awe for the Lord God your Maker. You are to bring Him your worship, your time, your very life. Anything else misses the mark (sin).

So what happens when you take your eyes off the target and begin to look elsewhere? You begin to look to yourself and others or to things for your security. What happens when those people, places or things let you down? You get frightened. What happens when you get scared? You seek security, protection, or a safe place.

Human Fear
Human Fear takes over and your ability to see God is diminished. Without God, you become even more frightened and on and on.

God created the creature "fear" to help you. He wanted you to fear Him with Holy Fear and have a healthy human fear of the things which might lead to your physical or spiritual death (a life without Him).

Adam and Eve had only Holy Fear, until the Fall. Then, with a broken fear, they hid in shame from God and dared not seek His presence. They now feared the very God that had made them, with a human fear instead of Holy Fear. We have been paying the price for this ever since!

The final word is in Ecclesiastes 12:13-14,

> Now all has been heard; here is the conclusion of the matter: Fear God and keep his commandments, for this is the whole duty of man. For God will bring every deed into judgment, including every hidden thing, whether it is good or evil.

True reverence toward God is shown by you in your obedience to Him. We will look at this more in Unit 6.

I remember the first *Joy Conference for Women* in 1994 was the most powerful experience I have ever had of the presence of a living God: One who knew me, and knew what I needed, but One who was expecting much of me, more than I thought I could possibly give. I did not sleep much that weekend. I was eight weeks pregnant and had constant morning sickness and bronchitis. But my insomnia was not a physical condition. I felt I was being "told" what to say and teach, which scriptures to reference, who needed special attention, and mostly that I was not in charge. This was His "show." I was humbled, humiliated, ashamed, awed, overjoyed, amazed, and most of all more afraid than I had ever felt in my life.

My friend Patty and I had the same due date. During the Conference, Patty began to miscarry. We prayed over her and the bleeding stopped. For the first time, I "knew" healing prayer, and the laying on of hands, worked, <u>really</u> worked. I also experienced that casual phrase in a not so casual way, "There but for the grace of God go I." I thank God neither of us miscarried. Our boys (born two weeks apart) are so precious, and I don't know what life would be like without them.

All weekend, I felt His presence and it was frightening to be that intimate with God.

For almost a year afterward, I pulled back. I felt depressed and separated from Jesus. I shut down intentionally. I was so scared. The second *Joy Conference* loomed ahead and whereas I knew I was supposed to "do it again," I quickly asked someone else to teach. The relief I felt was enormous. Now I wouldn't have to get so close, put myself or anyone else in danger, keep it safe, avoid the attacks. By then,

---

Seeds of Faith

2 Corinthians 4:6

2 Corinthians 3:3

But solid food is for the mature, who by constant use have trained themselves to distinguish good from evil.
Hebrews 5:14

So give your servant a discerning heart to govern your people and to distinguish between right and wrong. For who is able to govern this great people of yours?"
1 Kings 3:9

Do not be overcome by evil, but overcome evil with good.
Romans 12:21

the idea of inviting someone in to teach/lead the *Joy Conference* was set, and I was not going to say a word. I felt secure staying behind the scenes (hiding out) and even though I still didn't get any sleep at the Conference, I didn't feel God's presence as intently either. I know He was there. I saw His healing touch in people's lives. I saw Him using so many women for His purposes. But my "safety net" kept me at an arms length from Him. What a mistake!

Eventually, God showed me what I was up to. Then I prayed I would not be afraid to follow God's calling on my life, and that I would not allow my fear of Him to pull me away from His love for me. I allowed Jesus to be in charge.

He said, "Follow me, Allyson. Don't be afraid."

I prayed that I would have Holy Fear, full awe and reverence for God Almighty. I realized as Moses did, that I needed to tremble in His presence, take off my "shoes," my own covering, and come before Him on my knees, and <u>not</u> run away.

God wants union, <u>not</u> separation. So do I. My human fear registered danger in God's presence. I had to choose to over-ride that fear and ask Jesus to transform my fear into Holy Fear.

Do you have reverential fear of God? Does He ever cause you to tremble?

This fear will move you into action. It is not to permanently immobilize or freeze you as it did me. It is to get you to listen and hear what He has to say. Holy Fear draws you closer to a living God in a burning bush that speaks, even today.

GOOD FRUIT:
DISCERNMENT OF GOOD AND EVIL

Healthy human fear is aided by the Holy Spirit in the spiritual gift of discernment of good and evil. Evil exists. There are people, places and things that are evil. (*People of the Lie.*)

God wants us to avoid that which is evil and turn towards that which is good (of God). Our spirit seeks after the supernatural and can easily be drawn toward the dark, towards evil.

God wants to draw all men to Himself. He is Light and Truth. Therefore He equips you with all that is necessary to figure out good from evil. Evil is tricky, deceitful, sneaky, and can "con" the best of us. You need the Holy Spirit to advise you, guide you, and show you the way.

The Holy Spirit gives you the strength, if asked, to get away, flee, or avoid that which is not of God. He builds into you a capacity to be revolted, repulsed, or disgusted with evil. Likewise, God gives you the ability to be drawn to that which is lovely, pure, holy, and righteous... the characteristics of Jesus.

Satan wants to turn you around. He wants you to love that which is dangerous, scary, and horrible and loathe that which is good.

You are to avoid attaching or connecting to that which is evil. In order to grow this good fruit of security, you must mature in your decision-making to turn away from evil and focus on the good.

Good Fruit: Trust

What good news! Jesus is willing to protect you from harm, even from the evil one. To participate in the growing of this good fruit, you as a believer need to turn your fears over to Him. You need to hand Him all that you cherish, all that you desire. It involves trusting Him on the deepest level with all that matters to you.

Stop and ask Jesus to build up your trust in Him.

Day Three

Good Fruit: Freedom from Anxiety and Worry

Whatever you focus your thoughts on can slip into something you are worshipping. Jesus breaks this pattern of living out of Human Fear of God. He came so that you might be joined back with the Father and bring Him your sacrifice of praise and thanksgiving in Holy Fear (reverential awe) and bring Him a sacrifice of all of your human fears.

When you have this good fruit offered by the Lord, you can live each day, one at a time, choosing not to fret.

Exercise 4

In what ways do you revere with Holy Fear anything other than God? (**Key:** *Look at the impact fear has on your life especially in its forms of anxiety, obsessive thoughts, worry, and all other manifestations of fear.*) How much time and energy are you revering something other than God? Describe below.

Seeds of Faith

Finally, brothers, whatever is true, whatever is noble, whatever is right, whatever is pure, whatever is lovely, whatever is admirable—if anything is excellent or praiseworthy—think about such things.
Philippians 4:8

Humble yourselves, therefore, under God's mighty hand, that he may lift you up in due time. Cast all your anxiety on him because he cares for you.
1 Peter 5:6-7

Psalm 37:3-5

We demolish arguments and every pretension that sets itself up against the knowledge of God, and we take captive every thought to make it obedient to Christ.
2 Corinthians 10:5

Exercise 5

> *Dear Jesus,*
>
> *I will no longer spend hours and hours in worry. My time devoted to worry can be like a form of worship. I am basically saying, "This thing I am worried about is worthy of worship." (my time and thoughts focused on something).*
>
> *I will no longer let anxiety control my thoughts. I will let You "take captive every thought" (2 Corinthians. 10:5). I will be open to Your help in managing my thought life as You are in the process of renewing my mind.*
>
> *I will no longer let the emotion fear rule my day. I will be willing to let You be the one in charge of my emotions and with Your help, fear will not run my life.*
>
> *Because I renounce fear's impact on my time, my emotions and my mind, I am now able, with God's help, to live a life of freedom. I choose in my will to turn my life over to You, Jesus, and give You all my reverence, all my worship, all my thoughts, and all of my time to be under Your authority. In exchange, please give me Your perfect freedom.*
>
> *Through Your perfect love, Jesus, all fear is driven out (1 John 4:18), and all of its influence over my life is removed forever!*
>
> *Amen*

GOOD FRUIT: HEALTHY FEAR

God knows you will have fears. Fear is a creature that He made. Your fears can at times keep you safe. A healthy fear of danger keeps me from taking risks that are foolish. A healthy fear keeps me from going too fast in my car, for example. Holy Fear, as you've already learned, keeps you in reverence to God.

As it is His desire always to restore to health, I believe you can pray for His help with combating fear and all its forms that are destructive.

GOOD FRUIT: FREEDOM IN CAPTIVITY

The world says, "I am free and no one has an authority over me that I do not give them." True freedom for a Christian is to be a slave to Christ.

As I watched the return of the hostages who had been held in captivity in Lebanon for five or six years, it brought tears of joy to my eyes. There is nothing more joyful than the freeing of a captive who is now able to get back to life.

The hostages were interviewed upon their release and it was interesting to note what had kept them sane during their ordeal. Most spoke of keeping the memories alive of their loved ones (joy connections), the joy of reading found in books (connections to beauty, nature, others), and a spiritual connection that bound the men to something higher than their physical bodies. Joy Connections kept them alive and their spirits uplifted.

Exercise 6

Have there been times when you felt you were "being held captive", for example, in a relationship or a job or by fears? Describe one of those situations below.

What did it feel like when that "captivity" ended? Did you eventually feel joy?

Now that you have seen some of the god fruit of Eternal Security God wants to grow in your life, let's turn once again to see if there is any bad fruit needing pruning.

Seeds of Faith

You were bought at a price; do not become slaves of men.
1 Corinthians 7:23

Day Four

Bad Fruit

Exercise 7

Directions: Read over the list of bad fruits and check any that you need to have pruned in your life in order to grow the joy of eternal security, safety

- ☐ Worry
- ☐ Stress
- ☐ Phobias
- ☐ Deprivation
- ☐ Unholy Fear
- ☐ Anxiety
- ☐ Obsessions

Bad Fruit:
Allowing Satan to Stir Up the Fears.

1. As already discussed, Satan loves to steal your joy. His demonic forces will go to work when you have even the promise of true joy coming your way.

2. As you have also seen, God wants you to experience His joy.

If you combine these two basic premises, what you have is a formula for us to guard against the schemes of the evil one.

Let me explain through a personal story. My heart's desire for most of my life was to be a mother. God answered my prayer when I was 36 with a beautiful bundle of joy named Kelsey. My husband and I went through all the infertility procedures and like Elizabeth and Zechariah, we received the fulfillment of our dream. Kelsey's conception, however, was tinged with a combination of fear and hope.

I noticed during the pregnancy, especially in times of stress or physical trouble, my fears would escalate. "What if I lost the baby...or my marriage...or....?" I agonized over potential losses and spent many moments in anguish. At the same time, my husband was going through his own torment. He had lost his father at an early age and the thought terrified him of losing me or the baby. He began to pull away, disconnect from our relationship, increasing my fear of having to raise this precious child on my own. I feared his abandonment in life as he feared mine through death.

Seeds of Faith

Make a tree good and its fruit will be good, or make a tree bad and its fruit will be bad, for a tree is recognized by its fruit.
Matthew 12:33

I will never know the impact of all this fear on my daughter. I do know that at age six she tearfully shared a deep fear which came as no surprise. She feared her father and I would divorce, something which she had never heard us discuss except when she was in my womb. I have often prayed that there be a deep inner healing for her over the circumstances of her earliest days. (For more information regarding in utero prayer see Francis & Judith McNutt's book, *Praying for Your Unborn Child*. Robert DeGrandis also touches on this in his books, i.e., *Healing The Father Relationships* and *Intergenerational Healing*.) Through God's grace my husband and I were able to work through our fears and He secured our marriage.

Needless to say, Kelsey is a true joy connection, as is my second child, James, born four years later. As I was nursing Kelsey, especially late at night after very little sleep, I would ruminate about all the catastrophes that could happen. My exhaustion (as all new mothers know) made me almost delirious at times, and I could scarcely keep the fears at bay. Like a pack of wild dogs nipping at my feet, I'd knock one down only to find another in its place.

The Domino Effect
I see now that Satan and all his forces knew that he could easily steal the joy right out from under me by stirring up these fears. He knew that my joy connection to my children is so precious to me that losing them would create havoc and a great domino effect. Ultimately, I might give up on God as so many grieving parents do when the worst happens and their child dies or their marriages fail or other worst fears materialize.

Many marriages fall apart when something happens to a child. Again, Satan loves to destroy marriages, families, lives and most of all our connection to God, His Son, and His Holy Spirit.

You know you have a joy connection, even if it's an unhealthy one, if the thought of losing that person, place or thing brings great fear to your spirit. What does scripture say about this?

In Luke, Chapter 14, verse 26 , Jesus says, "If anyone comes to Me, and does not hate his father and mother, his wife and children, his brothers and sisters-yes, even his own life-he cannot be my disciple." If taken out of context, this verse could itself bring great fear because at first glance you can hear our Lord asking you to give up all your most precious relationships in order to be His disciple.

But put into its right context, Jesus is clarifying your priorities, not creating exclusive parameters which put back into context would make no sense. He wants you to be whole and live in healthy relationships: have a good marriage, strong friendships, or be an excellent parent. But He wants to be first, Lord over all.

Jesus continues in verse 33, saying, "In the same way, any of you who does not give up everything he has cannot be my disciple." Another tough message. Does He want me to get rid of everything, family, house, job, church, friends and walk away? The tough answer is, sometimes, "Yes." There have been many faithful saints who have heard God's call to do just that to serve Him. But for all of us, I believe He is saying, "Can you commit your life and every attachment you have made to Me? Can you put them all at my feet and walk away? Can you do as Abraham did with Isaac, and place your loved ones on My altar, willing to give them fully to Me?"

Luke 12:22-32

Serve the LORD with fear and rejoice with trembling.
Psalm 2:11

Finally, be strong in the Lord and in his mighty power.
Ephesians 6:10

The LORD is my shepherd, I shall not be in want. He makes me lie down in green pastures, he leads me beside quiet waters, he restores my soul. He guides me in paths of righteousness for his name's sake. Even though I walk through the valley of the shadow of death, I will fear no evil, for you are with me; your rod and your staff, they comfort me. You prepare a table before me in the presence of my enemies. You anoint my head with oil; my cup overflows. Surely goodness and love will follow me all the days of my life, and I will dwell in the house of the LORD forever.
Psalm 23

In Genesis, Chapter 22, verse 2 you see the greatest test Abraham ever faced. God tells him to sacrifice his son! God had promised Abraham he would have descendants and Abraham had fully trusted in God's promise. Now God was going to see if His servant loved Him more than his own son, Isaac. Abraham was obedient and God was faithful in providing a substitute sacrifice, a ram caught in the bushes.

This story is rich in personal application. In it you see a person of strong faith, trusting in God and loving Him above everything. Can I do that? I must if I am to grow Good Fruit pleasing to God.

Exercise 8

What do you need to hand to God? What is your greatest fear? The answer lies in that. Look closely. Spend a few minutes reflecting on this and journal here if you wish. (Note: If your fear involves losing something or someone, make a list of the losses you fear. When you're done, see if this is also a list of your needs and attachments.)

Exercise 9

Now, offer up in prayer all that you've just written and place it in the waiting hands of Jesus.

Bad Fruit:
Playing Hide and Seek with God

What is your hiding place? King David proclaimed that his hiding place, his protection, his covering was the Lord.

> ***You are my hiding place;***
> ***you will protect me from trouble***
> ***and surround me with songs of deliverance.***
>
> Psalm 32:7

We all have hiding places. Small children squeal as they play hide and seek. As we grow older, our hide and seek games change. We find new hiding places and hope that someone will come and find us or pray that no one will come and look.

Nothing in all creation is hidden from God's sight. Everything is uncovered and laid bare before the eyes of him to whom we must give account. (Hebrews 4:13)

What is your hiding place? Shopping, busy work, controlling others, reading, shyness, a bubbly personality, good works, the computer? The list could go on and on.

Exercise 10

Write about your favorite hiding places here:

Exercise 11

What or who are you hiding from? Why?

Seeds of Faith

There is no fear of God before their eyes.
Romans 3:18

Serve the LORD with fear and rejoice with trembling. Kiss the Son, lest he be angry and you be destroyed in your way, for his wrath can flare up in a moment. Blessed are all who take refuge in him.
Psalm 2:11-12

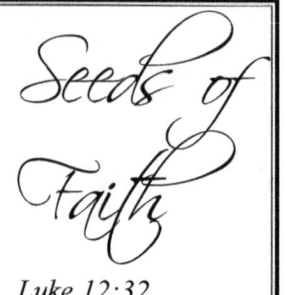

Luke 12:32

Luke 12:29

Therefore do not worry about tomorrow, for tomorrow will worry about itself. Each day has enough trouble of its own.
  Matthew 6:34

Cast all your anxiety on him because he cares for you."
  1 Peter 5:7

Bad Fruit: Worry and Anxiety

Security, Safety, Protection—all good fruit—come from God. This doesn't mean, however, that you won't have problems.

 **Joyful Christian folks don't have problems.**

Usually, quite the opposite is true. The difference is how you approach a problem in your life and the beliefs that you hold to be true.

"Consider it pure joy, my brothers, whenever you face trials of many kinds, because you know that the testing of your faith develops perseverance." (James 1:2-3)

Fear is one of the major roadblocks in your journey to joy and it is important to identify those roadblocks so that you can remove them.

Exercise 12

What are the fears in your life that are blocking your joy?
- ☐ Losing something dear to me
- ☐ Hurting someone else
- ☐ Not being loved for who I am
- ☐ Not having enough
- ☐ Not succeeding, etc
- ☐ Losing someone
- ☐ Not being adequate
- ☐ Not being worthy
- ☐ Not being loveable
- ☐ Not being wanted
- ☐ Other_____

Exercise 13

How much of the time do you spend in fear (worried, afraid, or concerned)?
- ☐ None of the time
- ☐ Some of the time
- ☐ Most of the time
- ☐ All of the time

Exercise 14

Does fear cause more problems in your life? Which area?
- ☐ Physical symptoms
- ☐ Emotional problems
- ☐ Relationship problems
- ☐ Work related problems
- ☐ School related problems
- ☐ Spiritual related problems
- ☐ Other_____

Exercise 15

Please explain:

Exercise 16

Make a choice today to take fear out of the center of your life and ask Jesus to stand there. Listen and He will tell you what other choices He wants you to make in each life area.

Directions: Look at these two circles and meditate for a while on the difference.

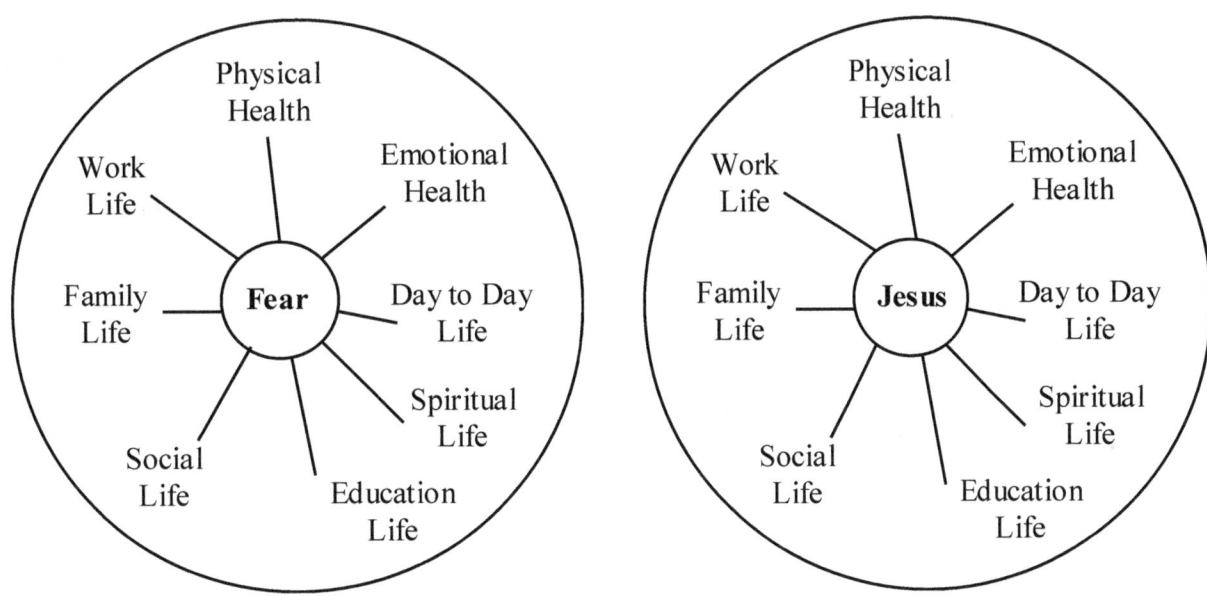

Therefore I tell you, do not worry about your life . . .
Matthew 6:25

The Lord is near. Do not be anxious about anything but in everything by prayer and petition with thanksgiving present your requests to God.
Philippians 4:5-6

BAD FRUIT: OBSESSIONS AND COMPULSIONS

Are you thinking more about a person, place or thing than you do about God, Jesus or His Holy Spirit?

Obsessions are recurring thoughts that become a controlling factor in day to day living. The thoughts repeat themselves and seem to take ownership over the thought world.

Sometimes they speed like an out of control train, racing across the mind. Sometimes they occur almost quietly, popping up when least expected or wanted.

Obsessions become Bad Fruit on our Tree of Life and can be a major roadblock to receiving God's joy.

They can become paired with an equally troublesome Bad Fruit called compulsions: the action or behavior to relieve the obsession. Carried to extremes, lives are severely damaged if not destroyed by habits, rituals and patterns that can dominate and cripple.

BAD FRUIT: PHOBIAS

Our word phobic (to be in great fear of, as to avoid) comes from the Greek "phobes" which means "to be in awe of, i.e., to revere." (*Strongs Complete Dictionary*) When a fear turns into a phobia, the person is consumed by the fear and cannot seem to break its hold over his or her life. Psychiatrists would say that this is the result of the person displacing their normal (healthy) fear or revulsion toward one thing onto something else. It is a defense, a protective device against that fear or revulsion. A hiding place.

In a strange way, this can become an idolatrous relationship between the person and the phobia, because it often does separate the person from God. When anything becomes central to our lives other than God, we are in danger of idolatry. This is true even of fears.

Our help is in the Lord. He is The Mountain Refuge, our Hiding Place, our Sure Foundation. In His Name is eternal security and by His Holy Name all fear trembles.

Exercise 17

Do you have phobic reactions to certain people, places, and things? Describe them here:

BAD FRUIT:
JOY-BLOCKING FEAR: (GOD WON'T ANSWER MY PRAYERS)

But the angel said to him: "Do not be afraid, Zechariah; your prayer has been heard. Your wife Elizabeth will bear you a son, and you are to give him the name John. He will be a joy and delight to you, and many will rejoice because of his birth." (Luke 1:13-14)

Like old Zechariah, everyone gets worried that needs will not be met.

Health, money, a relationship, a better job? We are all wanting in our lives, feeling needs that sometimes don't get filled the way we would like. Sometimes, in the long wait, we experience a loss of hope, and our joy is diminished. Instead we feel deprived, anxious, worried.

But God's promise is that you will have a kind of joy that is so real, it will fill you up and you need never feel deprived again. It may not happen in your time frame or according to your plan, but it is a promise that is to be believed. The question is, can you let go of your fear and have joy right now, while you are waiting?

Exercise 18

What need are you feeling may never be met? Where in your life do you feel deprived? Describe below.

Exercise 19

How has this affected your ability to feel the joy of Christ?

Fear blocks love, faith and joy. If you are in fear, you probably can't feel joy. Fear will steal your joy every time. Fear and its cousin anxiety are everywhere and we all experience it. But as Christians we have the strongest remedy possible. The joy of Christ is like a lighthouse beacon which calls to us in the blinding fog and lets us know that we need not fear. We're safe.

Seeds of Faith

But the angel said to them, "Do not be afraid. I bring you good news of great joy that will be for all the people. (11) Today in the town of David a Savior has been born to you; he is Christ the Lord."
Luke 2:10-11

Exercise 20

Write (or say) a prayer asking Jesus to remove any fears you may have at this time and ask Him to replace that fear with His joy.

> *Dear Jesus,*
>
> *You are my Hiding Place, my Fortress, my Strength. You are my Deliverer, my Champion, and Shield. I call on you Jesus as the Prince of Peace to restore my peace and be my security. Give to me the joy of your eternal protection and safety.*
>
> *I ask you Lord to*
>
>
>
> *Amen.*

BAD FRUIT: CONSTANT RISK TAKING

All life includes some risk. Taking risk is a part of faith itself. Risk-taking becomes Bad Fruit is when it is carried to extremes.

Promiscuous behavior, abusing alcohol and drugs, smoking during pregnancy, cheating on income tax, gambling, flirting with someone's spouse, etc. All of these and more are extreme risks.

Chronic risk-takers seem to lack normal, healthy fear. Just observe a teenager for 24 hours and count the risks. They throw caution to the wind and seem to forget about consequences. Impulse becomes the guide, tossing logic and wisdom out the door.

One fourteen year old recently told me, "I usually have four or five boyfriends at a time and I don't care what anyone says. I'll have sex anytime I want."

Thrills. Highs. Excitement. Risk becomes better than a drug. It is addictive and powerful and very scary to all whose lives are affected. The risk-taker seeks the danger and over-rides the built-in mechanisms for safety.

Gerald May, in his book *Addictions and Grace*, says there is an addiction to intensity. If you are pulled toward intensity and chaos, you need to ask Jesus to free you of this.

Exercise 21

Dear Jesus,

I renounce these tendencies toward risk-taking,

I ask you to restore in me healthy choices, thoughts and behaviors.

Amen.

Day Five

GROWING GOOD FRUIT

Exercise 22

"In order to grow good fruit, I need to develop these life skills and be..."

- ☐ Trusting in Jesus
- ☐ Bold and strong in the Lord
- ☐ Secure in my faith
- ☐ Risk-taking (in faith) not danger
- ☐ Able to ask for help from God and His people
- ☐ Discerning of good and evil
- ☐ Able to protect others when appropriate
- ☐ Cautious of Spiritual dangers
- ☐ Equally yoked with other believers
- ☐ Able to manage my personal power
- ☐ Reverent towards God
- ☐ Willing to stand firm in His full armor
- ☐ Standing firm in the assurance that Jesus gives me
- ☐ Alert and aware of evil
- ☐ Dependent on Jesus
- ☐ Hiding in Him
- ☐ A covering (protection) to my family
- ☐ Choosing to not be afraid
- ☐ Other

Exercise 23

Which three (3) do I most need in my life at this time?

1.

2.

3.

Exercise 24

How would you or your life be different if you had these three life skills?

Exercise 25 - PULLING UP WEEDS

Without these life skills you've identified, you may have been hiding out or making do. The following words describe this compensation. How would you honestly describe yourself?

"I am often …."

- ☐ A risk-taker
- ☐ Hiding out
- ☐ Hesitant
- ☐ Mistrusting
- ☐ Compulsive
- ☐ Scared
- ☐ A bully
- ☐ Panicky
- ☐ Fearful
- ☐ Foolish
- ☐ Over protective
- ☐ Obsessive
- ☐ Anxious
- ☐ Rash
- ☐ Unaware of danger
- ☐ A doubter
- ☐ Impulsive
- ☐ Naïve
- ☐ A "tough guy"
- ☐ Insecure
- ☐ Frightened
- ☐ Distracted
- ☐ Other

Exercise 26

Which three of these characteristics most block your ability to accept the safety, protection and security from Jesus?

1.

2.

3.

Exercise 27

Now look at the three words you chose in Exercise 26 and ask Jesus to change them into 3 new characteristics.

"I will now be…"

1. _____

2. _____

3. _____

Day Six

PREPARING THE SOIL OF THE SOUL: UPROOTING UNHOLY ROOTS

As you have read in this unit, Jesus wants you to be free of fears and to rest safely in His secure, loving arms forever. Eternal life provides ultimate security, right now!

In order to grow this good fruit, you need to give Him anything that roots your fears, insecurities and doubts.

Exercise 28

I need to give Jesus the following

☐ Specific fears (specify):

☐ Traumatic experience (specify)

☐ Thoughts (specify

☐ Beliefs (specify)

☐ Lies (that you have believed to be the truth)

Note: If you need more space, please use extra paper. This exercise should not be rushed.

Seeds of Faith

But blessed is the man who trusts in the LORD, whose confidence is in him. He will be like a tree planted by the water that sends out its roots by the stream. It does not fear when heat comes; its leaves are always green. It has no worries in a year of drought and never fails to bear fruit."
Jeremiah 17:7-8

Wait for the LORD; be strong and take heart and wait for the LORD. Psalm 27:14

Be strong and take heart, all you who hope in the LORD. Psalm 31:24

Search me, O God, and know my heart; test me and know my anxious thoughts. Psalm 139:23

Write Jesus a letter and ask Him to identify and then uproot the "unholy roots" keeping you from His gift of the good fruit of security, safety and protection. His Holy Spirit will let you know what needs healing.

Dear Jesus,

Amen.

Day Seven

A Change of Heart

Jesus freely gives us a new heart of security in Him and removes anything causing a spirit of fear.

Exercise 29

Mark how your heart is changing. Check all that apply to you.

My Old Heart Was	My New Heart Is
Anxious	Unafraid
Fearful	Courageous
Terror-filled	Secure
Tormented	Trusting
Timid	Other:
Other:	Other:
"An anxious heart weighs a man down, but a kind word cheers him up." Proverbs 12:25	"The LORD is my strength and my shield; my heart trusts in him, and I am helped. My heart leaps for joy and I will give thanks to him in song." Psalm 28:7

Exercise 30

How is the Lord changing your heart to make more room for His gifts of trust, security, faith and safety?

Exercise 31

If you are ready, pray the following prayer and see yourself placing on His altar or putting in the hands of Jesus the fears you know block your joy.

> *Dear Jesus,*
>
> *Lord, You are my Strong Rock. I long to find refuge from the storms of life in you, my Sanctuary, my Fortress, my Strong Tower. In You and You alone is my safety, protection and strength.*
>
> *I long always to be safe in Your strong arms from the evil one but there are fears and doubts that get in my way.*
>
> *I choose this day to revere only You. I choose this day to reserve for You my time and energy that I often put into worry and fear.*
>
> *I ask Your help, Oh Lord, to break old habits of reverencing anything other than You. I ask you to break the bonds that these habits have on me. Release me from these patterns of behavior and thinking, especially free me from worry, anxiety, fears of any kind (name them: _____) and from my obsessive thoughts that take my focus away from You.*
>
> *Thank you, Lord, for teaching me new ways to live and helping me to be free from destructive forces in my life. You are my Deliverer, my Strength, my Champion and Shield. You are the Prince of Peace.*
>
> *Fill me, then, with Your Holy strength, Your Holy protection and Your Holy peace. I pray this to You, Oh Lion of Judah.*
>
> *Amen. Alleluia. Amen.*

"Surely God is my salvation; I will trust and not be afraid.
The LORD, the LORD, is my strength and my song; he has become my salvation."

Isaiah 12:2

Self-Reliance versus Son-Reliance

You need to rely on the strength of Jesus Christ, the Son of God. How do I know He is strong?

Read about His time in the desert with Satan. Read about His agony in the Garden of Gethsemane. Read about His excruciating pain on the Cross. Then I think you will agree you have a strong and mighty Savior who is stronger and mightier than the "strong man" (Satan) any day! Praise God

The Spirit of the Sovereign Lord is on me, because the Lord has anointed me to preach good news to the poor. He has sent me to bind up the brokenhearted, to proclaim freedom for the captives and release from darkness for the prisoners, to proclaim the year of the Lord's favor and the day of vengeance of our God, to comfort all who mourn, and provide for those who grieve in Zion—to bestow on them a crown of ashes, the oil of gladness instead of mourning, and a garment of praise instead of a spirit of despair. They will be called oaks of righteousness, a planting of the Lord for the display of his splendor.

Isaiah 61:1-3

SOUL SEARCHING

As a result of the work I've done in this unit about growing the good fruit of safety and protection and freedom from fear:

MIND
What new beliefs or thoughts do I have?

What old beliefs am I ready to put on God's altar?

WILL
What new choices have I made?

What old choices can I give to God?

EMOTIONS
My feelings have changed in the following way:

What feelings or emotions am I giving to the Lord?

Unit Five

The Joy of Eternal Well Being:
Freedom in Sorrow, Loss, Pain, Suffering or Distress

    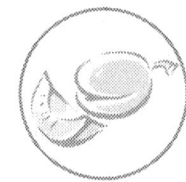 

Joy Choice # 5

Joy is choosing to give my suffering to Jesus, thus finding the comfort I need in hard times, through Him.

"Praise be to God and Father of our Lord Jesus Christ, the Father of compassion and the God of all comfort, who comforts us in all our troubles, so that we can comfort those in any trouble with the comfort we ourselves have received from God."
2 Corinthians 1:3-4

"God does not give us overcoming life—He gives us life as we overcome. The strain of life is what builds our strength. If there is no strain, there will be no strength. Are you asking God to give you life, liberty, and joy? He cannot, unless you are willing to accept the strain. And once you face the strain, you will immediately get the strength. Overcome your own timidity and take the first step. Then God will give you nourishment—"To him who overcomes I will give to eat from the tree of life…" (Revelation 2:7). If you completely give of yourself physically, you become exhausted. But when you give of yourself spiritually, you get more strength. God never gives us strength for tomorrow, or for the next hour, but only for the strain of the moment. Our temptation is to face adversities from the standpoint of our own common sense. But a saint can "be of good cheer" even when seemingly defeated by adversities, because victory is absurdly impossible to everyone, except God.

My Utmost for His Highest, Oswald Chambers, August 2

"I can wade Grief —
Whole pools of it —
I'm used to that —
But the least push of Joy
Breaks up my feet —"

Emily Dickinson

If the Lord is with us through life, we needn't fear for our dying confidence; for when we come to die, we shall find that "the Lord was there;" where the billows are most tempestuous, and the water is most chilly, we shall feel the bottom, and know that it is good: our feet shall stand upon the Rock of Ages when time is passing away. Beloved, from the first of a Christian's life to the last, the only reason why we don't perish is because "the Lord was there."

Morning and Evening, Charles Spurgeon, page 97

Day One

Even though there is a soft rain, you approach the orchard, anticipating your time with the Lord. He is sitting by the river, watching its peaceful, winding path. The sound of the water is soothing. Jesus draws you close and gives you a much needed hug. He hands you some small, smooth stones.

Skipping one across the river He says, "My fifth fruit is especially for you because of the hard times you have had in your life. This fruit is for my precious one who has suffered and has tasted from the cup of sorrows."

"I care for you so much, and I long to bring you comfort and relief. I will restore to you your sense of well-being and make you an 'Overcomer.'

I am known as *the Prince of Peace.*
I am *the Consolation of Israel.*
I am *the Hope of My People.*
I am *the Harbor of my people.*
I am *The Shepherd and Guardian of Souls*
I am *The Door of the Sheep.*
I am *The Good Shepherd.*
I am *your Fountain.*
I am *the Shiloh.*
I am *the Lord of Peace.*

"I have sent my Holy Spirit as the Comforter to strengthen you in times of pain and help your pain be transformed. Eating this fruit frees you <u>in</u> all distress, suffering, and heartache. Your cup of sorrows becomes mine. My cup of joy is now yours!"

"Remember, when you hurt and are in distress, say to yourself, 'I am chosen of God, holy and dearly loved.' You can have joy in the fellowship of sharing in My sufferings. All things dipped in the Blood of My Passion will be redeemed. Even if you should suffer for what is right, you are blessed."

"I desire for you to have well-being. One day there will be no more sorrow. Today, you can have joy in and through your suffering, because I am in you, My beloved."

Sit with the Lord as long as you like and enjoy your time alone with Him.
Share one of your deepest sorrows with Him.

Whatever you have learned or received or heard from me, or seen in me-put it into practice. And the God of peace will be with you.
Philippians 4:9

...to proclaim the year of the LORD'S favor and the day of vengeance of our God, to comfort all who mourn...
Isaiah 61:2

Praise be to the God and Father of our Lord Jesus Christ, the Father of compassion and the God of all comfort...
2 Corinthians 1:3

I, even I, am he who comforts you. Who are you that you fear mortal men, the sons of men, who are but grass...
Isaiah 51:12

GETTING TO KNOW JESUS

Jesus has shown you yet another wonderful aspect of who He really is.

Exercise 1

Read aloud the following list of names and put a check by the ones that you have already seen or heard:

"I know that Jesus is…"
- ☐ my Prince of Peace.
- ☐ the Consolation of Israel.
- ☐ the Hope of His People.
- ☐ the Harbor of My people.
- ☐ the Shepherd and Guardian of my Soul.
- ☐ the Door of the Sheep.
- ☐ my Good Shepherd.
- ☐ my Fountain.
- ☐ the Shiloh.
- ☐ my Lord of Peace.

Exercise 2

When you read His names, what aspect of His nature is Jesus revealing to you? Describe here:

GETTING TO KNOW GOD

The following names or titles for God reveal how He is seen throughout scripture as producing the good fruit of Eternal Well-Being.

"My Name Is…"	"I Am…"	"I Create…"
Yahweh-Shalom. the Lord sends Peace. Hope of Israel. Hope of His people. the Lord Our Peace. the Father of Compassion. the God of all Comfort.	Compassion Hope Comfort Peace	W E L L B E I N G

Getting to Know the Holy Spirit

Jesus says in John 14:26, "But the Counselor, the Holy Spirit, whom the Father will send in my name, will teach you all things and will remind you of everything I have said to you."

This Counselor, (or Comforter as some versions of this passage say) is the Holy Spirit. It is through His comfort that we survive and are sustained in all circumstances. He freely gives this comfort to all who call on the name of Jesus. As Christians, we are never promised a "comfortable" life. The Holy Comforter supplies the strength, guidance and endurance we need at the time we need it, when we call on Him.

It is through the compassion and love of Jesus that you can grow the good fruit of well-being, especially in hard times. Let's explore this fruit more closely.

Day Two

Good Fruit: Well-Being

Exercise 3

Directions:
Put an X next to the fruit that you still need to grow

- ☐ Healthy Grieving
- ☐ Compassion
- ☐ Comfort
- ☐ Endurance
- ☐ A New Dwelling

The Good Fruit: Well-Being

Do you have those moments, perhaps days, when all is well? You know: the bills are paid, the kids are healthy, the boss smiled, the traffic wasn't too bad and then you found a great parking space!

I call this "well-being." There is an aspect of life, a facet of the diamond called joy, where this sense of well-being is to be treasured. Billions are spent on the quest for this precious commodity; trips to the spa, the therapist, medications, the vacations, etc.

Seeds of Faith

If you have any encouragement from being united with Christ, if any comfort from his love, if any fellowship with the Spirit, if any tenderness and compassion, then make my joy complete by being like-minded, having the same love, being one in spirit and purpose.
Philippians 2:1

...The faith and love that spring from the hope that is stored up for you in heaven and that you have already heard about in the word of truth, the gospel that has come to you. All over the world this gospel is bearing fruit and growing just as it has been doing among you since the day you heard it and understood God's grace in all its truth.
Colossians 1:5-6

He is like a tree planted by streams of water, which yields its fruit in season and whose leaf does not wither.

Psalm 1:3

Even though I walk through the valley of the shadow of death, I will fear no evil, for you are with me; your rod and your staff, they comfort me.
Psalm 23:4

My comfort in my suffering is this: Your promise preserves my life.
Psalm 119:50

The stresses of day-to-day living can steal your well-being from under your nose. You are to stand firm and guard your being (life) from the thieves who would steal your joy and reduce you to a being of dis-ease, dis-comfort and dys-function (all bad fruit).

In God's Holy City, there is the promise of eternal well-being. Revelation 21:4 says, "He will wipe every tear from their eyes. There will be no more death, or mourning or crying or pain, for the old order of things has passed away." In the New Jerusalem, you will spend eternity with Jesus in a perfect state of well-being, restored to the original intention of your being. Adam and Eve originally had well-being. That was God's gift to His children.

The response to the loss of well-being for Adam and Eve is still your response today: fear, sorrow, shame, distance from God, distress, disappointment, struggle, etc. You have longed to return to a state of well-being.

Let's explore more about this fruit, whose possession brings joy and whose loss can lead you into despair.

All Will Be Well

Julian of Norwich is quoted as saying, "All will be well, all will be well, in all manner of things, all will be well." Unfortunately, the New Age movement has picked up this truth and repackaged it.

You know you are a "being." God breathed His breath of life into the nostrils of Adam and Eve and they became living beings. You have that same breath of life.

But what does it mean to have well-being, or to be a well being?

When a child is called into being, knit together by God in the mother's womb, that child is on its way to be a well-being. But along the way that child grows into a person who sins and who is sinned against. The cumulative effect of this sin is that the "being" God created no longer is a well-being, who has full and complete joy.

If you put all twelve of the "joy fruit" described in this book in one basket and gave it to someone, they would certainly say, "I have reached a state of well-being." That is God's plan for each of us. And if you abide (live) with Jesus, He will produce abundant fruit in you.

But what if you have filled your own basket or you are not willing or able to receive what Christ has to offer? What if you have designed your own method of achieving well being?

Exercise 4

What gives you a sense of well-being?

Exercise 5

What would you need or need to do to achieve a greater sense of well-being?

A Well in Your Being?
Did you know you have a "well" inside of you? Whenever you are thirsty, did you know you don't have to go far to satisfy your thirst?

One day when Jesus was hot and thirsty from His travels in Samaria, He stopped by Jacob's well to refresh Himself, as many other travelers had done for centuries.

Now it just so happened that a woman approached the well with her water pot at the same time Jesus wanted a drink. As He apparently had no cup or pot, He asked the woman for a drink, for He was thirsty. "May I have a drink?"

That simple request has echoed down the centuries.

A conversation is struck and out of it, like water from a rock, Jesus pours forth an eternal mystery. He tells her the obvious: that her water will only satisfy for a short while, but His water will satisfy for an eternity. It is "living water" He says. It comes from God. You will never thirst He says. It will become " a spring of water welling up to eternal life." (John 4:14) Wow! Like this woman, our thirst is an all-consuming craving and passion of the soul for complete union with God Himself, and the fullness of His Holy Spirit.

Seeds of Faith

If only you had paid attention to my commands, your peace would have been like a river, your righteousness like the waves of the sea.
Isaiah 48:18

Later, knowing that all was now completed, and so that the Scripture would be fulfilled, Jesus said, "I am thirsty."
John 19:28

When a Samaritan woman came to draw water, Jesus said to her, "Will you give me a drink?" John 4:7

The Spirit and the bride say, "Come!" And let him who hears say, "Come!" Whoever is thirsty, let him come; and whoever wishes, let him take the free gift of the water of life. Rev 22:17

A New Water Pot From The Potter's Hands

Like the Samaritan woman, I'm sold. How can I get some of this great stuff? I'll never be thirsty again or have to go in the hot sun to someone else's well to get a short-time supply.

Today, you and I just have to walk to the fridge or the bottled water dispenser in our air conditioned home with disposable cups ready at our fingertips. So how does this mysterious living water apply to our lives today?

Jesus later is recorded in John as saying, "...If anyone is thirsty, let him <u>come to me and drink</u>. Whoever believes in me, as the Scripture has said, streams of living water will flow from within him." (John 7:37-38)

So, believe in Jesus and get a flowing well or river of living water? Believe in Jesus and never go thirsty? Believe in Jesus and always be satisfied in the deepest place inside? Yes!

People talk about cravings, yearnings, desires, aches, deep thirsts. Jesus knew this about us because He too had desires. When this woman at the well believed in Him as her Messiah, He was so personally satisfied that He told His disciples <u>He</u> wasn't hungry any more.

By entering into a deeply personal and intimate conversation with this sinner, Jesus offered her His greatest gift: eternal life with God. That eternal life began the moment she received Him as Messiah. Immediately the living water was flowing in and through her!

She leaves her water pot at the physical well because now she **is** the water pot carrying the Good News to her townsfolk.

The living water of the Holy Spirit flows through her words as she gives testimony of the man she has befriended. Then, because of her testimony and His friendly visit with them, they believe in Him too. They became tributaries in the River of Life.

The Book of Revelation says, "...to him who is thirsty I will give to drink without cost from the spring of the water of life." (Revelation 21:6)

Are you the one who thirsts? A spiritually thirsty person might:

> **Seek to worship false idols**
> **Bow to the images engraved by others' imaginations**
> **Run to people, places or things to get a "drink"**

or, that same thirsty person might:

> **Turn to the One true God, fall to her knees and ask that all old sources of supply be relegated to their rightful places.**

God placed that thirst in you so that you would finally go to Him for refreshment.

"But why me?" You might ask.

"I'm just like the woman at the well—a life of poor choices. I've made my bed so now I have to lie in it, right?"

Jesus offered her the living water in spite of her many sins, even before she professed to believe in Him.

So how much more of that abundant living water will flow when you do believe! You become the Water Pot!

Let The River Flow
Your well-being comes from the "well" in your being. The water source in your being comes from the Holy Spirit abiding in you. The eternal life that springs or bubbles up in you from your innermost being gives you the fruit of well-being. It allows others to come and drink and meet Jesus at your well instead of Jacob's well.

I once imagined a garden inside of me. In the garden were fountains springing up out of the ground instead of flowers.

The fountain closest to me was collapsing into itself. The water was disappearing before my eyes. I panicked!

Jesus was standing next to this pitiful fountain, and I held out my right hand as if to show Him the problem.

Instantly, He held up His right hand and the entire landscape was filled with fountains of colorful water as far as the eye could see. Tall, leaping sprays of crystal clear water burst from the ground!

What joy I felt as I realized my mediocre fountain could and would run dry, but His fantastic fountain was without limit.

Seeds of Faith

As they make music they will sing, "All my fountains are in you." Psalm 87:7

Revelation 7:16-17

We have this hope as an anchor for the soul, firm and secure. It enters the inner sanctuary behind the curtain...
Hebrews 6:19

Therefore, among God's churches we boast about your perseverance and faith in all the persecutions and trials you are enduring. All this is evidence that God's judgment is right, and as a result you will be counted worthy of the kingdom of God, for which you are suffering.
2 Thessalonians 1:4-5

How is your well of living water? Is it flowing up and out like a river? Is it a joyous colorful fountain? Is it a deep well of sweet, fresh spring water? Or is it a dried up, barren or abandoned well that produces no good fruit?

Let's take a closer look at this good fruit of well-being.

GOOD FRUIT: A NEW DWELLING

How "well" you are depends upon where you <u>dwell</u>. You can either dwell in the presence of God (Unit 11) <u>or</u> you can <u>dwell</u> on yourself, your problems, your future, etc.

You live where you dwell. You choose where you dwell. Your being (that which is alive in you) can either be well where you dwell or it can be otherwise.

I believe you will be well when you <u>choose</u> to make your dwelling with the Lord. God wants you to ask Him into your "tent". Your tent (tabernacle or temple) is your heart. Jesus is called Emmanuel, God with us. He wants to live with you!

Jesus said to abide in Him. Abide means to dwell with and in Him. This is a major Kingdom principle: you will have well-being if your whole being <u>dwells</u> with Jesus, every day, all day.

Day Three

GOOD FRUIT: JOYFUL ENDURANCE

May those who delight in my vindication shout for joy and gladness; may they always say, "The LORD be exalted, who delights in the well-being of his servant." (Psalm 35:27)

Part of the Good Fruit of Well-Being comes from the endurance you develop in hard times. Jesus endured the cross because of the joy of heaven set before Him. The writer of Hebrews reminds us, *"Consider him who endured such opposition from sinful men, so that you will not grow weary and lose heart."* (Hebrews 12:3.)

You can endure just about anything if you become like Jesus and set your eyes, not on this plane, but the next. You need to develop the kind of endurance that sets joy before any situation.

GOOD FRUIT: HEALTHY GRIEVING

The loss of a special person by death or separation, the loss of a job, or the loss of a pet, the loss of one's health . . . these are all an integral part of life that cannot be avoided. Loss is a uersal, unavoidable experience, Christian or not, and sorrow is inevitable.

Jesus experienced loss because He too was human. He knows your pain. He is able to comfort you through your losses. His presence in your life *is* what brings pure joy. No man, woman or child should be able to take Christ's joy from you, even if they leave!

So, you need to grieve. And what does that mean exactly?

If you share your sorrows, you will be on the road to recovering your joy. Can you accept that your sorrow will turn to joy eventually in His time? If you are willing to let go, then God has something to fill up again. You keep hanging on and then there is no room for God to work in your life. You keep doing all the work in the struggle to get what you want. He could give it to you so much more easily.

What is taken away leaves a void. God fills the void with joy if you let him. You need to let him have the emptiness as His workplace, His canvas to paint a new picture, filled with joyful bright colors. Turn over the paintbrush to Him.

You are His "vessel" and He will fill you up again if you have been broken and emptied by some life circumstance.

Exercise 6

What loss in your life has temporarily taken your joy from you? What has happened since then?

Seeds of Faith

Blessed are those who mourn, for they will be comforted.
Matthew 5:4

Jesus wept.
John 11:35

...Now is your time of grief, but I will see you again, and you will rejoice, and no one will take away your joy." John 16:22

Shout for Joy, O heavens; rejoice, O earth; burst into song, O mountains! For the LORD comforts his people and will have compassion on his afflicted ones.
Isaiah 49:13

Exercise 7

Can I show my feelings of sadness, hurt, pain or sorrow?

☐ Always ☐ Sometimes ☐ Not Yet

Can I be with others when they are feeling these feelings without feeling ashamed or embarrassed? Or uncomfortable?

☐ Always ☐ Sometimes ☐ Not Yet

To be with someone in their grief is to be Jesus to that person. That is the good fruit of compassion, which means "with pain." The world desperately needs this good fruit on every Christian's tree of life.

The Compassion of Jesus

Soon afterward, Jesus went to a town called Nain, and his disciples and a large crowd went along with him. As he approached the town gate, a dead person was being carried out--the only son of his mother, and she was a widow. And a large crowd from the town was with her. When the Lord saw her, his heart went out to her and he said, "Don't cry." Then he went up and touched the coffin, and those carrying it stood still. He said, "Young man, I say to you, get up!" The dead man sat up and began to talk, and Jesus gave him back to his mother. (Luke 7:11-15)

Passion means pain, compassion means to enter someone's pain. Jesus does that. Jesus restores out of His compassion. He knows your hurts and longs to help you. His pain on the Cross gave you the miracle of new life, His gift to all who are spiritually dead. He restored joy to the grieving Mother who needed her son to take care of her. Jesus understood her pain and gave her back what was lost. He does not always raise the dead physically, but He does wish to restore or resurrect your sense of well-being and joy spiritually.

Exercise 8

Think of a time when Jesus gave you back something which you had "counted as lost". Describe it below.

Don't have a double loss: hang on to the Joy of Christ. Write a prayer asking Christ to <u>restore</u> you with His joy and <u>fill you up</u> to the brim until your sorrow is turned to joy.

Dear Jesus,

Amen.

GOOD FRUIT: COMFORT

When Jesus walked this earth, He showed great compassion for His fellow man. Much of the time He could be found caring for the distressed. His primary means of dispensing this compassion was with His words. His Sermon on the Mount offers such soothing words as "Blessed are those who mourn, for they will be comforted." (Matthew 5:4)

God's desire for you is that even in times of sorrow, pain, distress, troubles and loss, you would not lose your joy. Remember, joy is not the same as "happy" and does not depend upon circumstances.

Webster's definition of "well being" is "the state of being healthy, happy and free from want." But in the Bible, James encourages us by saying, "Consider it pure joy, my brothers, whenever you face trials of many kinds." (James 1:2.) There is a difference!

The *New Webster's Dictionary* defines comfort as:

1. Consolation, someone or something that brings consolation, well-being, contentment.
2. Someone or something that contributes to one's well-being.

There is also the sense of comfort meaning "rest", rest from the pain, rest from the agony. This is what Jesus brings to a needy world. He wants you to carry His comfort to the suffering. But you don't have to do that all alone.

The Holy Spirit as Comforter and Helper
The fourteenth chapter of John, verse 16 begins,
> "And I will ask the Father, and He will give you another Counselor, to be with you forever—the Spirit of Truth. The world cannot accept him, because it neither sees him nor knows him. But you know him, for he lives with you and will be in you. I will not leave you as orphans, I will come to you." (John 14:15-18)

Jesus says He will not leave you comfortless as an orphan.

Jesus promised His Holy Spirit, the Helper would be given to His believers for comfort, advice, strength, intercession with God and for encouragement. The Holy Spirit is the third person of the Holy Trinity and completes the Godhead. Just as this promise must have comforted the Disciples two thousand years ago, it still sends hope and comfort today.

It is through the indwelling (living inside of you) presence of the Holy Spirit that you can receive comfort even in times of pain and sorrow. In times of trouble it is important to invite the Holy Spirit <u>into</u> your problem. He will always come to your aid.

Good Fruit: The Sorrow of Conviction

If God is working in your life at all there will be times of another type of sorrow, the sorrow of conviction. This is beautifully written about in David's Psalm 51. We will look at this in Unit 6.

Day Four

> *Come Holy Spirit. Come Holy Comforter.*
> *I give you my pain, sorrow and any area of "dis-ease."*
> *Fill my life with your compassion, care and comfort.*
> *Thank you for your tender mercy touching my life and transforming my deepest pain.*
>
> *Amen*

> *For it is commendable if a man bears up under the pain of unjust suffering because he is conscious of God. But how is it to your credit if you receive a beating for doing wrong and endure it? But if you suffer for doing good and you endure it, this is commendable before God. To this you were called, because Christ suffered for you, leaving you an example, that you should follow in his steps. "He committed no sin, and no deceit was found in his mouth." When they hurled their insults at him, he did not retaliate; when he suffered, he made no threats. Instead, he entrusted himself to him who judges justly. He himself bore our sins in his body on the tree, so that we might die to sins and live for righteousness; by his wounds you have been healed.*
>
> 1 Peter 2:18-24

BAD FRUIT

Exercise 10

Directions: Read over the list of bad fruits and check any that you need to have pruned in your life in order to grow the joy of eternal acceptance:

- ☐ Unhealed Sorrow
- ☐ Struggle
- ☐ Misery
- ☐ Despair
- ☐ Depression
- ☐ Self-Pity
- ☐ Failure
- ☐ Distress
- ☐ Hopelessness

THE BAD FRUIT: UNHEALED SORROW

Sorrow in and of itself is not a bad fruit. Your life will have sorrow as well as joys.

Sorrow, however, can become a bad fruit if, like all of the broken emotions proceeding from Eden's fall, the soul is unable to return to the state God intended — joy and a sense of well-being.

The fruit on your tree will be sorrow, self-pity, despair, depression, and failure if you have not been able or willing to bring your soul to the Lord for healing and restoration.

Sorrow, by its very nature is filled with trap doors. Even people with strong faith may fall into a season of doubt, fear and despair as they experience a hard time in life. Saint Paul had a very hard life after his conversion. But he said that,

> "…we also rejoice in our sufferings, because we know that suffering produces perseverance; perseverance, character; and character, hope. And hope does not disappoint us, because God has poured out his love into our hearts by the Holy Spirit whom he has given to us." (Romans 5:3-5)

So the promise is that in your tribulations you will be building up your perseverance, character and hope in the Lord. Bad fruit is produced when your tribulations produce despair, hopelessness and sinfulness.

The sooner you turn to Jesus (as your Good Shepherd) to walk you through the "valley of the shadow of death" (Psalm 23), the sooner you will be out of harm's way of the trap doors of unhealed sorrow and tribulations.

Seeds of Faith

A good tree cannot bear bad fruit, and a bad tree cannot bear good fruit.
Matthew 7:18

John 16:20

The Fallout of Loss

Humans don't like to lose anything—other people, toys, games, car keys. Loss makes us angry. Loss makes us anxious. Loss makes us sad. Loss makes us give up hope. Loss produces bad fruit if not dealt with appropriately.

Our well-being suffers when we experience a loss and we can not recuperate. We need God's help to recover from a loss. Yet many turn angry faces away from Him in their seasons of sorrow. Alienation from God follows.

Exercise 11   SEASONS OF LOSS AND SORROW

Are you going through a season of loss now or have you been through one recently? Are you worried because you may lose something or someone? Spend a few minutes writing about this experience below. Make a list of all the losses.

Exercise 12

What feelings have you had in the experience you just wrote about?

- ☐ Sadness
- ☐ Worry
- ☐ Anger at Others
- ☐ Helplessness
- ☐ Frustration
- ☐ Hopelessness
- ☐ Numb; No Feelings
- ☐ Anger at Myself
- ☐ Anger at God
- ☐ Blame
- ☐ Despair
- ☐ Depression
- ☐ Disappointed
- ☐ Anxiety
- ☐ Panic
- ☐ Doubt
- ☐ Separation
- ☐ Self-hatred
- ☐ Other: _____

Note: Remember, the word <u>DANGER</u> has the word "Anger" imbedded in it.

Good Grief

These are the most common emotions of grieving over a loss or anticipated loss. Many have tried to describe this complicated, very personal experience, but I use these simple stages of the grief process:

Grief Cycle

1.	Get Ready	A loss is anticipated (anxiety) or occurs (shock; denial) "It can't happen!"
2.	React	Anger at myself or others; protest. "Why!" "No!"
3.	Go Inside	Sorrow, sadness, despair. "I'm lost!"
4.	Escape Anywhere	Detachment, rest, numbness. "I can't think about that now!"
5.	Go Forward	Acceptance, recovery—movement forward. "I'm accepting this now even though I still am sad sometimes."

The process is cyclical and unique to each person. Protest deals with the strong feelings of anger and denial about the loss: the "give it back to me" feelings.

Sorrow deals with the sadness, blues, depression, despair-like feelings which usually accompany a loss.

Detachment refers to the numbness that follows periods of loss. I believe this is a respite for the soul and is often accompanied by a period of inactivity, isolation or a need to be alone.

The Grieving Cycle described above exists on two levels.

Each day you can go through all stages and perhaps even within an hour you may experience all five stages.

Then if you were to stand back and look over a period of months, you may see that there were seasons of each stage. As a therapist, I look for movement, a fluid motion through the stages. When a person (or a family) is stuck in one stage for a time there is the danger of a prolonged and more complicated grieving. Remember, each person goes through the process in his or her own unique way and if allowed into the process, the Holy Spirit willingly and gently guides each step.

No book on <u>joy</u> would be complete if we did not talk about <u>sorrow and loss</u>. The two are closely related and walk through life hand-in-hand. I heard it said once that some folks drink from the Cup of Sorrow more than the Cup of Joy. This is hard to understand. Why would God give one person more sorrow than another?

Now if we are children, then we are heirs—heirs of God and co-heirs with Christ, if indeed we share in his sufferings in order that we may also share in his glory. I consider that our present sufferings are not worth comparing with the glory that will be revealed in us. Romans 8:17-18

In fact, everyone who wants to live a godly life in Christ Jesus will be persecuted... 2 Timothy 3:12

Neither do men pour new wine into old wineskins. If they do, the skins will burst, the wine will run out and the wineskins will be ruined. No, they pour new wine into new wineskins, and both are preserved." Matthew 9:17

Certainly many of God's saints have lives of suffering and even martyrdom. In the legacy of someone like Mother Theresa, we see that she knew and experienced more true joy than most. She said in her book, <u>Suffering Into Joy</u>, "Never let anything so fill you with pain or sorrow, so as to make you forget the joy of Christ risen." (Page 118)   She also said, "Today the passion of Christ is being relived in the lives of those who suffer. Suffering is not a punishment. God does not punish." (Page 96) She put her finger on a commonly held false belief or "lie" about suffering.

 **My suffering is always God's punishment.**

 **My suffering can produce True Joy, if I invite Jesus into the suffering.**

Some Suffering is of God
In Isaiah 53 you read about the revealed identity of Jesus as the Suffering Servant. We'll read more about this in Unit 9, but this chapter reminds you that if you are identified with Christ, you too will suffer, not only for yourself, but as a true servant would as he seeks the welfare of others.

Bitter or Sweet Wine
Sorrow, from the Greek word "lypes", means an experience of great stress, which brings physical, emotional or spiritual pain. (*Strongs Dictionary*)

Sorrow is a powerful force acting on the human soul. It can reshape or transform my soul in one of two directions: inward or upward.

Bad Fruit: Sorrow Turned Inward	*I can let it make me more <u>worldly</u> through self-pity and resentment and harden me to the Lord.*
Good Fruit: Sorrow Turned Upward	*I can let it produce a change in my mind, will or emotions that makes me spiritually sensitive and more Godly.*

Sorrow is the birthing pain of my restoration process and on the other side of the pain is the reward of a closer walk with the Lord. This is one path to true joy. Grapes have to be pressed, squished, smooshed, and flattened to get wine. Do you ever feel that life is doing that to you? But what is it producing — bitter or sweet wine? Are you whining to the Lord, "Woe is me!" Or, is there a true testimony of God's presence in your life by the way in which you <u>go through</u> sorrow, hardships and disappointments?

BAD FRUIT: STRUGGLE

When you strive and struggle with life, you just end up tired, frustrated and probably disappointed. You produce bad fruit when you try to tug and pull at a problem.

God wants to end your struggles in life, but He can't do that until you decide to let go first. It's like a knot. The harder you pull on both ends, the tighter the knot becomes.

Exercise 13

Are you struggling or having a tug-of-war with a problem? Write about this below.

Be still, and know that I am God...
Psalm 46:10

I can do everything through him who gives me strength. Phil 4:13

Then the woman, seeing that she could not go unnoticed, came trembling and fell at his feet. In the presence of all the people, she told why she had touched him and how she had been instantly healed. Luke 8:47

BAD FRUIT: MISERY

There is no need to describe the Bad Fruit of misery. Everyone has tasted this fruit at some point in life.

Do you want Misery or Mercy in your life?

Misery loves the company of Christ! Bring it to Him.

His mercy brings healing.
His mercy brings restoration.
His mercy brings love.
His mercy brings forgiveness.

A Word on Despair and Depression
Depression is big business. Psychotropic medication is found in almost every medicine cabinet in America. Medicine is good and doctors who administer it wisely are to be trusted.

However, if you are suffering from <u>despair</u>, no medicine can help. You need medicine for the spirit! Jesus Christ.

Despair means to feel as if you are "without spirit." It is a spiritual dis-ease. To have spiritual well-being, one must be renewed daily in the Spirit of God, by washing in the River of Life and drinking in its life-giving energy.

Your spirit needs nourishment. Otherwise, like your physical body, it will starve to death or die of thirst. Your spirit gets hungry and thirsty. Begin to recognize the signs and symptoms of spiritual malnourishment. Basically, all of the Bad Fruits are the result of a spiritual eating disorder.

Beware: Despair Kills. Feed your spirit and return to the joy of well-being.

Day Five

Growing Good Fruit:
Cooperating with the Gardener

Exercise 14

"In order to have well-being, I need to be more…"

- ☐ Patient
- ☐ Loyal to God (faithful)
- ☐ Persevering
- ☐ Forgiving of God
- ☐ Forgiving of Myself
- ☐ Open to my feelings
- ☐ Accepting of support
- ☐ Hopeful
- ☐ Accepting of my grieving cycle
- ☐ Other: _____

Exercise 15

How would you honestly describe yourself?

"I am often…"	Always	Sometimes	Never
Restless			
Discontented			
Angry			
Blocked			
Filled with self-pity			
Impatient			
Stuck in an unending grief			
Numb			
Depressed			
In despair			
Unable to accept help			
Willing to give up too soon			
Grouchy			
Other			

Exercise 16

Which of these characteristics are getting in the way of you having a sense of well-being in your life?

1. _____
2. _____
3. _____

How?

I will be like the dew to Israel; he will blossom like a lily. Like a cedar of Lebanon he will send down his roots Hosea 14:5

Day Six

PREPARING THE SOIL: UPROOTING UNHOLY ROOTS

As you have read in this Unit, Jesus wants you to have well-being, through His comfort and compassion in times of trial and sorrow.

Are there "unholy" roots deep in the soil of your soul blocking this healthy fruit?

For example, one client felt that she had so many problems in her life because she was inherently BAD, doomed from the start as an abused child to live a life of misery. Every time she felt joy or even a little happiness in her life, the feeling carried with it a twin feeling of impending doom, as if a "black cloud" was always bound to rain on her parade at any moment. It always had so why not think it was her destiny? She had a long history of sorrow, so where was the joy?

Of course, she grew up hearing that God was always going to punish her and that she didn't deserve good things or good feelings. At age 40, she was still living each day with the lie that joy was not hers to receive. Therefore, she questioned every time she felt joyful or happy. In her therapy, she learned to question the rigid beliefs that had kept her in misery most of her life. She began to allow the uncomfortable moments of joy to replace the more familiar feelings of misery.

Exercise 17

Some examples of unholy roots might be:

- ☐ Negative attitudes (specify one) _____
- ☐ False beliefs about suffering
- ☐ Something learned which needs unlearning (specify one) _____
- ☐ Hopelessness or depression (specify) _____
- ☐ Self-pity
- ☐ Unresolved grief
- ☐ Unmet dreams and expectations
- ☐ Other moods, attitudes which produce bad fruit and are displeasing to God (specify): _____
_____
_____
_____

Exercise 18

Stop and pray: Ask the Holy Spirit to show you what needs to be uprooted so He can replace it with His own deep Holy roots.

> **Dear Jesus,**
>
>
>
>
>
>
>
>
>
> **Amen.**

Exercise 19 — UPROOTING FALSE BELIEFS

Was there a time when you thought that suffering in your life was a punishment of God? Write about that experience and your beliefs here:

Exercise 20

What did you think that God was punishing you for?
- ☐ Because of a sin I've committed: _____
- ☐ Because of a sin committed against me: _____
- ☐ Because I feel unworthy of God.
- ☐ Because I didn't believe in Him enough.
- ☐ Because I:_____

Seeds of Faith

He was despised and rejected by men, a man of sorrows, and familiar with suffering. Like one from whom men hide their faces he was despised, and we esteemed him not. Surely he took up our infirmities and carried our sorrows, yet we considered him stricken by God, smitten by him, and afflicted. Isaiah 53:3-4

Exercise 21

What is your belief about God and punishment and suffering?
- ☐ He will never forgive me.
- ☐ He loves others, not me.
- ☐ Other: _____
- ☐ He is mean.
- ☐ He is not involved in my life.

_____

Exercise 22

What beliefs about <u>yourself</u> came from this experience? "I am . . . "

_____
_____

Exercise 23

What beliefs about <u>others</u> arose from this experience? "Others are . . ."

_____
_____

Exercise 24

What beliefs about <u>God</u> came from this experience? "God is . . ."

_____
_____

Now ask the Lord to reveal the truth and to root out the lies from this memory.

Exercise 25

When you are ready, answer these questions.

What is the truth about <u>myself</u> that I can now see in this experience?

_____
_____

Exercise 26

What is the truth about <u>others</u>?
___
___

Exercise 27

What is the truth about <u>God</u> that is revealed in this experience?
___
___

Unmet Dreams and Expectations: The Sorrow of Disappointment
Your joy may be shaken when you have hoped and dreamed for something or put all your expectations and desires into one "basket" and then feel as if all is lost.

Exercise 28

Have you had an experience of unmet expectations, broken dreams, failures, disappointments? Write about one of these below, especially one that you know needs healing (blocks you from having well-being).

Exercise 29

What false beliefs about yourself came from this experience?

- ☐ I'm unlovable in this way:_____
___

- ☐ I'm inadequate in this way:_____
___

- ☐ I'm unworthy in this way: _____
___

Other: _____
___

Exercise 30

What false beliefs about others arose from this experience?
- ☐ People can't be trusted.
- ☐ People are out to hurt me.
- ☐ People are selfish
- ☐ People are inadequate
- ☐ People are cruel.
- ☐ Other: _____

Exercise 31

What false beliefs about God came from this experience?
- ☐ God is untrustworthy
- ☐ God is unloving
- ☐ God is unmerciful
- ☐ God is harsh
- ☐ God is vengeful
- ☐ God is uncaring
- ☐ Others: _____

Now pray for God to show you the truth in this experience and to separate the lies by His perfect Truth. (You may want to look back at your previous answers with the eyes of Christ.)

Exercise 32

When you are ready, answer the questions below:

What is the truth about <u>yourself</u> from this experience?

_____
_____
_____

Exercise 33

What is the truth about <u>others</u>?

_____
_____

Exercise 34

What is the truth about <u>God</u> that is revealed in this experience?

_____
_____
_____

Exercise 35

Now, as the Holy Spirit guides you, offer to Jesus all that you think is blocking you from the joy of well-being.

Dear Jesus,

You are my Good Shepherd, my Shiloh, and the Lord of my Peace. You are my Place of Repair. You bring me consolation and hope when all seems hopeless.

Lord, my soul cries out to you and I long for all to be well. But dear Jesus, there are things which keep me from having the well-being you offer me (name them):

My prayer dear Lord is:

Amen.

Day Seven

A CHANGE OF HEART

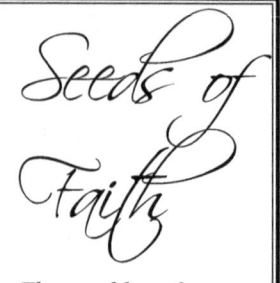

Seeds of Faith

The troubles of my heart have multiplied; free me from my anguish.
Psalm 25:17

For troubles without number surround me; my sins have overtaken me, and I cannot see. They are more than the hairs of my head, and my heart fails within me.
Psalm 40:12

A happy heart makes the face cheerful, but heartache crushes the spirit.
Proverbs 15:13

I have great sorrow and unceasing anguish in my heart.
Romans 9:2

A cheerful heart is good medicine, but a crushed spirit dries up the bones.
Proverbs 17:22

All the days of the oppressed are wretched, but the cheerful heart has a continual feast.
Proverbs 15:15

Hearts long for well-being—a total person where all is well in body, soul and spirit. If the heart, your innermost being, is well with the Lord, then all is indeed well. When your heart is one with the Lord, you have well-being. (John 7:38) To be one with Jesus is to have His Heart.

How is Jesus changing your heart to be more like Himself even when all is not well in your external circumstances?

Exercise 36

Mark all boxes that describe the changes that you are allowing Jesus to make in your spirit.
Mark how your heart is changing. Check all that apply to you.

My Old Heart Was:	**My New Heart is Becoming:**
☐ Despairing	☐ Cheerful
☐ Aching	☐ Hopeful
☐ Anguished	☐ Peaceful
☐ Crushed	☐ Resilient
☐ Sorrowful	☐ Laughing
☐ Other:_____	☐ Happy
☐ Other:_____	☐ Enduring
☐ Other:_____	☐ Other:_____
"How long must I wrestle with my thoughts and every day have sorrow in my heart? How long will my enemy triumph over me?" Psalm 13:2	"Therefore my heart is glad and my tongue rejoices; my body also will rest secure." Psalm 16:9 "Above all else, guard your heart, for it is the wellspring of life." Proverbs 4:23

Soul Searching

As a result of the work I've done in this unit:

MIND
What new beliefs or thoughts do I have?

What old beliefs am I ready to put on God's altar?

WILL
What new choices have I made?

What old choices can I give to God?

EMOTIONS
My feelings have changed in the following way:

What feelings or emotions am I giving to the Lord?

Unit Six

The *Joy* of Eternal Righteousness:
Freedom from Sin and disobedience

  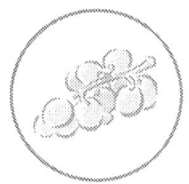 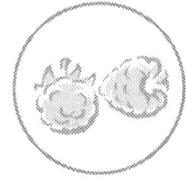 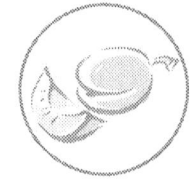 

Joy Choice # 6

Joy is choosing the gift of Jesus' righteousness.
I am free in Christ from the bondage of sin.
I choose joy in the doing of God's will.

"So, my brothers, you also died to the law through the body of Christ, that you might belong to another, to him who was raised from the dead, in order that we might bear fruit to God."
Romans 7:13

"Jesus cannot come and do His work in me as long as there is anything blocking the way, whether it is something good or bad. When He comes to me, am I prepared for Him to drag every wrong thing I have ever done into the light? That is exactly where He comes. Wherever I know I am unclean is where He will put His feet and stand, and wherever I think I am clean is where He will remove His feet and walk away."

My Utmost For His Highest, Oswald Chambers, August 22

"God is determined to have His child as pure, clean and white as driven snow, and as long as there is disobedience in any point of His teaching, He will allow His Spirit to use whatever process it may take to bring us to obedience."

My Utmost for His Highest, Oswald Chambers, June 30

No good tree bears bad fruit, nor does a bad tree bear good fruit. Each tree is recognized by its own fruit.

Luke 6:43-44

Day One

In the cool of the evening, Jesus has prepared a fire with the dead and broken branches strewn on the ground. The flames shoot upward in brilliant shades of blue, yellow and red. As you approach, the heat intensifies, and you hesitate to get too close. He rises to greet you and plucks an interesting fruit from the nearest branch on the tree.

"My sixth fruit is so important and lovingly comes from God, Our Father. This is the fruit of Righteousness and it gives Him great joy when you eat of this fruit.

In God's Word, you will see:

I am *the Righteous One.*
I am *your Sanctification.*
I am *your Redeemer.*
I am *the Lamb that was slain*
I am *the Passover.*
I am *the Just Judge.*
I am *Christ, your Passover.*
I am *the King of Righteousness.*
I am *the Holy One of God.*
I am *the Ransom for all.*
I am *the Friend of sinners.*

I am *the Stone of Stumbling and*
I am *a Stone cut without Hands.*
I am *a Merciful and Faithful High Priest.*
I am *the Mediator.*
I am *the Righteous Servant.*
I am *the Intercessor.*
I am *a Righteous Branch.*
I am *the Launderer's Soap.*
I am *the Refiner.*
I am *the Purifier.*
I am *the Propitiation.*
I am *your Righteousness.*

I want to free you from your slavery to sin so that you may wear My white linen robe of righteousness before Our Father. I am your Advocate with the Father, and I willingly give you My clean slate from sin as you come into My Father's presence.
Forevermore, <u>you</u> can then say these words about yourself:

"I am set free from sin and am a slave to righteousness."
"I am a prisoner for the Lord."
"I am becoming the righteousness of God."
"I am chosen in Him before the creation of the world to be holy and blameless in His sight."

"I am the temple of the living God."
"I am created to be like God in true righteousness and holiness."
"I am a slave to God."
"I am dead to sin but alive to God in Christ Jesus!"
"I am the Lord's freedman."

"You are already clean because of My Blood and the words I have spoken to you. You will be called the Holy People, the Redeemed of the Lord, and you will be called Sought After, the City No Longer Deserted. You are to be holy because I, the Lord, am holy. I have set you apart from the nations to be My own. I want you for My own! You bring Me such joy."

Sit for a while and talk with the Lord about this fruit of Righteousness.
Allow the truth of His words to soak into your spirit and renew your soul.
Read the words again and again.

...and be found in him, not having a righteousness of my own that comes from the law, but that which is through faith in Christ-the righteousness that comes from God and is by faith. Philippians 3:9

GETTING TO KNOW JESUS

Jesus has just revealed even more about Himself. This is a side of His character that makes some run away and hide. All need the strong Jesus, the loving Jesus, the saving Jesus, the Jesus of truth and comfort. But, do you really want to embrace the Jesus who calls you out of sinful living?

Read aloud the names just revealed and ask yourself if you know Jesus personally by these names:

Exercise 1

"I know that Jesus is...:

my Righteous One.
my Sanctification.
my Redeemer.
my Lamb that was slain.
my Just Judge.
my Passover.
my Stone of Stumbling.
my Christ, My Passover.
my King of Righteousness.
my Launderer's Soap.
my Refiner.
my Purifier.
my Propitiation.

my Holy One of God.
a Stone cut without Hands.
my Merciful and Faithful High Priest.
my Mediator.
my Righteous Servant.
my Intercessor.
my Righteous Branch.
my Righteousness.
my Ransom for all.
my Advocate (with the Father.)
a friend of sinners (like me.)

Exercise 2

What do these names reveal to you about Jesus?

GETTING TO KNOW GOD

The following names or titles for God reveal how He is seen throughout scripture as producing the good fruit of Eternal Righteousness.

"My Name Is…"	"I Am…"	"I Create…"
Yahweh-M'Kaddesh.	Holiness	R
Yaweh-Makkeh.	Patience	I
Yaweh-Tsid Kenu.	Righteousness	G
Sanctifier.	Sanctification	H
the Lord and Judge of All the Earth.	Perfection	T
the God of Holiness.	Power	E
Refiner.	Jealous	O
Purifier.	Forgiveness	U
the Lord the Judge.	Mercy	S
Holy One.	Grace	N
Just Lord.		E
Righteous Father.		S
Judge.		S
Lawgiver.		
the Great and Terrible God.		
the Lord Doth Sanctify.		
the Lord is Righteous.		
Governor.		
the Lord which sanctifies you.		
Consuming Fire.		

But when the kindness and love of God our Savior appeared, he saved us, not because of righteous things we had done, but because of his mercy. He saved us through the washing of rebirth and renewal by the Holy Spirit, whom he poured out on us generously through Jesus Christ our Savior…
Titus 3:4-6

GETTING TO KNOW THE HOLY SPIRIT

The Holy Spirit is sent by God as a guarantee that the Son will return. He is The Promise mentioned in Galatians 3:14. He convicts the believer to be aware of sin and then empowers you to turn towards holiness and righteousness. He gives freedom to you, the believer, from sin and its wage, death. He makes you holy.

The fruit of the righteous is a tree of life, and he who wins souls is wise. Proverbs 11:30

....They will be called oaks of righteousness, a planting of the LORD for the display of his splendor. Isaiah 61:3

For all have sinned and fall short of the glory of God, and are justified freely by his grace through the redemption that came by Christ Jesus. Romans 3:23-24

Day Two

Good Fruit: The Joy of Righteousness

"What, then, was the purpose of the law? It was added because of transgressions until the Seed to whom the promise referred had come. The law was put into effect through angels by a mediator." (Galatians 3:19)

Exercise 3

<u>Directions:</u>
Put an X next to the fruit that you still need to grow.

- ☐ Conviction
- ☐ Purification
- ☐ Repentance
- ☐ Obedience
- ☐ Clean Heart
- ☐ Freedom from Sin
- ☐ God's Forgiveness
- ☐ Holiness

Good Fruit: Righteousness

I am a sinner and I am often disobedient. Now that Jesus is my Lord and Savior, I know when I "fall into sin" and it <u>always</u> steals my joy.

Scripture says in Romans 3:10, "...There is no one righteous, not even one." I can <u>not</u> save myself. The revealed truth that Jesus is my only hope to be pure enough and cleansed from my sin to stand before God's throne, gives my soul the assurance it needs.

I don't like to think of God being angry, but throughout the Bible, His wrath is revealed. Like a little girl who hates when her Daddy is upset, I squirm when I think of my Heavenly Father being angry with me. It is my sin and disobedience which makes God angry. He chooses not to abide in the presence of my sin. If I truly desire (and I do) His presence in my life, I must be put back in right-standing. I could try all day long to do this for myself, but it will get me nowhere.

I can not wipe my slate clean by myself. I can not purify my life, my actions, or my soul by myself. I am not able.

God knows this. He gave a solution so wonderful that it could only have come from Him. You see, in His early Laws, He demanded a blood sacrifice to remove sin. The Jewish people were faithful to offer animals as substitutions for their own lives being sacrificed on the altar. But even these burnt and sin offerings didn't do the trick. Man continued to sin and God continued to be angry with their sin.

So, He sent His only Son to be the animal (Lamb) to be sacrificed (slain) as the final and permanent solution to the problem. Jesus, the Lamb, was sent to be the fulfillment of the Law about sacrificial atonement. God wiped out <u>all</u> of our sins and the penalty for them was paid. Then He said if we would believe His Son was all we needed, the gift of Eternal Life would be ours and our presence in His throne room would be anticipated. He's waiting for us. Our name is written in the Lamb's Book of Life. What joy!

So, if this is all true, why do I still disobey? Why do I still sin? Why do I still let my own nature steal my joy? How can I ever be righteous?

What is Righteousness?
The *New Webster's Dictionary and Thesaurus* gives the following synonyms for the word RIGHTEOUS: chaste, commendable, conscientious, decent, equitable, ethical, good, honorable, just, pure, right, scrupulous, virtuous, worthy, devout, godly, pious, religious, saintly. The antonyms are interesting as well: amoral, corrupt, immoral, licentious, unethical, impious, irreligious.

"Righteousness" is not in the dictionary but the definition from <u>Webster's</u> of "righteous" (an adjective) is: conforming to or in conformity with the moral law. If you look to the definition of the verb, "to right" something, it strikes home in that it means "to restore."

Isn't that what God wants? To restore you to your intended state of being, purpose, and life? To stop the war and have peace reign between you and Himself?

But in order to do that He had to give you something you lost through Adam and Eve. Your nature has become "fallen" and corrupt, immoral, etc. No matter how hard you try you can never get back to the "right" standing (correct, true, perfect) with God that Adam and Eve once enjoyed. He wants you back but can't take you back with dirt on your hands (or heart).

So, as promised, He sent Messiah. Through Jesus He sent a gift package. It's yours to open. It contains something very special as all gifts that are "...good and perfect...coming down from the Father of the heavenly lights..." (James 1:17) What's in this package? God's righteousness. Now if you stumble over this word, keep reading.

Seeds of Faith

Nothing impure will ever enter it, nor will anyone who does what is shameful or deceitful, but only those whose names are written in the Lamb's book of life.
Revelation 21:27

If we confess our sins, he is faithful and just and will forgive us our sins and purify us from all unrighteousness.
1 John 1:9

Your statutes are my heritage forever; they are the joy of my heart.
Psalm 119:111

Blessed is he whose transgressions are forgiven, whose sins are covered. Blessed is the man whose sin the LORD does not count against him and in whose spirit is no deceit. Psalm 32:1-2

Godly sorrow brings repentance that leads to salvation..." 2 Corinthians 7:10

God is righteousness. This fundamental truth is critical to our faith. He is always right, always moral, always good. He doesn't have to do anything to be more of anything. He is all and needs no more. "...In Him there is no darkness at all." (1 John 1:5)

Secondly, anything coming into His presence needs to be in this same state of righteousness. So, God sent the One who never sinned, Jesus, to take your place as the required sacrifice or (atonement), so that you might be joined in a relationship once again with Him. Righteousness is God's very expensive gift: it cost Him one Son. His only Son.

This is the Good News. You are made clean and can therefore enjoy communion with God Himself. But this can only happen through faith and belief in Jesus Christ. God gives the fruit of righteousness to those who believe in His Son.

For more information on this please read the letter of Paul to the Romans.

GOOD FRUIT:
THE SORROW OF CONVICTION/GODLY SORROW

Did you know God feels sorrow, too. You can grieve His Holy Spirit when you sin and disobey God.

And Jesus felt sorrow when His friend Lazarus died. "Jesus wept." (John 11:35) He experienced the kind of sorrow discussed in Unit 5.

But Jesus also feels sorrow today when you forget His "needs". "...Give me a drink..." (John 4:7), He says.

Oswald Chambers says about this, "A person who has forgotten what God treasures will not be filled with joy." (*My Utmost for His Highest*, January 21)

A Christian pastor came to me like a person would go to a priest. He confessed he had been molesting his step-daughter. The words from his mouth were the words of a man convicted of his sin. But his actions showed something else. He "seemed" to be sorrowful for his actions but upon further discussion he seemed more sorrowful that he had been caught in his misbehavior and sorrowful over the consequences for himself. He seemed sorrowful for the mistakes made that led his sin to be uncovered. The ugly secret was out. There appeared at first to be a sense of disgust, not in the sin, but with the consequences for himself.

What was missing? A sense of remorse about his daughter, a sense of his family's pain he had caused by his sin, or a sense of the need to be forgiven. He continued to focus solely on his own needs, his own feelings, his own dysfunction, and his own problems resulting from being brought into the Light of Truth.

He was missing "Godly sorrow," a good fruit that leads to repentance. True <u>Repentance</u> unblocks joy. Godly sorrow produces repentance. You are entering the phase of gardening that I avoid...You have to dig in the soil and pull out the thorns and weeds. Jeremiah 4:3-4 says,

> ..Break up your unplowed ground and do not sow among thorns. Circumcise your hearts, you men of Judah and people of Jerusalem, or my wrath will break out and burn like fire because of the evil you have done-burn with no one to quench it.

This is not a superficial process. Go deep. Dare to let the Lord be your Gardener, uprooting that which blocks your joy of righteousness.

Day Three

A Basket of Good Fruit

Receiving God's gift of righteousness begins to produce more good fruit in the Christian: purification, sanctification or holiness, forgiveness, and freedom from sin. God's desire is for a clean heart and His righteousness is the only way to clean the house of my spirit: the temple of God.

Here are more good fruits that grow from righteous living.

The Fruits of Righteous Living

> Blessed are the poor in spirit, for theirs is the kingdom of heaven. Blessed are those who mourn, for they will be comforted. Blessed are the meek, for they will inherit the earth. Blessed are those who hunger and thirst for righteousness, for they will be filled. Blessed are the merciful, for they will be shown mercy. Blessed are the pure in heart, for they will see God. Blessed are the peacemakers, for they will be called sons of God. Blessed are those who are persecuted because of righteousness, for theirs is the kingdom of heaven. Blessed are you when people insult you, persecute you and falsely say all kinds of evil against you because of me.

Matthew 5:3-11

Seeds of Faith

You heavens above, rain down righteousness; let the clouds shower it down. Let the earth open wide, let salvation spring up, let righteousness grow with it; I, the LORD, have created it.
Isaiah 45:8

Rejoice in the LORD and be glad, you righteous; sing, all you who are upright in heart!
Psalm 32:11

The Fruits of Righteous Living

Peace	I'm at peace with God, no longer warring against His plan for my life. Walking in obedience to my Father.
Access	I can now walk prayerfully into the throne room of God with my praise, my thanksgivings, my intercessions, my petitions.
Hope	I have the hope of the Glory of God in Jesus.
Endurance	Strength for the journey holding my Father's hand.
Reconciliation	Back in right standing in the Father's heart.
Eternal Life	Uninterrupted life with the Father.
Grace	His loving pardon and favor that lifts me up.
His Blessing	Total acceptance of the true "me" in Jesus.
Union	One with God, saved from His wrath at the Judgment.
Kingdom	The Kingdom of Heaven is near.
Comfort	Holy Spirit's strength and compassion for the journey.
Satisfaction	Full and complete joy in all circumstances.
Mercy	The tender forgiveness of my Father.
Inherit the Earth	The inheritance of a prince or princess.
See God	The greatest honor is to be in the Father's presence.
Called Sons of God	He changes my name and inheritance.
Reward	Great rewards in Heaven and the taste of those rewards in this life.
Joy	All of the above!

GOOD FRUIT: REPENTANCE

Is your ground untilled? Then it is time to rethink what you have or are doing and return to God. Joel says in Chapter 2:12-13, "Even now, declares the Lord, return to me with all your heart, with fasting and weeping and mourning. Rend your heart and not your garments. Return to the Lord your God, for he is gracious and compassionate, slow to anger and abounding in love, and he relents from sending calamity." He's a loving God. This is a call to personal repentance from deep within your soul. God is calling you to turn towards Him.

Repentance bears good fruit. "Produce fruit in keeping with repentance." (Matthew 3:8) It is the turning or changing of your mind and heart that yields a changed life.

Baptism is a reminder of your need to have repentance of sin as a daily bath. Remember, you are cleansed by the Blood of Jesus at your Salvation, but you need to bring your life to Him continually for housecleaning.

I desire to do your will, O my God; your law is within my heart.
Psalm 40:8

Jesus replied, "Let it be so now; it is proper for us to do this to fulfill all righteousness..."
Matthew 3:15

Blessed are those who hunger and thirst for righteousness, for they will be filled.
Matthew 5:6

Exercise 4

Circle the words in the bubbles in the chart above that you would like the Lord, the "Launderer's soap" to cleanse.

Sobriety Test
Repentance is a pathway to the River of Life. The path is narrow. We need to be "sober" in spirit to stay on the path. It's a pathway to bearing good fruit. Jesus came to fulfill all righteousness. He opens the door, walks down the path and shows you the way-carries you if necessary. You must come to the River and jump in!

Day Four

BAD FRUIT

"...The shouts of joy over your ripened fruit and over your harvests have been stilled. Joy and gladness are taken away from the orchards; no one sings or shouts in the vineyards: no one treads out wine at the presses, for I have put an end to the shouting." (Isaiah 16:9-10)

Exercise 5

Directions: Read over the list of bad fruits and check any that you need to have pruned in your life in order to grow the joy of eternal righteousness:

- ☐ Sin
- ☐ Disobedience
- ☐ Idolatry
- ☐ Unhealthy Guilt and Shame
- ☐ Regret

BAD FRUIT: SIN

Sin comes from the Greek word "hamartano" which translates "to miss the mark." (*Strongs Dictionary*)

Sin is missing God's mark for the target of your life, who He wants you to be, and what His goal or bulls-eye is for you. His target is not always your target, right?

When you sin, you therefore miss the central being or position in your development that God wants. Missing the mark can produce bad fruit on your Tree of Life.

Nothing steals your joy quicker than your own sin or the sin of others. This is true day to day as well as in the big picture, when Paul says "the wages of sin is death." (Romans 6:23) Spiritual death is permanent separation from God. All will face physical death. But believers are given a "pass" card to spiritual death.

Seeds of Faith

For when we were controlled by the sinful nature, the sinful passions aroused by the law were at work in our bodies, so that we bore fruit for death. Romans 7:5

The ax is already at the root of the trees, and every tree that does not produce good fruit will be cut down and thrown into the fire. Matthew 3:10

For the wages of sin is death, but the gift of God is eternal life in Christ Jesus our Lord. Romans 6:23

If we claim to be without sin, we deceive ourselves and the truth is not in us. 1 John 1:8

The LORD detests men of perverse heart but he delights in those whose ways are blameless. Proverbs 11:20

The list of possible sins would fill this book. We will focus on a few areas of bad fruit: disobedience produced by a rebellious will, idolatry, unhealthy guilt, shame, and regret.

You will focus on your own sins in this Unit and then look at the effect of the sins of others in Units 8 and 9.

Exercise 6

The following, Psalm 51, was written by King David as he asked God's forgiveness for his sins and sought a clean spirit and relationship with Him. Blank spaces have been inserted for you to <u>fill in details</u> with your own story.

>   *Have mercy on me, (name) _____, O God,*
>   *according to your unfailing love; according to your great compassion*
>   *blot out my transgressions. Wash away all my iniquity and cleanse me from my sin.*
>
>   *For I know my transgressions, and my sin is always before me.*
>   *Against you, you only, have I sinned (list your sins)_____*
>   *and done what is evil in your sight, so that you are proved right*
>   *when you speak and justified when you judge.*
>   *Surely I was sinful at birth, sinful from the time my mother conceived me.*
>   *Surely you desire truth in the inner parts;*
>   *you teach me wisdom in the inmost place. (The truth about me is _____*
>   *_____).*
>
>   *Cleanse me with hyssop, and I will be clean; wash me, and I will be whiter than snow.*
>   *Let me hear joy and gladness; let the bones you have crushed rejoice.*
>   *Hide your face from my sins and blot out all my iniquity (list the bad fruit produced by your sin)*
>   *_____.*
>
>   *Create in me a pure heart, O God, and renew a steadfast spirit within me.*
>   *Do not cast me from your presence or take your Holy Spirit from me.*
>   *Restore to me the joy of your salvation and grant me a willing spirit, to sustain me.*
>
>   *Then I will teach transgressors your ways, and sinners will turn back to you.*
>   *Save me from bloodguilt, O God, the God who saves me,*
>   *and my tongue will sing of your righteousness.*
>   *O Lord, open my lips, and my mouth will declare your praise.*
>   *You do not delight in sacrifice, or I would bring it;*
>   *you do not take pleasure in burnt offerings.*
>   *The sacrifices of God are a broken spirit;*
>   *a broken and contrite heart, O God, you will not despise.*
>
>   Psalm 51:1-17

He did evil because he had not set his heart on seeking the LORD. 2 Chronicles 12:14

Who can say, "I have kept my heart pure; I am clean and without sin"? Proverbs 20:9

And this is his command: to believe in the name of his Son, Jesus Christ, and love one another as he commanded us. 1 John 3:23

Their land is full of silver and gold; there is no end to their treasures. Their land is full of horses; there is no end to their chariots. Their land is full of idols; they bow down to the work of their hands, to what their fingers have made. Isaiah 2:7-8

Hebrews 12:3-11

Bad Fruit: Disobedience

All children disobey. A perfectly "good" child is not normal. Good parents discipline disobedience. Discipline means to teach the right way.

When you disobey, God your Father wants to teach you the right way. He sent Jesus to instruct you in His way. Bad fruit is produced when you walk off the path and choose to disobey His way.

Everyone has a will in their soul. The will is the decision-maker. Deciding to disobey is rebellious and is sinful.

A rebellious will has roots in the sins of pride, arrogance, and self-righteousness. Rooted in the self, the will chooses to conduct itself in personal, social, and civil situations against God's sovereignty. The consequences of these actions develop bad fruit when the will's choices are not under God's authority.

Partial obedience is still disobedience. When you obey and follow His will, God takes care of the consequences. When you partly obey, the consequences are of your own making.

Exercise 7

Can you think of an area in your life where you are sinning through disobedience? What have been the consequences? Please describe.

Bad Fruit: Idolatry

God knows that men like idols-something to worship, usually something that can be seen, touched, owned, or acquired. To worship a God that you cannot see requires more faith. A person, a statue, a building, or an object is easier to believe than an unseen God.

Moses warned his people that God commanded them to destroy their idols and put no other God first in their lives. He is a "jealous God."

In direct disobedience and rebellion, they made the golden calf. God allowed them the Ark of the Covenant and they turned it into an idol as well.

Jesus broke the power over all idols, then and now. To maintain idols in your life is to sin and produce much bad fruit.

Exercise 8

What are the idols in your life that are keeping you from worshipping the One True God with all your mind, all your heart, and all your strength? (Matthew 22:37) (Examples: any person, place, or thing which has highest priority in your life.) Please Describe:

BAD FRUIT: UNHEALTHY GUILT AND SHAME

Much has been written on guilt and shame in the past fifteen years. Spiritually speaking, these are God made mechanisms to keep you on the path of righteousness. They are both creatures of God and have a good purpose.

When broken, all of God's creations malfunction. Guilt can become a bad fruit when it strangles and cuts the life-force off inside of you. Likewise, unhealed shame crushes your joy.

BAD FRUIT: REGRET

Regrets, too are a normal part of life. With "20-20 hindsight" you see what could have, would have and should have been or done. The "if only's" in life can truly steal your joy.

Healthy regret allows a person to learn from experience and take new courses of action. Regret involves grieving what might have been but will never be.

Seeds of Faith

You shall not make for yourself an idol in the form of anything in heaven above or on the earth beneath or in the waters below. You shall not bow down to them or worship them; for I, the Lord your God, am a jealous God, punishing the children for the sin of the fathers to the third and fourth generation of those who hate me, but showing love to a thousand generations of those who love me and keep my commandments. Exodus 20:4-6

Let us fix our eyes on Jesus, the author and perfecter of our faith, who for the joy set before him endured the cross, scorning its shame, and sat down at the right hand of the throne of God. Hebrews 12:2

They exchanged the truth of God for a lie, and worshiped and served created things rather than the Creator-who is forever praised. Amen.

Romans 1:25

Unhealthy regret lingers, cuts deep into the soul and causes a person to be unhappy with what is. Regret becomes bad fruit when sorrow, conviction, and forgiveness don't remove the regret but deepen it somehow.

Sarah's Story
An example comes from a woman who left her marriage after seventeen years in hopes for a happier life. Her children and husband continued long after the divorce to blame her for all of life's problems, most of which were brought on by their own choices (drug and alcohol problems, problems with the law and IRS, etc.). Her return to her faith was fervent and sincere. As time went on however, she became deeply depressed and suicidal. She repeated this phrase, "I've done something unforgivable."

Her regret over her choices cycled in an unending circle of self-loathing and unworthiness before God. This was fed by strongholds of feeling deeply unacceptable, fed by early life experiences.

Her regrets produced much bad fruit which her children continued to eat for sometime.

It was truly a vicious cycle. No one in the family was growing good fruit and the roots of despair and bitterness grew deeper. Unwilling to hand over her regrets to the Lord, the fruit continued to rot. It saddens me to not be able to write a happy ending to this story.

I have heard that St. Ignatius of Loyola almost committed suicide until his spiritual director reminded him to release his repented sins and regrets once and for all-thankfully, that's all God requires.

Growing Good Fruit — *Day Five*

Exercise 9

"To grow the good fruit of righteousness, I need to become more:"

- ☐ Ethical
- ☐ Obedient to God
- ☐ Disciplined
- ☐ Honest
- ☐ In control of my self
- ☐ Repentant
- ☐ Accepting of authority
- ☐ Sincere
- ☐ Virtuous
- ☐ Meek
- ☐ Able to make hard choices
- ☐ Able to set goals and achieve them
- ☐ Just and fair to others
- ☐ Remorseful when appropriate
- ☐ Other:

Exercise 10

Which three (3) of the characteristics listed in the previous Exercise would help you grow the good fruit of righteousness in your life?

_____
_____
_____

Please Explain:

Exercise 11 - Pulling Up Weeds

How would you honestly describe yourself?

- ☐ Rebellious
- ☐ A hypocrite
- ☐ Strong willed
- ☐ Rigid
- ☐ Self-indulgent
- ☐ Unfair
- ☐ Ashamed
- ☐ Unethical
- ☐ Unjust
- ☐ Willful
- ☐ Impure
- ☐ Guilty
- ☐ Disobedient
- ☐ Other:

Exercise 12

Which of these personal characteristics are blocking your ability to follow God's authority in your life?

_____
_____
_____

Explain how?

Exercise 13

Write a short prayer asking Jesus to help you remove those characteristics which are blocking your ability to follow God's authority in your life:

> *Dear Jesus,*
>
> *You are my Sanctification and my Righteousness. You are my Mediator, my Intercessor and Just Judge.*
>
> *But Lord, as hard as I try, I keep stumbling and falling flat on my face. I want so badly to please you and yet I struggle with myself in the following ways (name them):*
>
>
> *My prayer dear Lord is:*
>
>
> *Amen.*

Day Six

PREPARING THE SOIL OF THE SOUL: UPROOTING UNHOLY ROOTS

Jesus offers you Himself as righteousness with God. You offer Him your sin and disobedience. Not a fair trade on your part, but that doesn't stop Him.

Now would be the time to hand Him any deviant behavior, a vice, any behavior displeasing to God that leads you away from Him.

Exercise 14

I need to give Jesus the following

_____
_____
_____
_____

The "unholy root" most commonly found blocking the good fruit of righteousness is sin. But in working this unit, something else may have been revealed to you (eg. unworthiness, anger, lack of self acceptance).

Exercise 15

Ask Jesus to help identify and then pluck out the unholy roots blocking this good fruit and causing bad fruit instead.

Seeds of Faith

For the wages of sin is death, but the gift of God is eternal life in Christ Jesus our Lord.
Romans 6:23

Hebrews 6:7-8

James 1:18-21

Day Seven

A Change of Heart

A true conversion to become more like Jesus takes place in your heart. Jesus died to make these changes possible; to bring you the fruit of righteousness and the joy that glorifies God.

Exercise 16

Read over the following list and check those ways in which the Lord is changing you in your spirit home.

My Old Heart Was:	My New Heart Is:
Unwilling	Steadfast
Murderous	Contrite
Wicked/Unrepentant	Just
Perverse	Pure
Obstinate	Obedient
Lustful	Willing
Rebellious	Honorable/Trustful
Willful	Ethical
Unclean	Righteous
Stubborn	Moral
Adulterous	Sober
Corrupted	Meek
Unrepentant	Upright
Other:_____	Other:_____
"The good man brings good things out of the good stored up in his heart, and the evil man brings evil things out of the evil stored up in his heart. For out of the overflow of his heart his mouth speaks." Luke 6:45	"For this is what the high and lofty One says-he who lives forever, whose name is holy: "I live in a high and holy place, but also with him who is contrite and lowly in spirit, to revive the spirit of the lowly and to revive the heart of the contrite." Isaiah 57:15

As your new (born-again) heart is transformed into the likeness of Jesus, you will reap a bountiful harvest of the good fruit of righteousness.

Prayers of a Righteous Man
James reminds us in Chapter 5, verse 16, "Therefore confess your sins to each other and pray for each other so that you may be healed. The prayer of a righteous man is powerful and effective." (James 5:16)

Find someone you can trust and confess your sins in prayer. A priest, a pastor, or a prayer partner, or spiritual director will do.

Exercise 17

Now, let's pray for the good fruit of Righteousness.

Dear Jesus,

You are Righteousness. Without You I can never wipe my slate clean. Without You, I would still be a slave in the market place of sin. You bought me and the price You paid was Your life. Thank You, Jesus.

Your death gives me freedom from the consequences of my disobedience. You have also satisfied our God and by Your love I am now pleasing once again to my Maker. I can rest assured that my sin nature is now ineffective and I am free to live a life pleasing to God.

I don't have to strive to live by the Law, because You have given me a new Law of Love, Lord Jesus.

I'm cleaned by Your Blood and I am truly reconciled. I accept that my state of alienation from God is forever changed, and I am eternally grateful for Your gracious gift to me. You are my Redeemer, my Advocate, and my Mediator. Bless you King of Righteousness!

Amen.

Soul Searching

As a result of the work I've done in this unit:

MIND

What new beliefs or thoughts do I have?

What old beliefs am I ready to put on God's altar?

WILL

What new choices have I made?

What old choices can I give to God?

EMOTIONS

My feelings have changed in the following way:

What feelings or emotions am I giving to the Lord?

Unit Seven

The Joy of Eternal Completion:
Freedom from Dissatisfaction and Self-Pity

    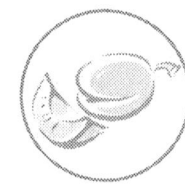 

Joy Choice # 7

Joy is choosing to be made complete
by the love of Jesus and by the Holy Spirit who fills my cup
with contentment, satisfaction and perfection.

*"And God placed all things under his feet and
appointed him to be head over everything for the church,
which is his body, the fullness of him who fills everything in every way."*
Ephesians 1:22-23

"Ask the Lord to put awareness of Himself in you, and your self-awareness will disappear. Then He will be your all in all. Beware of allowing your self-awareness to continue, because slowly it will awaken self-pity, and self-pity is satanic . . . Simply ask the Lord to give you Christ-awareness, and He will steady you until your completeness in Him is absolute."

My Utmost For His Highest, Oswald Chambers, August 20

Then Jesus declared, "I am the bread of life. He who comes to me will never go hungry, and he who believes in me will never be thirsty...I am the living bread that came down from heaven. If anyone eats of this bread, he will live forever. This bread is my flesh, which I will give for the life of the world."

John 6:35, 51

Day One

The orchard ground is covered by a sweet dew. Spread before you is a blanket, a jug of wine and a loaf of bread. A basket of the juiciest fruits is overflowing.

"Join me in a picnic," says Jesus as you enter your wooded sanctuary today. "I have prepared this meal in your honor." He lifts a cup and fills it to the brim. His jovial mood is contagious.

Jesus reaches for another ripened piece of fruit and says, "These fruits I have given you might satisfy you enough, My beloved, but I have more. God made you to be full and complete, but you must learn to empty yourself so that **I** can fill you.

Listen, as I tell you who I am and how I can satisfy you:

I am *the Bread Of Life*.
I am *the Hidden Manna*.
I am *the Portion and the Cup*.
I am *the True Vine*.
I am *the First and the Last*.

I am *the Alpha and the Omega*.
I am *the Beginning and the End*.
I am *the Heir of all things*.
I am *the Shoot*.
I am *the Branch*.
I am *He who fills all in all*.

"When the earth was created and reached completion, a Sabbath rest was proclaimed. At the day of your completion in Me, I became your *Lord of The Sabbath, your Finisher, your Completer*. I announced this on the Cross. The world has nothing to offer you, My beloved. I alone know your heart's desire, and I alone can satisfy you."

Fulfilled and complete, you can say:

I am an heir of God and a co-heir with Christ.
I am blessed in the heavenly realms with every spiritual blessing in Christ.
Your satisfaction brings me great joy!

As you join Jesus in the feast He has prepared just for you, allow yourself to soak in the abundance. Sit for a while in His Presence, thanking Him for supplying all your needs.

For God was pleased to have all his fullness dwell in him...
Colossians 1:19

For in Christ all the fullness of the Deity lives in bodily form, and you have been given fullness in Christ, who is the head over every power and authority.
Colossians 2:9-10

And my God will meet all your needs according to his glorious riches in Christ Jesus.
Philippians 4:19

GETTING TO KNOW JESUS

In this meditation, you met a wonderful side of Jesus that comes when you have chosen to walk with Him for awhile.

Read over the list again and find the names that you know personally. Check all the ways that Jesus has personally shown Himself to you in your spiritual journey.

Exercise 1

"I know Jesus is..."

my Bread of Life.
my Hidden Manna.
my True Vine.
my First and Last.
my Alpha and my Omega.
my Beginning and my End.
the Branch.

He who fills all in all (in me.)
the Heir of all things (for me.)
my Lord of the Sabbath.
my Finisher.
my Completer.
my Portion and my Cup.
the Shoot.

Exercise 2

As you read these names, what is Jesus telling you about Himself?

GETTING TO KNOW GOD

The following names or titles for God reveal how He is seen throughout scripture as producing the good fruit of Eternal Completion.

"My Name Is..."	"I Am..."	"I Create..."
Yaweh-Jireh.	Sufficiency	C
El Shaddai.	Provision	O
Poverty.	Goodness	M
the Sword of Excellency.	Intervention	P
the First.	Care	L
the Last.		E
the Feeder of Israel.		T
Jealous.		I
the Lord will Provide.		O
		N

GETTING TO KNOW THE HOLY SPIRIT

The Holy Spirit is the *"living water"* Jesus gives us to drink. He is an abundant source of supply that will never end. He pours Himself into places of desolation to satisfy the deepest thirst. He ushers in all completion in and through Jesus.

Day Two

GOOD FRUIT:
THE JOY OF ETERNAL COMPLETION

God made you just like a potter uses clay to form an empty vessel. If you let Him, He fills up that vessel or cup. If you let Him, He provides all you need. But being "empty" is uncomfortable, painful at times and so you rush to fill yourself. Dissatisfaction is rampant in this world as people scramble to fill the emptiness.

God wants you to pour yourself out so <u>He</u> can fill your cup. He sent Jesus to complete or top off any joy you can possibly find on this earth. It says in John 15, verse 11, "I have told you this so that my joy may be in you and that your joy may be complete."

Without Him, you end up in ruin and desolation with wasted, useless, and vain attempts to fill what God intended to fill Himself, (with Himself.) The Greek and Hebrew definitions help us see the true meaning of scripture. To "fill" means to make complete, to satisfy, to be full, to slake thirsts or appetites, to fill entirely, to quaff to satiety, and satisfaction itself. (*Strongs Complete Dictionary*)

Your best attempts at filling your own cup leave that cup half empty. When allowed to participate, Jesus has your cup running over. Psalm 23 says, "my cup overflows." Can you say that?

With joy you will draw water from the wells of salvation.
Isaiah 12:3

He who did not spare his own Son, but gave him up for us all-how will he not also, along with him, graciously give us all things?
Romans 8:32

Command those who are rich in this present world not to be arrogant nor to put their hope in wealth, which is so uncertain, but to put their hope in God, who richly provides us with everything for our enjoyment.
1 Timothy 6:17

Genesis 1:11

Genesis 3:6-7

1 John 2:16

Why would the Creator of the entire uerse care if you are satisfied in this way? Because it pleases Him. Because then you will come with a grateful heart and offer Him thanksgiving and praise. And the more you do that, the more full your cup becomes!

How have you tried to fill your own cup? Let's take a closer look!

Turn to the beginning of the Bible to Genesis, Chapter One. There we find the Spirit of God busy at work, creating. After all, He is called the Creator. And what are His materials? Water, light, dry land and seeds. He created the stuff to provide for you before there was even a "you" to provide for! He liked the fruit trees with little seeds tucked in the fruit to make more fruit trees. What a nifty idea!

In fact, He seemed to like His creature, the seed, so much He gave humans "seeds" as well. He gave you the desire to eat of the fruit trees and to be satisfied by them. He plants His seeds (His Word) in you and patiently awaits their sprouting. Then as you mature, others may pick the fruit from your branches and so on. You are fruitful and multiply as commanded.

Forbidden Fruit
Of course, everyone knows the most famous fruit tree story ever told. Adam and Eve were from the get-go a pretty interesting couple. They walked with God on a daily basis. They knew His will clearly enough as they were in His presence with full provision, full security, and fullness of all that life could offer. Yet there was <u>something in them that craved more</u> and thus they ate of the Tree of Knowledge of Good and Evil, the forbidden fruit from the forbidden tree. Before they could eat of the Tree of Life too, and become immortal, God stopped them.

> *And the LORD God said, "The man has now become like one of us, knowing good and evil. He must not be allowed to reach out his hand and take also from the tree of life and eat, and live forever." So the LORD God banished him from the Garden of Eden to work the ground from which he had been taken. After he drove the man out, he placed on the east side of the Garden of Eden cherubim and a flaming sword flashing back and forth to guard the way to the tree of life.*
>
> Genesis 3:22-24

Great News of Abundance
Now, when you turn to the very last chapter in the Bible, Revelation 22:1-2 tells you that the City of God is a beautiful place, abundant, and rich in provision. And in this city is a river *"whose streams make glad."* This river flows from God's throne and is *"the water of life."* It is crystal clear implying absolute purity. The Lamb (Jesus) is at its source. Again, perfect, eternal provision. So why are you ever worried or dissatisfied? He's got you covered!

> *A shoot will come up from the stump of Jesse; from his roots a Branch will bear fruit. The Spirit of the LORD will rest on him-the Spirit of wisdom and of understanding, the Spirit of counsel and of power, the Spirit of knowledge and of the fear of the LORD-and he will delight in the fear of the LORD. He will not judge by what he sees with his eyes, or decide by what he hears with his ears...*
>
> Isaiah 11:1-3

God provided all you need. Jesus is the "shoot." He is the Branch. He sent the Spirit to continue the provision to all who believe.

Seeds of Faith

Hope deferred makes the heart sick, but a longing fulfilled is a tree of life.
Proverbs 13:12

The trees of the Lord are well watered, the cedars of Lebanon that he planted.
Psalm 104:16

Perseverance must finish its work so that you may be mature and complete, not lacking anything.
James 1:4

Do not conform any longer to the pattern of this world, but be transformed by the renewing of your mind. Then you will be able to test and approve what God's will is-his good, pleasing and perfect will.
Romans 12:2

Exercise 3

<u>Directions:</u>
Put an X next to the fruit that you still need to grow.

- ☐ Christ-Awareness
- ☐ Perfection
- ☐ Enough
- ☐ Finishing
- ☐ Spirit-filled
- ☐ Satisfaction
- ☐ Fulfillment
- ☐ Poverty in Spirit

GOOD FRUIT: CHRIST-AWARENESS

The methods used in this workbook intentionally draw you into self-awareness or self-examination. Like most therapeutic healing models, this type of process may heal some areas and soothe some emotional pain, but it does not guarantee <u>true healing</u>. So, at this stage in our journey together, you need to be aware that your goal is not to stay in self-awareness but to move into Christ-awareness.

Oswald Chambers cautioned against this very thing in *My Utmost for His Highest* (August 19). He says:

> God intends for us to live a well-rounded life in Christ Jesus, but there are times when that life is attacked from the outside. Then we tend to fall back into self-examination, a habit that we thought was gone. Self-awareness is the first thing that will upset the completeness of our life in God, and self-awareness continually produces a sense of struggling and turmoil in our lives. Self-awareness is not sin, and it can be produced by numerous emotions or by suddenly being dropped into a totally new set of circumstances. Yet it is never God's will that we should be anything less than absolutely complete in Him . . . If we come to Him (Jesus) asking Him to produce Christ-awareness in us, He will always do it, until we fully learn to abide in Him.

GOOD FRUIT: PERFECTION

God wants you to be <u>perfect</u>. But you say, "But I'm not perfect or holy!" But in the Bible, perfect means to be <u>filled, complete, full or whole, healed, and healthy and holy</u>! Wow!

The New Testament says specifically that Jesus has the way to do this. It is through a relationship with Him.

By receiving Him, your life is made full, complete, and whole. That means you are <u>healed</u> of all brokenness from sin and spiritual wounds. That means you become <u>healthy</u> in mind and spirit, and that the end result is that you are made, through Him, set apart and pleasing to God. That is what "holy" means.

> **God is always complete (full, perfect, whole, healthy, holy).**
>
> **Fullness of joy means to be completed in God, by God; to be one with Him; His possession...*and you have been given fullness in Christ, who is the head over every power and authority.***
> **Colossians 2:10**
>
> **He wants you to reverently and meekly seek Him for completion. Then you will be perfect.** *Be perfect, therefore, as your heavenly Father is perfect.*
> **Matthew 5:48** .

You can't receive this kind of healing, (completing your joy) other than through a perfect union with God's Son.

So, listen to what this really means:

When you are in mourning, when you are at your lowest spiritually, when you feel the emptiest, when you feel the loneliest, when you feel the most depressed, when you are being picked on and persecuted in some way, when you are broken and shattered, **that's** precisely when God says, "OK, now come to Me, ask Me, make a request, lean on Me, trust Me, don't be afraid." As soon as you let go and do that, guess what can happen?

MIRACLES! MIRACLES!

Say it with me, "I believe in MIRACLES!" If you turn your life over to God you <u>can</u> expect miracles.

But just as he who called you is holy, so be holy in all you do; for it is written: "Be holy, because I am holy."
1 Peter 1:15-16

Hebrews 9:12-14

2 Corinthians 9:10

We proclaim him, admonishing and teaching everyone with all wisdom, so that we may present everyone perfect in Christ.
Colossians 1:28

...so that the man of God may be thoroughly equipped for every good work.
2 Timothy 3:17

I have brought you glory on earth by completing the work you gave me to do.
John 17:4

You've been examining the road blocks to a stronger, more perfect union with God. You've worked hard, as a farmer would toil all day in the hot sun. You may have begun to feel the healing touch of the Holy Spirit as you cleanse your inner life. But you have a little more work to do.

It's not enough to understand intellectually the things which block your joy. It's not enough to feel emotionally the pain, the sorrow, or the emptiness of your inner being. You must lay it all at His feet.

GOOD FRUIT: ENOUGH

God is "enough" and He makes you enough. It is true that you (by yourself) are never enough. Beloved, is this a question that has haunted you, "Am I enough-good enough, smart enough, pretty enough, etc?"

You are not enough until a divine presence of an eternal being is living inside of you. You are miraculously made "enough" in the eyes of the only One that matters!

Jesus gives you worth and restores you to "enough-ness".

His Cross did this for you. His death completed you.

Like Jesus, you have to come to the end of you and been born again. This new life is the provision of all that you need to be enough. You only have to accept it. True conversion comes when you bring your lacking, your depletion, your emptiness and in exchange, He gives you enough.

Jesus emptied himself down to the last moments of His earthly life. You too have to follow His example and be made full by being made empty. What a paradox! You have to be empty to be full.

> **I am made full when I am empty.**
> **Then I receive complete union with God the Father.**
> **Jesus accomplished full and complete removal**
> **of sin to give us full and complete union with God,**
> **which gives us full and complete joy!**

Good Fruit: Finishing

I've just mowed half the backyard. I'll finish it later, it's too hot; I'm too tired; I have other things to do.

My husband often says, "Half measures gain us nothing." To complete a project, to finish a job, to come to the end of the book: unfinished things can steal my joy!

God finished His creation and then declared the Sabbath rest. He didn't stop until He finished the job. Jesus announces from the Cross, *"It is finished."* (John 19:30) He is the Author and Finisher of our faith, our lives, our joy.

To be like Jesus, you too must be a finisher, a completer, and an accomplisher of His mission for your life. The good fruit of the completed task or finished product mirrors the hope you have of moving from glory to glory until you become like your Maker (not gods, but completed and lacking in nothing).

Do you ever get in your own way? Do you trick yourself, procrastinate, block God's attempts to help you be a finisher?

Do you fear success? Do you deem yourself incapable? Do you "bite off more than you can chew" and therefore set yourself up for incompleteness in your life?

To be a finisher is to be like Christ who accomplished His work in our lives once for all on the Cross.

Such a high priest meets our need- one who is holy, blameless, pure, set apart from sinners, exalted above the heavens. Unlike the other high priests, he does not need to offer sacrifices day after day, first for his own sins, and then for the sins of the people. He sacrificed for their sins once for all when he offered himself.
Hebrews 7:26-27

The thief comes only to steal and kill and destroy; I have come that they may have life, and have it to the full.
John 10:10

Romans 12:3-8

1 Peter 4:7

There are different kinds of gifts, but the same Spirit. There are different kinds of service, but the same Lord. There are different kinds of working, but the same God works all of them in all men. Now to each one the manifestation of the Spirit is given for the common good.
1 Corinthians 12:4-7

Psalm 107:35-37

Day Three

Good Fruit: Spirit-Filled

One of the ways God promises to fill you is to pour His Holy Spirit into your life. The sign that the Spirit is present in the believer is the presence of His "gifts." Every believer has at least one.

The Bible tells you there are many gifts of the Holy Spirit!

1. Prophecy	10. Encouraging
2. Distinguish between true and false prophesy	11. Contributing
	12. Performing acts of mercy
3. Instruction, teaching	13. Giving aid
4. Speaking in tongues	14. Helping
5. Interpretation of tongues	15. Administration
6. Knowledge	16. Healing
7. Wisdom	17. Performing miracles
8. Caring for the needy	
9. Serving	

God has placed in you unique gifts that are to be used to help others. Your fulfillment of life will come through the use or expression of these gifts as you bring Jesus into the world.

Exercise 4

Read over the list above and pick up to five (5) that you have. Put their numbers here:

_____   _____   _____   _____   _____

Exercise 5

Are you open to exploring the ways God has gifted you?
   Yes_____No_____

Are you willing to build your gifts to their highest potential?
   Yes_____No_____

Are you willing to regularly express (use, show) your gifts?
   Yes_____No_____

GOOD FRUIT: SATISFACTION

At the Last Supper, the night before He died, Jesus took bread and wine and fed His disciples. This same celebratory meal is served every day all around the world and is known as the Mass, the Eucharist, Communion, or the Lord's Supper.

Jesus became the Bread of Life. Jesus offers to feed your spirit and make you full. Jesus gives you the Cup of His Blood that was shed for you. All of this is mystery, to be accepted by the faithful.

So there remains a tension between your hunger and fullness, your thirst and satisfaction.

This mysterious status of your spirit is kept in check by the Holy Spirit. He fills the hearts of the faithful and monitors the condition of your spirit.

Jesus went into the desert "full of the Holy Spirit" (Luke 4:1). He was full before He attempted to become empty. His emptiness allowed Him to hear from His Father, feed even more richly on His Word, and face the enemy with power and strength. Spiritual food gave His spirit strength just as it does yours.

Believers are already indwelt with the Holy Spirit, but you can ask Him to fill more and more of you each day "to do the work He has given us to do".
The Book of Common Prayer,

People get hungry and thirsty. God made you that way in your body, and He made you that way in your spirit. He built into you a deep hunger for Himself to "draw all" to Him.

People have a thirst for that which is true and good. This state of spiritual neediness is what brings you to the Heavenly table prepared long ago. We will explore more of this in Unit 11.

Do not work for food that spoils, but for food that endures to eternal life, which the Son of Man will give you. On him God the Father has placed his seal of approval.
John 6:27

For my flesh is real food and my blood is real drink.
John 6:55

They all ate the same spiritual food...
1 Corinthians 10:3

Isaiah 58:11

From the fullness of his grace we have all received one blessing after another.
John 1:16

You prepare a table before me in the presence of my enemies. You anoint my head with oil; my cup overflows.
Psalm 23:5

...so that you may eat and drink at my table in my kingdom and sit on thrones, judging the twelve tribes of Israel.
Luke 22:30

2 Corinthians 9:8

Psalm 107:9

Come to the Table

*That part of me
That looks to heaven,
Searches for You-
Longing for a glimpse
Of Your perfect face.*

*My core, my center
Where You are welcome
To live and move
And turn
My being into
That which
Only You can
Fully see.*

*Hunger pangs, Great thirst. My spirit
Craves your loving nourishment as a
Baby longs for its mother.
You invite me to come to Your table and be fed.*

*Come Lord Jesus.
Wrap around and hold me
My spirit seeks to
Dance with You as
Its partner.
What a beautiful waltz!*

GOOD FRUIT: FULFILLMENT

Fulfillment occurs when you can say, "For the moment <u>I am</u> OK. I am <u>doing</u> what God wants me to do. I am <u>full</u> of His peace, love and joy."

Exercise 6:

Think about the various jobs, careers, projects, or ministries that you have pursued and ask yourself, "Which ones felt right, felt joyful, left me feeling a sense of peace or goodness within me?" Use the space below to write about one experience.

Exercise 7

On the other hand, which ones felt wrong in that you often ended the day feeling anxious, miserable, stressed, lonely, unfulfilled. Briefly describe one of these experiences.

Exercise 8

Prayer: Ask the Lord to show you His direction in your life for His glory and your fulfillment. The following prayer may help you get started. Journal what He shares with you.

Prayer of Abandonment

*Father, I abandon myself
Into Your hands;
Do with me what You will
Whatever You may do,
I thank You.
I am ready for all,
I accept all.
Let only Your will
Be done in me and in
All Your creatures.
I wish no more than this, O Lord.*

*Into Your hands
I commend my soul.
I offer it to You
With all the love of
My heart.
For I love You, Lord.
And so I need to give
Myself, to surrender
Myself into Your hands
Without reserve, and
With boundless confidence,
For You are my Father.*

Anonymous

...equip you with everything good for doing his will, and may he work in us what is pleasing to him, through Jesus Christ, to whom be glory for ever and ever. Amen.
Hebrews 13:21

LORD, you have assigned me my portion and my cup; you have made my lot secure.
Psalm 16:5

Psalm 107:9

"I am the Alpha and the Omega," says the Lord God, "who is, and who was, and who is to come, the Almighty.
Revelation 1:8

GOOD FRUIT: POVERTY IN SPIRIT

It is in my <u>in</u>completeness, my poverty, or in my total lacking that I have room for Christ. If I fill myself up, why do I need Him?

Jesus says on the Mount, "Blessed are the poor in spirit." (Matthew 5:3) It is precisely when you are without, then He can bless you, pour Himself into you and fill your cup. And what can He pour into you?

Exercise 9

What fills your cup? What do you need from Jesus?

His Will
His Hope
His Strength
His Love
His Joy
His Worth
His Excellence
His Self-control
His Peace
His Patience
His Goodness
His Kindness
His Faithfulness
His Gentleness
His Riches
His Serenity
His Understanding
His Spirit

There is no end to Him. He is the Alpha and Omega, the Beginning and the End. His ability and desire to fill your cup is not a matter of supply. It's a matter of yielding to Him instead of a false belief that you or someone else can make you complete.

 **To be complete, full and whole I must rely on myself or someone or something (food, alcohol, sex, spending, a person, a program, etc.)**

 **Only Jesus can make me full and complete.**

I need to be poor in spirit, which means empty, no more, used up, or unworthy to become more. Rich in spirit means filled, complete, whole. Eternity is a state of all things being complete, done, or finished. No more projects to complete. No more messes to clean up. No more lists to do. In fact there isn't as much "doing" as there is "being". Doesn't that sound great!

Day Four

BAD FRUIT
Exercise 10

Directions: Read over the list of bad fruits and check any that you need to have pruned in your life in order to grow the joy of completion.

- ☐ Addictions
- ☐ Dissatisfaction and Self-pity
- ☐ Full of Myself
- ☐ Co-dependency

Seeds of Faith

...for he satisfies the thirsty and fills the hungry with good things.
Psalm 107:9

Romans 11:36

Each tree is recognized by its own fruit. People do not pick figs from thornbushes, or grapes from briers.
Luke 6:44

You will eat, but you will not be satisfied; your stomach will still be empty. You will store up but save nothing, because what you save I will give to the sword. You will plant but not harvest; you will press olives but not use the oil on yourselves, you will crush grapes but not drink the wine.
Micah 6:14-15

2 Corinthians 9:6

BAD FRUIT: ADDICTIONS

One good thing that has come out of the field of psychology and medicine in the past fifty years is the study of addictions and the fallout of addictive behavior. If you have lived with an addiction or with someone who has one, you know personally the bad fruit that comes with it. You've tasted this fruit and know how poisonous it can be to body, spirit and soul.

So why do addictions exist and continue to torment millions of lives? From a spiritual viewpoint, addictions have been defined as "trying to fill the emptiness on the inside with some person, place or thing from the outside."

This is not a new phenomenon. Noah turned to alcohol after the Ark reached dry land. His mission had filled his days for countless years! What could possibly top that? A few beers?

I have no answer to why people turn to self-destruction to fill the emptiness. It is one of the greatest paradoxes of our existence. Why destroy the vessel just because it is empty or broken? Is it the pain? Is it a way to self-medicate?

Addictions usually have an element of looking for fulfillment in "all the wrong places". The destructive elements are the "wrong places" (sex, chemicals, work, relationships, etc.) because they bring us further and further away from God. Further and further into our prideful search for our own solutions. Further and further away from true joy.

BAD FRUIT: DISSATISFACTION AND SELF-PITY

Complain, complain, complain. When I get on a roll it almost feels good. But it brings <u>no</u> good fruit. It brings me down a dark path into self-pity and despair.

Joy is the ability to be content in any circumstance. Bad fruit is produced when you focus on the deprivation you feel, the lacking sensations, the depletion you have created in your own personal resources. Negativity and scarcity thinking can be addictive, too.

Dissatisfaction, malcontent, and unhappiness tend to feed on each other and affect others profoundly. Others eat of this bad fruit and spread the bad taste to the next fellow. Whole organizations can be contaminated in a short time by one person's bad fruit of dissatisfaction. <u>Beware</u>...if someone passes you their bad fruit, reject it for your own health. You wouldn't take bad fruit from the grocery except if the grocer has deceived you by packaging a few pieces of good fruit on top. Let the buyer beware!

BAD FRUIT: FULL OF MYSELF

This type of bad fruit grows with roots of pride and arrogance. Someone who is "full of him or herself" can not be full of the Lord. John the Baptist says you must decrease so Jesus can increase.(John 3:30) When there is much of you, there is little room for Jesus to squeeze in.

Arrogance sees only the self as the best source of completion. Blinded by this deception, that you are fulfilled, satisfied and perfect in your own self, you may actually believe this lie. Psychology calls this narcissism. Jesus was put to death at the hands of those who were "full of themselves". People hurt Him still every day when they seek to fill themselves and then take all the glory.

Exercise 11

What fills your cup? Check all that apply.

- His Will
- His Hope
- His Strength
- His Love
- His Joy
- His Worth
- His Excellence
- His Self-control
- His Peace
- His Patience
- His Goodness
- His Kindness
- His Faithfulness
- His Gentleness
- His Riches
- His Serenity
- His Understanding
- His Spirit, and on and on

Exercise 12

If you checked anything in Exercise 11, describe below the effect this has had on your life and the life of those you love.

Psalm 107:33-34

You cannot drink the cup of the Lord and the cup of demons too; you cannot have a part in both the Lord's table and the table of demons.
1 Corinthians 10:21

Psalm 119:57

I will save you from all your uncleanness. I will call for the grain and make it plentiful and will not bring famine upon you. I will increase the fruit of the trees and the crops of the field so that you will no longer suffer disgrace among the nations because of famine. Ezekiel 36:29-30

BAD FRUIT: CODEPENDENCY

Codependency is the sacrificing of your own self and ULTIMATELY your own joy in your relationships to other people, to your job, to your family, or to your church, IN ORDER TO RECEIVE MORE self-esteem, security or self-worth, or in the hopes that eventually you will feel joyful.

I was raised in a family where service to the church was a normal and expected part of life. My father taught Sunday School for 35 years. I fell into his footsteps proudly. He was involved in the church leadership, and so was I. I saw much good fruit from this in my early life.

Like many people in their twenties, I had left the church for a while, too busy to bother. But when things turned sour, I discovered my spiritual bankruptcy. I headed for the place I thought would soothe my soul, a church. My joy reserves were depleted, and I sat in church like I sit in the drive-through, waiting for someone to fill my belly!

I was tremendously needy and yet no one could have guessed as much. I presented myself to my new church as the happy volunteer extraordinaire!

I began to attract a following. People began to see me as the "leader" that could bring this struggling little church out of its pattern of infighting and conflict. The cherished image of leader was comfortable to me and filled my emptiness.

I gave more and more. The more I gave, the more I felt loved, respected, and admired. This hooked me. I felt I was really accomplishing something in God's Name. But the tide turned and like anyone who tries to make changes, I began to be blamed, accused of wrongdoing, called a liar, a thief and a cheat. I was none of these to be sure except that I fell for a lie that became my truth:

The more I do, and give, the more full and complete satisfaction I'll receive. True Joy will return and all my problems will end.

I was living a lie. This lie is often called codependency and is the opposite of God-dependency. My needs were being met and for awhile, I was satisfied.

I remember, after a particularly painful meeting at the church, walking out and saying to God, "After all I have done for them!" (The battle cry of the co-dependent.)

I was devastated and angry. What had I done to them to deserve this? I spent another year in denial that this was really happening - that the same people who had liked me one minute were talking behind my back the next. I began to pull away. Crash and burn. I went to therapy and took a good hard look at my codependence.

But under my codependent behavior was a deep spiritual hunger and thirst that I didn't even know existed. When therapy alone did not "fill my cup", I began to see my neediness in a positive light, something of God and not totally a dysfunction. My therapist, an atheist, did the best thing possible: she identified my emptiness and neediness. However, she was not connected to the Source! I had to go elsewhere and guess where I went? Back to a church! This time I didn't volunteer for anything for two full years.

Exercise 13

Are there codependency issues in your life? Write about them here.

Seeds of Faith

The Spirit and the bride say, "Come!" And let him who hears say, "Come!" Whoever is thirsty, let him come; and whoever wishes, let him take the free gift of the water of life.
Revelation 22:17

Psalm 126:5-6

Day Five

GROWING GOOD FRUIT

Exercise 14

"In order to the grow good fruit of completion, I need to become more…" (Check all that apply.)

- ☐ Orderly
- ☐ Generous
- ☐ Responsible
- ☐ Receptive/open
- ☐ Thrifty
- ☐ Dependable
- ☐ Diligent
- ☐ Organized
- ☐ Determined
- ☐ Willing to be content
- ☐ Excellent
- ☐ Efficient
- ☐ Able to receive
- ☐ Able to say "No"
- ☐ Able to finish what I start
- ☐ Able to hold on
- ☐ Able to initiate
- ☐ Able to set limits with others
- ☐ Able to set limits on myself
- ☐ Able to "empty myself" out
- ☐ Other:_____

Exercise 15

"I need to be able to…" (Check all that apply.)

- ☐ Wait to get my needs met
- ☐ Stick with something in spite of opposition, setbacks
- ☐ Face unpleasantness, discomfort or frustration without giving up
- ☐ Wait for gratification Able to not have it "my" way
- ☐ Compromise, or negotiate
- ☐ Live up to responsibilities, be dependable.
- ☐ Honor promises, can be counted on
- ☐ Make a decision and follow through
- ☐ Be courageous enough to take action
- ☐ Set realistic goals for myself and others
- ☐ Be content with the way things are.
- ☐ Other:

Exercise 16 – PULLING UP WEEDS

Without the skills and attributes listed above, you may have settled into being "less" rather than "more" How would you honestly describe yourself?

Read over the following chart and check all that apply to you.

"I am …"	Always	Some times	Never
Envious			
Unreliable			
Overly busy			
Addicted			
Jealous			
Unresponsive to others			
Wishy-washy			
Disorganized			
Lazy			
Tardy			
Sloppy			
Inconsistent			
Covetous			
Stingy			
Extravagant			
Lonely			
Deprived			
Competitive			
Judgmental			
Full of regrets			
Depleted			
Codependent			

"I am …."	Always	Some times	Never
Greedy			
Changing jobs			
Changing friends			
Changing churches			
Changing mates			
Breaking promises			
Irresponsible			
Not a carry-through person			
Making excuses or alibis			
Setting unrealistic goals and expectations			
Procrastinating			
Unable to make commitments			
Exploring possibilities and options and then no action			
Mediocre			
Incomplete in this way: _____			

I pray that out of his glorious riches he may strengthen you with power through his Spirit in your inner being, so that Christ may dwell in your hearts through faith. And I pray that you, being rooted and established in love, may have power, together with all the saints, to grasp how wide and long and high and deep is the love of Christ, and to know this love that surpasses knowledge-that you may be filled to the measure of all fullness of God. Ephesians 3:16-19

Exercise 17

Pick three of these characteristics (from Exercise 16) that get in the way of your having the joy of completion in your life:

_____
_____
_____

Exercise 18

Describe how these block or get in the way of this type of good fruit growing in your life.

Day Six

PREPARING THE SOIL OF THE SOUL: UPROOTING UNHOLY ROOTS

As you have read, Jesus makes you complete and full. He is your completion.

As you have worked through this unit, the Holy Spirit may have helped you "see" the deeper root to this type of joy being blocked in your life. Take some time to let the Holy Spirit shine the light of truth on any memories regarding the following areas that need uprooting.

Exercise 19

Check those that apply to your life:

- ☐ Deprivations (experienced any time in life)
- ☐ Losses
- ☐ Dissatisfactions
- ☐ Negative Attitudes
- ☐ Other: _____

Jesus gives you His all. Give Him yours. Ask Him to remove the deepest "unholy root" that is preventing this good fruit from flourishing in your life. (Please describe)

Exercise 20

Often our relationship status can affect our level of joy. Look over the following list and indicate where you are now.

- ☐ Single
- ☐ Married
- ☐ Separated
- ☐ Divorced
- ☐ A parent with (#)_____ children
- ☐ Living with someone that I am not married to
- ☐ Childless
- ☐ Living alone

How does what you checked above affect the joy in your life? Please Explain. (Would you feel more or less "complete" if things were different?)

Exercise 21   KILL JOYS

Sometimes our current life circumstances can affect our ability to receive joy. These may be situations that you have no control over, like what part of the world you were born in or who is in your family. Other situations you do have more control over, but something may be blocking you from doing anything about it, i.e., where you work, financial problems, etc.

Read over the following list of issues that can stand between you and your joy, and indicate if there are any situational blocks to your joy.

- ☐ Financial issues (e.g., I don't have enough money. I'm obsessed, fearful about money.)
- ☐ Time issues (e.g., I'm too rushed, stressed, burdened, always late, etc.)
- ☐ Issues concerning children (e.g., My children are disappointments; I have failed as a parent, etc.)
- ☐ Job or career issues (e.g., I'm not successful enough; I hate my job, etc.)
- ☐ Family issues (e.g., My family doesn't accept me; I come from the wrong race, color, etc.)
- ☐ Social issues (e.g., I have no friends; I don't measure up, etc.)
- ☐ Health issues (e.g., I'm overweight, depressed, too thin, too tall, too short, etc.)
- ☐ Relationship issues (e.g., I'm not loved or accepted in my relationships; I'm all alone, etc.)
- ☐ Traumatic event (e.g., I'm a victim of a crime, auto accident, etc. I've lost a loved one, etc.)
- ☐ Legal issues (e.g., I'm over my head in legal matters; I'm afraid I might go to jail, be sued, etc.)
- ☐ Other:_____

Write about the items you checked above and how they affect your joy.

Exercise 22   People, Places, and Things

Your acceptance of the fullness of Christ can be blocked when you are consumed by people, places or things which steal your joy. Check any that apply to you.

- ☐ Alcohol or drug related problem
- ☐ Food problem
- ☐ Sex or pornography problem
- ☐ Spending, gambling problem
- ☐ Negative self-talk, believing your own doubts about yourself
- ☐ Prejudice problem
- ☐ Abuse (physical, verbal, sexual, spiritual)
- ☐ Stress problem
- ☐ Guilt or shame problem
- ☐ No commitments or priorities
- ☐ Low self-acceptance
- ☐ Needing to be in control
- ☐ Loss: past, present or anticipated
- ☐ Work related problem
- ☐ Relationship problem
- ☐ Other_____

Exercise 23

At this time in your life, which three items checked (in Exercise 22) are affecting you the most in your ability to receive the fullness of joy from Christ? Be honest and elaborate if you wish.

Seeds of Faith

This is the day the LORD has made; let us rejoice and be glad in it.
Psalm 118:24

Offer these to the Lord when you are ready.

THE JOY OF BEING BALANCED

Holy balance means all eight areas of your life are in a healthy proportion and you maintain this balance on a daily basis.

1. Spiritual Life
2. Emotional Life
3. Physical Life
4. Work Life
5. Educational Life
6. Social Life
7. Practical Life
8. Family Life

Joy TRUTH

At the end of the day, you may be physically tired but you will not feel depressed or stressed if that day has been balanced. Instead you will feel joyful. You will look forward to the day when you wake up if it has been planned as a balanced one.

Exercise 24

Draw a normal day in your life:

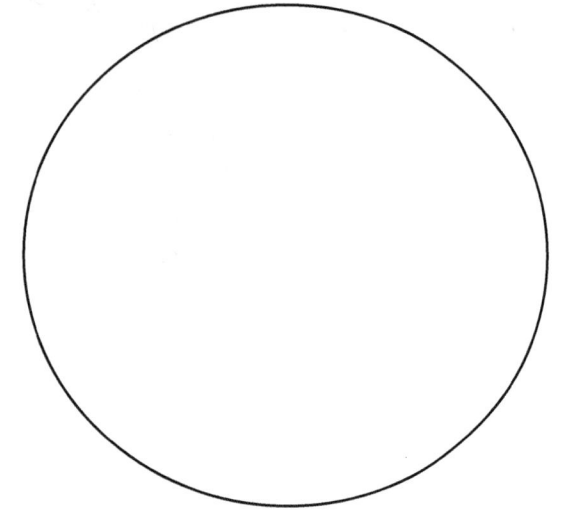

What steps do you need to take to restore a healthy balance to your life?

Exercise 25

Listed below are the life areas that should be in balance. Check the boxes that best describes your life now.

	Needs Healing	OK for Now	Complete in Christ
My Sexual Self			
My Intellectual Self			
My Spiritual Self			
My Playful/Child-like Self			
My Practical Self			
My Learning Self			
My Working Self			
My Physical Self			
My Creative Self			

Dear God,

I am needy and my desire is to be full and complete in You.

Your Son died to finish a work in me and He will complete this task if I let Him. As I become less, You become more.

I am empty. I have deep places within me of poverty.

I ask You now to feed me with the Spiritual food I need for my daily journey. Fill me, Holy Spirit, with all I need so that I can go into the world in readiness and completion. Put my life into a Holy Balance.

I give You thanks for being my all in all, my Portion and my Cup and the provider of my life. You are Jesus, my Lord.

Amen.

Day Seven

A Change of Heart

It is in our Lord's nature to complete and make whole. The fruit of completion and perfection comes from Jesus only.

As you have let Him work in you, your spirit (heart) has been re-evaluating priorities and perspectives. You may have noticed a new attitude-a new view with the eyes of the heart.

Exercise 26

Check all the words below that describe the changes in your spirit

My Old Heart Was	*My New Heart Is*
Dissatisfied	Empty (yet full)
Ungrateful	Whole
Divided ("half-hearted")	Solid
Grudging	Satisfied
Greedy	Content
Unhappy	Grateful
Grumbling	Thankful
Complaining	Hungry
Other:_____	Other:_____
"I thought in my heart, "Come now, I will test you with pleasure to find out what is good." But that also proved to be meaningless." Ecclesiastes 2:1	"Delight yourself in the LORD and he will give you the desires of your heart." Psalm 37:4

BEWARE: A GREAT LIE

 **Joy LIE**   I can "self-activate."

What is the truth?

 **Joy TRUTH**   **Jesus is the fulfiller. Jesus is the actualizer. Jesus is the activator of our wholeness. You participate with Him in your completion.**

Units One to Seven have shown you how to grow good fruit by having a relationship between Jesus and your self. As you move into Unit Eight, you will shift your focus on union with others and the joy this brings.

Jesus
The Source of Perfect Joy
⇩
He gives me full and complete joy
⇩
He heals me, makes me whole
⇩
I am becoming healthy
⇩
I am becoming holy and perfect

Soul Searching

As a result of the work I've done in this unit:

MIND
What new beliefs or thoughts do I have?

What old beliefs am I ready to put on God's altar?

WILL
What new choices have I made?

What old choices can I give to God?

EMOTIONS
My feelings have changed in the following way:

What feelings or emotions am I giving to the Lord?

Unit Eight

     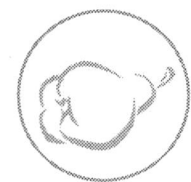

THE *Joy* OF ETERNAL INTIMACY:
FREEDOM FROM BROKEN RELATIONSHIPS

  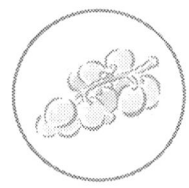 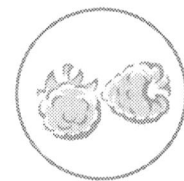 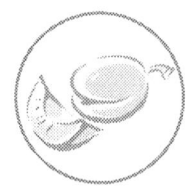 

JOY CHOICE # 8

**Joy is choosing the power of the Holy Spirit
in my intimate relationships and union with others.
It is freedom from and in broken relationships.**

"...And the two will become one..."
Ephesians 5:31

"Our Lord is so obviously uncompromising with regard to every human relationship because He knows that every relationship that is not based on faithfulness to Himself will end in disaster."

My Utmost for His Highest, Oswald Chambers, July 30

"We believe in the Holy Spirit, the Lord, the giver of life, who proceeds from the Father and the Son."

The Nicene Creed, *Book of Common Prayer*, p. 358

Day One

Jesus is dressed in beautiful white clothes. The very air is dancing. He embraces you and says,

"My beloved, I desire to be in a relationship with you. My next fruit is my gift for your relationships with others, especially the difficult ones. I have sent my Holy Spirit to give you special fruit to help restore broken relationships and bring joy to you. In relationship with Me you will never be lonely again.

I am your Bridegroom, and I long for you to have healthy relationships in this world and the next. I have paid the bride price for you. You are My betrothed. As I place the cup of wine before you, will you drink it in acceptance of me? My Father and I have written the marriage contract, and I will be faithful as your Spouse. All your needs are accounted for. My love is my covenant with your Father and His with you. The wedding feast is planned, and the rejoicing is near for My glorious Bride will soon be unveiled for all to see!

I have gone to prepare a place for us in My Father's home. I want you to get ready, for I promise I will return for you soon. Then we will be united as one for all eternity! I desire that you minister to My lambs and represent Me in all your relationships."

As you eat of this fruit of healthy relationships with others, you may say about yourself:

"I am the Bride of Christ.
I am reconciled to God and am a minister of reconciliation.
I am a fellow citizen with the rest of God's people in His family.
I am a holy brother or sister, partaker of a heavenly calling.
I am a part of the Body of Christ.
I am a friend of Jesus!"

"I can bring you joy in your relationships as you bring Me joy in our relationship to each other."

Jesus hands you a marriage contract which He has signed.

Marriage Contract from Jesus

My Beloved,

Here is my betrothal covenant to you. I promise to love you until the end of time. I want you to be my Bride for all eternity and I will never leave you nor reject you. I want you to have full and complete joy. You are so special to me and I want to draw you close.

As my Bride you need to let go of all your worries, cares or concerns. Leave all to me. I will provide all you need. You will never be alone again. I will be with you always. I alone can meet your every need and fulfill the deepest longings of your heart for love and companionship. My angels guard you day and night and nothing can harm you. Love Me. Rest in Me. Joy in Me. Delight in My love as I delight in you. Trust in Me. Share all of your life with Me and give Me the joy of sharing all with you. See Me in everything.

I, the Bridegroom rejoice over you. I have called you to Myself. I have paid the Bride price and have gone to prepare a place for you. But do not worry. I am coming soon and we will be together always. Keep watch. Stay prepared. Flee temptation. Resist the Devil. Trim your wicks and fill your lamps with oil! Put on your wedding garment, your jewels and your crown. My wedding garment for you is without spot or blemish. You will wear it in our wedding chamber. There you will have joy unspeakable. You will look upon Me as I am, face to face, for you shall be like Me.

No one knows the hour or the day of my return. Only my Father knows. But when the trumpet sounds, I will return on the clouds and no one will separate us again. I want to share our new home together so that where I am you may also be.

Blessed art Thou, O Lord who causes the Bridegroom to rejoice with the Bride. I am Jesus, the Bridegroom of your soul and I sign this Ketubah with My Blood.

Shalom,
Amen

Jesus

(For more information about Jesus as Messiah contact CJF Ministries at www.cjf.org)

GETTING TO KNOW JESUS

Jesus reveals Himself in relationships because He is always in relationship. He is the Son of God, His Father and He says you have the same relationship with God and can call Him "Daddy". Here are a few of the revealed relationships in scripture.

Relationships

Jesus	You
Shepherd	Flock (sheep)
Bridegroom	Bride
Servant	One who is served
Friend	Friend
Teacher	Student
King	Daughter/Son
Son	Brother/Sister
Savior	Saved
Husband	Wife
Covenant Maker	Covenant Receiver

GETTING TO KNOW GOD

The following names or titles for God reveal how He is seen throughout scripture as producing the good fruit of Intimacy and healthy relationships.

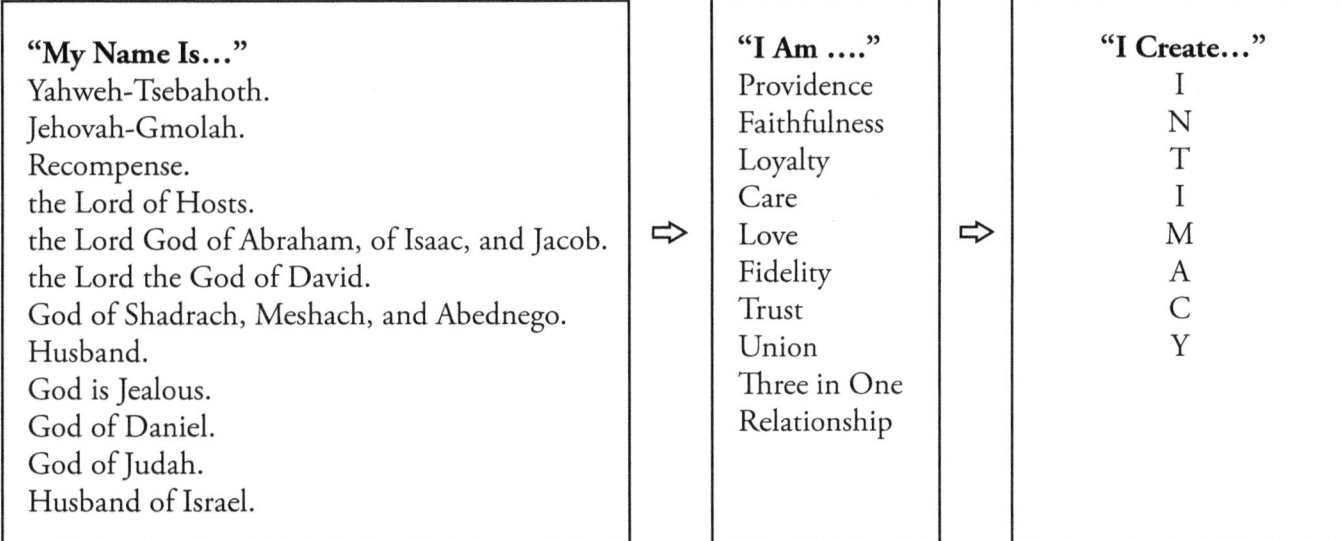

"My Name Is…"
Yahweh-Tsebahoth.
Jehovah-Gmolah.
Recompense.
the Lord of Hosts.
the Lord God of Abraham, of Isaac, and Jacob.
the Lord the God of David.
God of Shadrach, Meshach, and Abednego.
Husband.
God is Jealous.
God of Daniel.
God of Judah.
Husband of Israel.

⇒

"I Am …."
Providence
Faithfulness
Loyalty
Care
Love
Fidelity
Trust
Union
Three in One
Relationship

⇒

"I Create…"
I
N
T
I
M
A
C
Y

I am the vine; you are the branches. If a man remains in me and I in him, he will bear much fruit; apart from me you can do nothing.
John 15:5

To love him with all your heart, with all your understanding and with all your strength, and to love your neighbor as yourself is more important than all burnt offerings and sacrifices.
Mark 12:33

Getting to Know the Holy Spirit

The Holy Spirit is God's Spirit and is in relationship with God the Father and God the Son. He gives Love to you for you to share with others. He grows nine special fruit in you to help you in relationships. He unifies believers, producing the good fruit of fellowship, as He prepares the Bride of Christ for the return of the Bridegroom.

Day Two

Good Fruit: The Joy of Intimate Relationships

Exercise 1

Directions:
Put an X next to the fruit that you still need to grow.

- ☐ Intimacy
- ☐ Harmony
- ☐ Humility
- ☐ Reconciliation
- ☐ Love
- ☐ Forgiveness of others
- ☐ Healthy relationships
- ☐ Unity & Accord
- ☐ Companionship
- ☐ Attachment
- ☐ Union in Marriage

Good Fruit: Healthy Relationships

We were created by God to be relating creatures. God put in all of us the desire and the capacity to seek relationships with Himself and others. In fact, relationships are a key source of God's joy.

In this unit, you will look at the issue which is on most people's minds some part of every day: the relationships with others.

Relationships come in all shapes and sizes: Marriage, family, friendships, and co-workers, to name a few.

On the Day of Pentecost, Jesus came into a relationship with all believers through the indwelling of the Holy Spirit.

Together, with God and Jesus, the Holy Spirit helps you to fulfill the desire of your heart: to be in a healthy relationship with God and others. Right relationship with others is itself a fruit of a right relationship with God.

Let's look at the good fruit of the joy of healthy, intimate relationships

Good Fruit: Attachment

Critical moments in a person's life occur between conception and birth. Our first human connection is made at conception. The moment a woman "knows" she is pregnant is the first moment of reception or rejection.

All babies should be received (welcomed, accepted) by their parents. It is crucial that the child begins "knowing" he or she is wanted as early as possible.

When a child is sent home from the hospital, the parents carry the baby in a "receiving blanket". This is symbolic of their love, protection and covering they will provide. The baby's "job" is to receive that love. The parents' job is to give it. Ultimately, that baby will learn to give as well.

Of course the greater symbolism is that the parents' reception into loving arms mirrors God the Father's loving embrace of each of us as His children. He is the great Receiver who wraps us up in love and acceptance.

The parents' ability to receive sets up the child's ability to receive the love of God (and others) in the future.

God received you at your New Birth when you received His Son. Your baptism symbolizes this wonderful reception. When Jesus was baptized, God sent His Holy Spirit to signify the Divinity of His Son, and said "this is My Son whom I love; with him I am well pleased." (Matthew 3:17 .) He received His Son and He receives you as well as His beloved!

Seeds of Faith

While they were there, the time came for the baby to be born, and she gave birth to her firstborn, a son. She wrapped him in cloths and placed him in a manger, because there was no room for them in the inn. Luke 2:6-7

And a voice came from heaven: "You are my Son, whom I love; with you I am well pleased." Mark 1:11

After this, Jesus and his disciples went out into the Judean countryside, where he spent some time with them, and baptized. John 3:22

But the fruit of the Spirit is love, joy, peace, patience, kindness, goodness, faithfulness, gentleness and self-control. Against such things there is no law. Galatians 5:22-23

Once received, the baby responds. This response becomes attachment, bonding or connection. Some babies are able to attach even when there is no reception by the mother or father. But the good fruit of attachment and then healthy relationship is usually formed from a give and take between child and parent (or significant others).

Exercise 2

Ask Jesus to come into your earliest moments and heal you where you need healing in your ability to attach, bond, or connect.

Probably more books are written, more magazine articles, more self-help seminars, and more counseling occurs around the subject of human relationships than any other topic.

Human conflict is the stuff of great literature. The pain in relationships, especially broken ones, is splattered on every talk show from dawn 'til dusk. Why? Why do we care so much about the art of relating to others?

The image of God is the capacity for relationship. You are seeking to return to the likeness and image of God. He wants a relationship with you. Old and New Testament stories tell of a God who sought after an adulterous "wife" and never gave up. Intimacy and relationships are not words found in the Bible and yet the essence of these two words flows in and out of chapter and verse. Surely if our God desires us to be in relationship, He would provide the means to accomplish this lofty goal, right?

Healthy Relationships Require Healing
To be healthy (perfect, whole, complete, full) you need to bring your relationships to the maker of all Relations. Jesus is the Relationship Doctor and the sign always reads, "The Doctor is In."

He can heal (mend) the relationships between people as he can heal the broken hearted.

As you know, this is no small task.

Help is on the Way!
God knows you can't keep relationships alive and healthy alone. He sent His Holy Spirit to be your Helper. The good news is that when you turn your relationships over to Him, the Holy Spirit has certain signs to let you know He's at work.

Suddenly, where I once was impatient, the Holy Spirit gives me patience. Where once was impulsiveness, there is now self-control. Where there once was meanness, vengeance, coldness, there is now gentleness, kindness, and goodness. Where there was a fading sense of connection, He brings a basket of good fruit: peace, love, joy, and faithfulness! How? Because God is "hesed," everlasting faithfulness, love and tender mercies.

The "fruit" of the Holy Spirit help you in conflicts with others and can actually prevent broken relationships. What power!

Exercise 3

Which of the Holy Spirit's special fruit do you need now in your relationships? Check all that apply.
- ☐ Love
- ☐ Joy
- ☐ Peace
- ☐ Patience
- ☐ Kindness
- ☐ Goodness
- ☐ Faithfulness
- ☐ Gentleness
- ☐ Self-control

Exercise 4

Ask the Holy Spirit to increase His special relationship fruit in you today.

Gifts of the Holy Spirit that help in Relationships
In addition to the fruit of the Holy Spirit, He also disperses to the body of Christ precious gifts. These gifts or charisms are to empower the Christian to spread the Gospel and minister to God's people. They are God's special allowance to us to "be" Christ to the people in our lives and to protect His kingdom.

Exercise 5

Go over the list and pick the ones that you feel God is calling forth in you.
- ☐ Encourage others
- ☐ Heal the sick
- ☐ Help people work together
- ☐ Share
- ☐ Serve
- ☐ Teach
- ☐ Wisdom
- ☐ Help anyone who needs help
- ☐ Kindness
- ☐ Lead others

Knowing your gifts can help you increase the good fruit in your life. Ask your church or Christian book store for materials about the Gifts of the Holy Spirit. (More in Unit 12.)

Exercise 6

Ask the Lord to help you open the gifts He is giving you. Sit for a while looking at your gifts from the heart of God.

Seeds of Faith

Good Fruit: Accord, Harmony, and Unity

"If two of you on earth agree..." Matthew 18:19

Jesus encouraged agreement, accord and unity in His disciples and followers. He teaches that this too is an attribute of His own relationship with His Father. This unity and agreement in His Name signifies being unified under His will. Remember, His Name means all that He is, stands for, and can give.

Unified with Jesus, your relationships are more likely to succeed and your decisions with others are more likely to be in God's plan.

The bad fruit of discord and strife can be produced when accord and unity are not your top priority. This does not mean you have to agree with everyone totally. It means you must at times compromise, negotiate, give up some need or expectation and place them on God's altar. This sacrifice will often lead to a greater accord and a higher level of functioning in your relationships. And it will always lead to a greater peace in your heart.

Another aspect of accord is harmony. When all the instruments in an orchestra blend they make harmonious music. If more families sought harmony, their children would be thriving. Churches that seek to be in one accord are living testimonies to the body of Christ and the power that is the Holy Spirit.

Exercise 7

Do you have unity, accord and harmony in your relationships?

	Never	**Sometimes**	**Always**
Marriage			
Family			
Work			
Friendship			
Church			
Others			

Exercise 8

Ask the Lord what you need to do to restore or increase the harmony in each of these relationships.

Day Three

GOOD FRUIT: INTIMACY

Some relationships are more intimate than others. Intimacy is a sharing of the "inner man" with someone else. It is a state of relationship that provides a deep knowing, a "seeing" into the true self. Intimacy may include a physical sharing, emotional sharing, intellectual sharing, creative sharing, spiritual sharing, etc. Few relationships short of marriage offer an opportunity to have all shared. The closest may be your intimacy with God, discussed in Unit 11.

Intimacy requires many life skills which allow you to "touch and feel" another in a powerful way. All again are bringing you closer to the likeness and image of God Himself, who desires you to seek Him, know Him, and let yourself be seen by Him.

Exercise 9

Do you have an intimate connection which brings you joy? Describe this relationship in the space below.

Exercise 10

Ask the Lord to show you what is blocking your intimacy with others.

GOOD FRUIT: UNION IN MARRIAGE

The scripture most often quoted about marriage is "...and the two will become one..." (Ephesians 5:31)

Think about that. Two people becoming one. Even identical twins are separate individuals. Even a baby in the womb is unique from its mother. And yet, when God joins two people in the sacrament of marriage, He does the impossible.

Seeds of Faith

Ephesians 5:21-25

Genesis 2:24

Revelation 19:6,7

Seeds of Faith

For this reason a man will leave his father and mother and be united to his wife, and they will become one flesh. The man and his wife were both naked, and they felt no shame. Genesis 2:24-25

As a young man marries a maiden, so will your sons marry you; as a bridegroom rejoices over his bride, so will your God rejoice over you. Isaiah 62:5

This type of holy union is a mirror image of the union God himself has in the Trinity: God the Father, God the Son, and God the Holy Spirit. It is also replicated in the union Jesus wants with his Bride, the Church. This is an intense longing on God's part to be united with the one He loves—you!

Man's desire to be united with someone, then, is part of being made in the likeness and image of God and hence the desire to return to that state of perfection, completion, wholeness, and oneness.

Exercise 11

Invite the Holy Spirit to be a part of your marriage today.

GOOD FRUIT: HEALTHY SEXUALITY

One of God's special creatures is human sexuality. Since Adam and Eve brought on the collision between this creature and the creatures shame, fear and desire, it is no doubt a far cry from what God intended it to be. Much of Man's brokenness is manifested in sexuality. Couples trying to return their sexual intimacy to the Garden may feel they are trying to paddle a boat upstream.

Sexuality has been described as the openness to allow another to "touch" you, which really includes touching the heart and mind as well as the body. My husband calls this "3-D" sex—and if you think about it, God wants all three parts of us connected to all these parts of Himself—Trinity to trinity. He wants to be known completely with "yada" knowledge.

Exercise 12

Invite the Holy Spirit into your sexuality. Ask for His healing touch to those areas that you know are not healthy, including shame, false beliefs and sin.

Note: Recommended book on this subject: **The Gift of Sex** by Clifford and Joyce Penner.

GOOD FRUIT: COMMITMENT IN MARRIAGE

Commitment means that by my will, I am choosing to spend the rest of my life with this person. I am choosing to surrender my right to change my mind and "undecide" or rethink this decision. Every time things don't go my way or I don't "feel" the same way anymore, my right or impulse to "unchoose" is given to God. It is sacrificed to Him. In return, He gives me the creature called commitment. Our God is a God of commitment (covenant.)

If God "unchooses" for me, then so be it. If my partner "unchooses" for me, then God help me to endure it.

In any case, I will rely on God. True, sacramental marriage is a daily invitation to the Holy Spirit to abide in the commitment. He can make it happen when my human strength runs out.

Exercise 13

Call on the Holy Spirit to stand guard over your Godly commitments and to help you discern God's will. Invite Him again today to seal your marriage vows.

GOOD FRUIT: PEACE

Jesus says, "Peace I leave with you; My peace I give you. I do not give to you as the world gives." John 14:27

Most of the time, you can work through problems and conflicts in relationships and get to the other side, right? But when you can't, it is comforting to know that your Lord desires you to call on His Name and calm the rough waters by saying "Peace!." (Mark 4:39)

Then you become a peacemaker like Jesus!

Seeds of Faith

Judges 2:1

Psalm 105:8

Isaiah 61:8

Malachi 2:10-16

Blessed are the peacemakers, for they will be called sons of God.
Matthew 5:9

Now I rejoice in what was suffered for you, and I fill up in my flesh what is still lacking in regard to Christ's afflictions, for the sake of his body, which is the church.
Colossians 1:24

Exercise 14

Do you seek peace in your relationships (work through conflicts, resentments) and work at open communication and forgiveness?

	Never	**Sometimes**	**Not Yet**
Your spouse			
Your children			
Your friends			
Your Parents			
God			
Others			

Exercise 15

Ask Jesus to show you how to be like Him in times where there is no peace. What would He do?

GOOD FRUIT: FORGIVENESS OF OTHERS

Our God is a forgiving God. Jesus preached forgiveness. If there is one tool in your box of gardening tools that can help you produce good fruit it is forgiveness.

And yet, it is the hardest thing to do sometimes when there is deep hurt, trauma or abuse.

Here are some truths about forgiveness.

1. Forgiveness is a choice. I choose to forgive even if I don't "feel" like forgiving.
2. Forgiveness is not condoning another's behavior, letting someone "off the hook" or giving permission for the behavior to continue.
3. Forgiveness is in God's nature and He sent His Holy Spirit to help us to forgive. He abides in the words, "Please forgive me" or I forgive you".
4. Forgiveness does not mean the relationship must continue. Forgiveness allows the changes necessary to improve the relationship or end it if necessary.

Exercise 16

Describe a time that you chose to forgive someone even though it may have been difficult.

GOOD FRUIT: MERCY

The Bible says God is rich in mercy. His mercy endures forever. It is great. It is abundant. He delights in mercy. Jesus' mercy is tender. (Luke 1:78)

This divine attribute is yours when you lean into Jesus and call upon His Name. Mercy may be easy until someone hurts you. When blended with forgiveness and justice, mercy can be shown to those who hurt you.

Exercise 17

Prayer: Who needs your mercy? Ask Jesus to let His mercy flow through you today.

GOOD FRUIT: LOVE

Jesus says to "Love one another" (John 13:34). He didn't say, "love some of the people, some of the time."

Love is an action word. Love, like forgiveness is a choice.

Love is the fruit of the Holy Spirit when you invite Him into the very midst of your human relations. God is love.

Without love, true intimacy is impossible. Love opens the door to your heart and allows another to enter in. It is a state of vulnerability in the presence of risk. It is a choice to allow that risk into your life.

Love is the very nature of God, so allowing love into your relationships is allowing God to be present.

Accept one another, then, just as Christ accepted you, in order to bring praise to God.
Romans 15:7

Blessed are the merciful, for they will be shown mercy.
Matthew 5:7

Greater love has no one than this, that he lay down his life for his friends. You are my friends if you do what I command. John 15:13-14

Love springs from God's heart to yours. God's love fills your heart. It flows into your relationships with others.

God's love is alive and does not come back void (like God's Word) (Isaiah 55:10-12). Love flows out of each vessel God has filled with Himself. If resentment or bitterness fills you instead, then there is no room for love.

Love can flow even towards difficult people. Are there areas in your life where love is blocked? Then this helps identify an area of healing you need.

Exercise 18

Ask God to "unclog the pipes and turn on the faucet" so His love will flow freely to you and then to others.

GOOD FRUIT: FRIENDSHIP

Jesus is our Friend. His gospel message is a call to a deep friendship with Him.

Some of my most precious relationships on Earth are my Brothers and Sisters in Christ. If you have not eaten of this sweet fruit, I encourage you to open your life up to Christian friendships.

Companion loosely means "bread for the journey." Christian friends are people who walk the road of life side by side and share the Bread of Life, who is Jesus.

Companionship is the rich fruit of a true friendship and again has the elements of intimacy and love discussed earlier. Your friendships, if they are to be deep and meaningful, also need the help of the Holy Spirit. He can mend the broken places of misunderstandings, betrayals, hurts and disappointments. He can also increase the peace, love, and joy when invited to live in a friendship.

Now let's look at the Bad Fruit that can crop up in your relations, get in the way of healthy intimacy, and block the joy of union with others.

There are many. I have chosen the ones that seem to be the most prevalent in our culture.

Day Four

BAD FRUIT

Exercise 19

Directions: Read over the list of bad fruits and check any that you need to have pruned in your life in order to grow the joy of eternal intimacy

- ☐ Broken Relationships
- ☐ Loneliness
- ☐ Vengeance
- ☐ Discord
- ☐ Unforgiveness

BAD FRUIT: BROKEN RELATIONSHIPS

As mentioned earlier, healthy relationship skills begin as early as the womb. A disengaged, detached or absent parent may plant the seeds in the child for the bad fruit of broken relationships.

The child's need to be united intimately with another will go unmet. What would be a source of joy becomes a lifetime of struggle. Relationships become burdensome, painful, dysfunctional, and ultimately bearing no good fruit. Strife kills.

This problem is often generational, meaning you can go back in the previous generations and trace the bad fruit. Look back at your family tree for stories of abandonment, divorce, infidelity, abuse, neglect, etc. and you may be able to explain the nature of the relationships in your own life. This is no accident or coincidence. We will look at intergenerational healing a little later.

Relationships break for many reasons. The Bad Fruit of broken relationships refers to a pattern of ended relationships over a period of time or a pattern of unhealthy relationships.

"If anyone does not remain in me, he is like a branch that is thrown away and withers; such branches are picked up, thrown into the fire and burned."
John 15:6

Seeing a fig tree by the road, he went up to it but found nothing on it except leaves. Then he said to it, "May you never bear fruit again!" Immediately the tree withered.
Matthew 21:19

Seeds of Faith

Scorn has broken my heart and has left me helpless; I looked for sympathy, but there was none, for comforters, but I found none.
Psalm 69:20

Hebrews 12:14-15

Each heart knows its own bitterness, and no one else can share its joy.
Proverbs 14:10

Exercise 20

Do you have such a pattern?

☐ yes ☐ no ☐ unsure

Exercise 21

Ask the Holy Spirit to show you what broken relationships He wants you to bring for healing.

BAD FRUIT: UNFORGIVENESS AND BITTERNESS

One of Jesus' main teachings is about unforgiveness. His most precious gift to us is His mercy and forgiveness.

Health is restored to relationships when there is forgiveness. The Bad Fruit of broken relationships is produced when there is unforgiveness.

Jesus told Peter to forgive seventy times seven. (Matthew 18:22) In other words, keep forgiving no matter what. His last words included, "Father, forgive them, for they do not know what they are doing." (Luke 23:34)

Unforgiveness is a choice and has far reaching effects. The flow looks something like this:

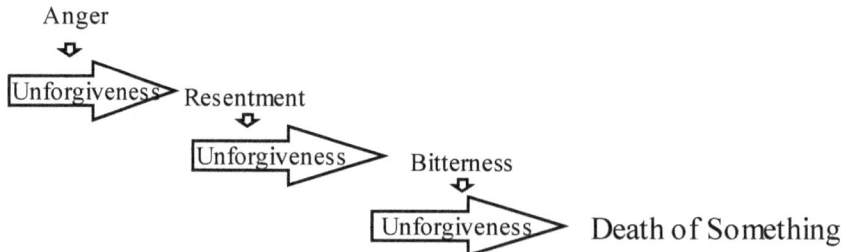

Bitterness is the effect on the soul of a pattern (over time) of choosing not to forgive. It is usually driven by a need to protect oneself from hurt, disappointment or fear. Bitterness is not as much a bad fruit on our tree, but a condition of rotting roots. Bitterness destroys relationships and the people in them. The Bible says we must get rid of roots of bitterness.

In preparation for growing good fruit, let's uproot any bitterness that may be destroying you from the inside out.

Exercise 22 — BITTER ROOTS

Describe a relationship (old or current) which is being affected by bitterness.

What needs to be forgiven?

Exercise 23

Write a letter to Jesus asking for His help in uprooting this bitterness from your soul and allowing new good fruit to grow.

> **Dear Jesus,**
>
>
>
> **Amen.**

Get rid of all bitterness, rage and anger, brawling and slander, along with every form of malice.
Ephesians 4:31

Dear children, let us not love with words or tongue but with actions and in truth.
1 John 3:18

Bad Fruit: Loneliness

Isolation, alienation, loneliness. These words mark our times and plague our world.

Loneliness is the fruit of disconnection and broken attachments. Someone can be married, have a family, belong to a church and still be incredibly lonely.

The danger with this state of relationship to others is the potential for the person's spiritual connection to break as well. The person who feels disconnected from friend and neighbor is also likely to feel disconnected from God. It is the "chicken or the egg" syndrome. Spiritual bankruptcy can also lead to broken human relations and vice versa, creating a vicious downward spiral into a dark and lonely place.

Once there, a person has a difficult time reaching up, asking for help, connecting with anyone at all and the cycle continues.

Exercise 24

Do you have a problem with loneliness?

- ☐ always
- ☐ some of the time
- ☐ never

Exercise 25

Jesus is your Friend who will never leave you or reject you. Invite Him into your loneliness and see what He does. Listen to what He tells you, and record it here.

BAD FRUIT: VENGEANCE

Your wounded soul may seek retribution. You may seek to settle the score, get vengeance, or get your way in the end. Jesus has settled all of the scores. Trust in Him to take your personal "trash" bag to the dump.

How? You repent of your own sins and turn away, toward new behaviors. You forgive those who have offended you. You forgive yourself for your own reactions to hurts. You forgive God if you have resentment against Him.

Exercise 26

Ask God to help you dump all that is in this list into the trash can.

Hatred
Vengeance
Bitterness
Irritation
Unforgiveness
Jealousy
Anger
Frustrations
Resentment

You "bind" or bring into your true self, the aspects of Christ that helped Him deal with people and his earthly relationships.

His Love
His Will
His Purpose
His Mind
His Truth
His Grace

Steps for Healing Relationships:
1. You seek Jesus' Love to fill you so that if yours is insufficient, His will suffice.
2. You seek His Will. What does He want for your relationships? It may not be the same as your will.
3. You seek His Purpose for this relationship, and the issues that present themselves in it.
4. You seek His Mind, replacing all of your false beliefs, all of the lies that have bound you to not see yourself or the other person as God would see you.
5. You bind yourself to the Truth, to Jesus' version of reality which again is contrary to all lies and to your perceptions from which spring your faulty attitudes.
6. You desperately need His Grace. Jesus pours into you enough of what you need on a daily basis to get through each day and it is entirely enough. *My grace is sufficient for you…* (2 Corinthians 12:9)

Now, you are ready. Clothed with Christ, you can enter into any relationship and any difficulty that may arise out of it.

Father Mike Hesse in Destin, Florida, says that there are three ways taught in the gospel that Jesus Himself dealt with extremely difficult relationships. I call them Door Number One, Two and Three.

Door #1: Turn and Walk Away
Jesus was in His hometown. He spoke to the people in the synagogue and announced that He was the Messiah. In Luke's Gospel, beginning in Chapter 4, verse 14, when the crowd turned against Him, Jesus walked right through and left, not turning back or making any strong overtures to try to "work things out." I believe He forgave them all.

Door #2: Stand and Confront
The second example comes from the Gospel of Matthew 21:12-13, when Jesus cleanses the Temple. Here you see Jesus with strength and righteous anger confronting a wrong and standing up for what is right. Popularity was not His goal.

Door #3: Stay and Give it your all
The third example is His last and most important in that He stayed quiet when confronted, gave those He was in conflict with the "upper hand" and allowed them to put Him to death. He probably will not ask you to physically die, but He may ask you to offer your life on the altar in other ways (e.g. give up a dream, let go of expectations, sacrifice a need, want or desire).

God may ask of you any of these three responses to difficult relationships:

1. Turn and walk away (in forgiveness).
2. Stand and confront (with forgiveness).
3. Stay and give it your all (through forgiveness).

I repeat, God may ask of you: not your friends, spouse, children, therapist, parents, etc. I will always tell a client that the choices in difficult relationships must include God. I take seriously the marriage vows "let no man (or woman) put asunder." If someone is contemplating divorce or separation it is not my job to play God as many professionals are prone to do. The answer will come in prayer!

Exercise 27

Lord, which door do you choose for me in this extremely difficult relationship? Spend some time in prayer to see which "door" He wants to open. Remember, *Jesus is the door* (John 10:7).

Day Five

GROWING GOOD FRUIT

Exercise 28 — INTIMACY IN RELATIONSHIPS: TOOLS...

Relationships require skills. The following list is just a sampling of the life skills needed to grow the good fruit of healthy relationships.

"I need to learn…" (Check all that apply to you.)

- ☐ To bond, connect, attach, affiliate
- ☐ To forgive
- ☐ To communicate (ideas, opinions)
- ☐ To express feelings
- ☐ To touch, hug, kiss
- ☐ To be sexual
- ☐ To include
- ☐ To take turns
- ☐ To share
- ☐ To manage others appropriately
- ☐ To bless others
- ☐ To give
- ☐ To affirm others
- ☐ To give up being right
- ☐ To give affection
- ☐ To receive affection
- ☐ To seek fellowship
- ☐ To be interdependent
- ☐ To include God in relationships
- ☐ To let others "know me"
- ☐ To struggle (have conflict) successfully
- ☐ To receive love
- ☐ To be available
- ☐ To listen (silently) and not interrupt
- ☐ To show interest
- ☐ To nurture others
- ☐ To be vulnerable
- ☐ To show mercy
- ☐ To be gentle
- ☐ To control anger and settle conflicts appropriately
- ☐ To be humble
- ☐ To say "I'm wrong"
- ☐ Other:

Seeds of Faith

Be completely humble and gentle; be patient, bearing with one another in love.
Ephesians 4:2

It always protects, always trusts, always hopes, always perseveres.
1 Corinthians 13:7

Exercise 29

How would you honestly describe yourself?

"I am often …"	Always	Sometimes	Never
Controlling			
Hostile			
Inhospitable			
Isolating			
Abusive			
Avoiding of relationships			
Dominant			
Victimized			
Unavailable to others			
Callous			
Rejecting			
Indifferent			
Rude			
Unmerciful			
Selfish			
Inappropriate			
Disrespectful			
Other: _____			
Other: _____			

Exercise 30

Pick three of these characteristics which get in the way of healthy relationships or contribute to broken relationships in your life?

1.

2.

3.

How?

If you keep on biting and devouring each other, watch out or you will be destroyed by each other.
Galatians 5:15

Day Six

PREPARING THE SOIL OF THE SOUL: UPROOTING UNHOLY ROOTS

The Holy Spirit creates intimacy and connection between people. He wants this good fruit to grow in your relationships. He is unity.

What "unholy roots" are firmly planted in the soil of your soul that are creating broken or unhealthy relationships? A common unholy root is called the "root of bitterness" which is grounded in unforgiveness. But there may be others, like unholy unions which are blocking healthy intimacy in your life.

Exercise 31

Check all that apply:

- ☐ Unforgiveness
- ☐ Bitterness (see Exercise 22)
- ☐ Unholy unions (e.g. previous sex partners out of marriage, infidelities, etc)
- ☐ Poor choices
- ☐ Unhealed memories
- ☐ Other

Describe in more detail.

Exercise 32

Write a prayer letter to Jesus asking Him to remove these unholy roots.

Dear Jesus,

Amen.

Day Seven

A CHANGE OF HEART

Relationships that are healthy in the Lord produce the fruit of intimacy. Jesus changes us in our hearts to create the open doorways for healthy relationships to happen. All of the other good fruit (Units 1-7) come together to help us have healthy relationships. For example, you need Truth, Security, Righteousness, and Acceptance to sustain intimacy with others.

Exercise 33

How is the Lord changing your heart in this important aspect of your life of intimate relationships?

My Old Heart Was	My New Heart Is
Rageful	Merciful
Violent	Gentle
Destructive	Kind
Hateful	Affectionate
Vengeful	Nurturing
Lonely	Loving
Unforgiving	Dependable
Resentful	Loyal
Bitter	Compassionate
Lustful	Quiet
Adulterous	Other:
Other:	Other:
"Do not hate your brother in your heart. Rebuke your neighbor frankly so you will not share in his guilt." Leviticus 19:17	"Instead, it should be that of your inner self, the unfading beauty of a gentle and quiet spirit, which is of great worth in God's sight." 1 Peter 3:4

Unit Nine will help you to go deeper into your soul's need for God's healing touch. All healing happens in relationship: God to you; you to others; you with yourself.

Note: It is imperative that you allow His healing to occur, for the people you love eat the bad fruit on your tree!

Soul Searching

As a result of the work I've done in this unit:

MIND
What new beliefs or thoughts do I have?

What old beliefs am I ready to put on God's altar?

WILL
What new choices have I made?

What old choices can I give to God?

EMOTIONS
My feelings have changed in the following way:

What feelings or emotions am I giving to the Lord?

Unit Nine

The *Joy* of Eternal Health:
Freedom from the Disease of the Soul

  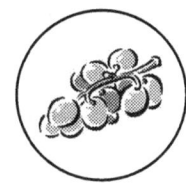 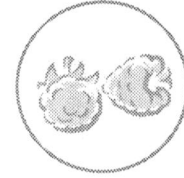  

Joy Choice # 9

**Joy is choosing to be made whole
through the healing and restorative power of Jesus Christ.**

I said, "O LORD, have mercy on me; heal me, for I have sinned against you."
Psalm 41:4

Why are you downcast, O my soul? Why so disturbed within me? Put your hope in God, for I will yet praise him, my Savior and my God.
Psalm 42:11

"We need to seek the Healer, not just the healing; the Savior, not just freedom."

Francis MacNutt, *Deliverance from Evil Spirits*, p. 214, 1995 Chosen Books

"Sometimes God heals us in a single prayer, but ordinarily it requires a gradual series of prayers, combined with the human advice, love, wisdom of friends, and the spiritual director we all need to mature into the full measure of our life in Christ."

Francis MacNutt, *Deliverance from Evil Spirits*, p. 249, 1995 Chosen Books

The Spirit of the Sovereign LORD is on me, because the LORD has anointed me to preach good news to the poor. He has sent me to bind up the brokenhearted, to proclaim freedom for the captives and release from darkness for the prisoners, to proclaim the year of the LORD's favor and the day of vengeance of our God, to comfort all who mourn, and provide for those who grieve in Zion-to bestow on them a crown of beauty instead of ashes, the oil of gladness instead of mourning, and a garment of praise instead of a spirit of despair. They will be called oaks of righteousness, a planting of the LORD for the display of his splendor."

Isaiah 61:1-3

Day One

Today you come quietly to the orchard. Your basket of memories is full of broken promises, broken hopes, and broken dreams. To carry the basket is hard. It is heavy and tiresome. You've become so thirsty, but the water you've tasted is bitter and doesn't quench the ache in your soul.

Standing by the river, Jesus is playfully throwing sticks into the water. He calls you to come and play. Hesitantly, you lay your basket down and join Jesus in the fun. Finally, exhausted from the laughter, and thirsty from the exercise, the two of you scoop up handfuls of water. It tastes incredibly sweet! As you lay on your backs in the cool green grass, the shade of the great tree brings soothing relief. The leaves on the tree bring the respite you need.

"My dear one, you are My charge, and I have good in store for you. I long to lead you beside quiet waters and in green pastures to restore your soul. I desire that any memories you have that have limited you in any way be healed. Some memories in your soul are like poison to your body, and I am the antidote. This fruit I now give you is the joy of restoration and of healing. It is your soul I desire to restore to health.

I am *the Great Physician*.
I am *your Deliverer*.
I am *the Anointed*.
I am *the Servant*, whose suffering and wounds bring you healing.
I am *the Almighty, which Is and which Was, and which Is to Come...*

I am *a Shadow from the heat*.
I am *the Place of Repair*.
I am *the Sun of Righteousness with healing in its wings*.
I am *Him who healed them all*.

"My blood I shed at my death washes away your woundedness and restores your soul to the way I intended it to be from the beginning. By my wounds you have been healed. You see, I have great plans for you. Whenever you are broken down, I long to build you up. Then you can say:

"I am one of God's living stones and am being built up as a spiritual house."

"My fruit for you, my little lamb, is your Restoration, to prepare you for eternity with My Father. What a joy you are to Him!"

"I share in your sufferings and sorrows. I know them all. The more you know Me and the pain I carried, the more you and I become one. Let me have all of your pain. Let Me have all of your sorrows. Let Me have all of your suffering. I take on My Cross not only all of your sins and shame, but the ways the sins of others have hurt you. I will restore your soul."

"But My beloved, you must let loose. I will not grab hold of your pain unless you let Me. Do not hold on any longer to what hurts you. I want to give you freedom. This is My gift. Open your hand, let Me take what you don't need, and then you can receive what I have to offer. Your healing gives me joy!"

Sit quietly in His presence and continue to hear what He has to say to you. Bring a painful memory to Him and wait for His reply.

He makes me lie down in green pastures, he leads me beside quiet waters, he restores my soul. He guides me in paths of righteousness for his name's sake.
Psalm 23:2-3

GETTING TO KNOW JESUS

What has Jesus just told you about Himself? Repeated below are the names Jesus revealed to you under the tree. Read them aloud and check those that are already familiar to you.

Exercise 1

"I know that Jesus is..."

- ☐ my Great Physician.
- ☐ my Deliverer.
- ☐ my Anointed.
- ☐ the Servant, whose suffering and wounds bring me healing.
- ☐ the Almighty, which Is and which Was, and which Is to Come...
- ☐ my Shadow from the heat.
- ☐ my Place of Repair.
- ☐ Him who healed them all.
- ☐ the Sun of Righteousness with healing in its wings.

As you read this list, do you feel His healing touch? Here is a Savior who is ready to heal you. Here is Jesus, a loving, merciful, giver of wholeness and perfection. He is the only way your soul can be fully restored.

Exercise 2

Describe below what these names tell you about Jesus. As you familiarize yourself with Him, you will become more like Him. Pray that these aspects of His character will take root and grow good fruit in you, too.

Then your light will break forth like the dawn, and your healing will quickly appear...
Isaiah 58:8

GETTING TO KNOW GOD

The following names or titles for God reveal how He is seen throughout scripture as producing the good fruit of Eternal Health.

"My Name Is...."	"I Am...."	"I Create...."
Yahweh-Rophi. Jehovah-Ropheka. the Lord, the Physician. thy Healer. I am the Lord that healeth thee.	Wholeness Health The repair The cure The mending The recovery Wholesomeness	R E S T O R A T I O N

GETTING TO KNOW THE HOLY SPIRIT

The Holy Spirit is the spirit of power behind <u>all</u> healing and resurrection. He is the Helper that lives in the words, "I forgive you." or "Will you forgive me?"

He is the One that anointed the Messiah to "...bind up the brokenhearted, to proclaim freedom for the captives and release from darkness for the prisoners..." (Isaiah 61:1) The Holy Spirit gives "...beauty instead of ashes, the oil of gladness instead of mourning, and a garment of praise instead of a spirit of despair..." (Isaiah 61:3) This produces everlasting joy.

Seeds of Faith

The Spirit of the Lord is on me, because he has anointed me to preach good news to the poor. He has sent me to proclaim freedom for the prisoners and recovery of sight for the blind, to release the oppressed...
Luke 4:18

He himself bore our sins in his body on the tree, so that we might die to sins and live for righteousness; by his wounds you have been healed.
1 Peter 2:24

Fruit trees of all kinds will grow on both banks of the river. Their leaves will not wither, nor will their fruit fail. Every month they will bear, because the water from the sanctuary flows to them. Their fruit will serve for food and their leaves for healing.
Ezekiel 47:12

Day Two

Good Fruit: The Joy of Eternal Health

Let's take a look at the good fruit of inner healing that Jesus wants you to have from the Tree of Life. It is through His healing touch that you can be made whole, which is God's desire for you..

Exercise 3

Directions:
Put an X next to the fruit that you still need to grow.

- ☐ Forgiveness of Others
- ☐ Willingness to be Healed
- ☐ Forgiveness of God
- ☐ Renewed Spirit
- ☐ Restoration
- ☐ Forgiveness of Self
- ☐ Healing of Memories

And a woman was there who had been subject to bleeding for twelve years. She had suffered a great deal under the care of many doctors and had spent all she had, yet instead of getting better she grew worse. When she heard about Jesus, she came up behind him in the crowd and touched his cloak, because she thought, "If I just touch his clothes, I will be healed." Immediately her bleeding stopped and she felt in her body that she was freed from her suffering. At once Jesus realized that power had gone out from him. He turned around in the crowd and asked, "Who touched my clothes?" "You see the people crowding against you," his disciples answered, "and yet you can ask, 'Who touched me?'

But Jesus kept looking around to see who had done it. Then the woman, knowing what had happened to her, came and fell at his feet and, trembling with fear, told him the whole truth. He said to her, 'Daughter, your faith has healed you. Go in peace and be freed from your suffering.' - Mark 5:25-34

Rocky Times / Rocky Soil

Over the years I have had fourteen Springer Spaniels. My dear friend Sally gave me a puppy named Sugar, and I fell in love with these brown and white dogs that shed and love to sit in every mud puddle they can find. I usually have two of them at a time to keep each other (and me) company.

When I lived in California, before I remarried, I spent many hours on the beautiful Malibu beaches walking Sugar. But she needed a friend, and so I let the animal shelter know that I would gladly receive discarded Springers. Then, God sent Rocky into my life.

Rocky was eleven years old and had been dropped at the pound. The family that raised him didn't want him swimming in their pool. My heart broke as I took this orphan into my home. Like many orphans, Rocky was an angry dog, and if dogs feel bitterness, he had plenty of it.

He'd snarl at you if you went near him, and he was <u>really</u> ungrateful for all I was doing. I decided to leave him alone and hoped his heart would soften.

I was late for work, rushing to an important meeting, when I noticed Rocky scratching his ear and crying. Putting my briefcase down, I knelt near him and gently looked in his ear. It was the first time he had let me touch him in the three days he had lived with me.

To my horror, hidden under the tangled, matted hair in his ear, were open sores and a massive infection. Again, my heart sank as I realized the neglect of the former owners. Rocky now sensed I meant no harm, and I spent the next hour cleaning out his diseased ear. There was a gentle peace that fell over us both as I washed and cleaned and prayed.

In time, Rocky's ear healed, but the transformation of his character was even more profound. From that moment when he allowed me to touch him, he became <u>my</u> dog and I his <u>master</u>. He adored me and hardly left my side. Something had happened on the inside and his trust of me grew. His eyes could now look to me, and I saw the true dog Rocky was meant to be.

He was still pretty ornery sometimes. The dog catcher knocked on my door one day and said, "Hey, Lady, is that your old Springer? Can you come get him out of the front seat of my truck? He's growling at me and won't let me get in!" The poor man had tried to put Rocky in the back of his truck but Rocky liked to ride in the front seat. He promised not to ticket me if I'd just get Rocky out!

Seeds of Faith

And wherever he went-into villages, towns or countryside-they placed the sick in the marketplaces. They begged him to let them touch even the edge of his cloak, and all who touched him were healed.
Mark 6:56

Good Fruit: The Willingness to be Healed

There was a time in my life when I was just like Rocky. There was so much hurt in me. I thought if I just kept everybody away, I wouldn't get hurt again. Like Rocky, I was fiercely independent and filled with bitterness.

Then, one day someone introduced me to Jesus. At first, I wouldn't admit I needed Him, because I really didn't know Him. But when, like Rocky, painful circumstances brought me to my knees, Jesus didn't hesitate to minister to me. Just one touch of the Master's hand was all it took. No, I wasn't healed in a flash, but I've never turned back from seeking His help.

Like Rocky, I felt a profound love, trust and a new desire to worship and praise the One who had touched me. Like Rocky, I became a new person who still falls into my old ways, especially when I want to sit in the front seat! But now I am never far from my Master's side, and I know He will never leave me.

Tender Mercies
As I remember old Rocky, I remember how I had to approach him that day. You see he was truly afraid of me. He didn't know that I desired to help him heal. I had to approach him slowly and my touch had to be tender.

That word, tender, leads you to the words of Isaiah, Chapter 53. Isaiah is prophesying about the Suffering Servant and he describes a Messiah that is not exactly what the Jews expected. "He grew up before him like a tender shoot . . ." (Isaiah 53:2) We see this word "tender" describing his youthful state. We see over and over in the New Testament mention of the tenderness of Jesus. His "tender mercy" is the way in which His healing and delivering hand touches our lives today. As King David appealed to God's tender mercies to "blot out" all of his transgressions in Psalm 51, verse 1 , you come to the Lord appealing to His tender nature rather than, of course, his wrath or anger. In fact, your very salvation depends on His tender mercy.

So, like Rocky, you need the tender healing touch of the Savior. And like Rocky, you have areas that are hidden from view that need His help.

EXPERIENCING JOY

The Soil of the Soul

Isaiah 53 returns you to the tree. This time you are going to look at what lies under the ground, the soil of the soul. Isaiah says the Messiah will be "like a root out of dry ground." (Isaiah 53:2). This may refer to his humble birth and lowly background, certainly not the birth of the king they expected. But I also see that this refers to the way Jesus can spring up in <u>your</u> parched, dry ground, when you are barren or without sustenance to keep yourself refreshed. Jesus comes into your soil (soul) and brings the water of life, the Holy Spirit, to your parched ground and gives your roots what you need to grow good fruit. He heals your soul. (Psalm 41:4)

Let's take a look below ground at this thing you can't see or X-ray, but that you know exists, the soil of the soul.

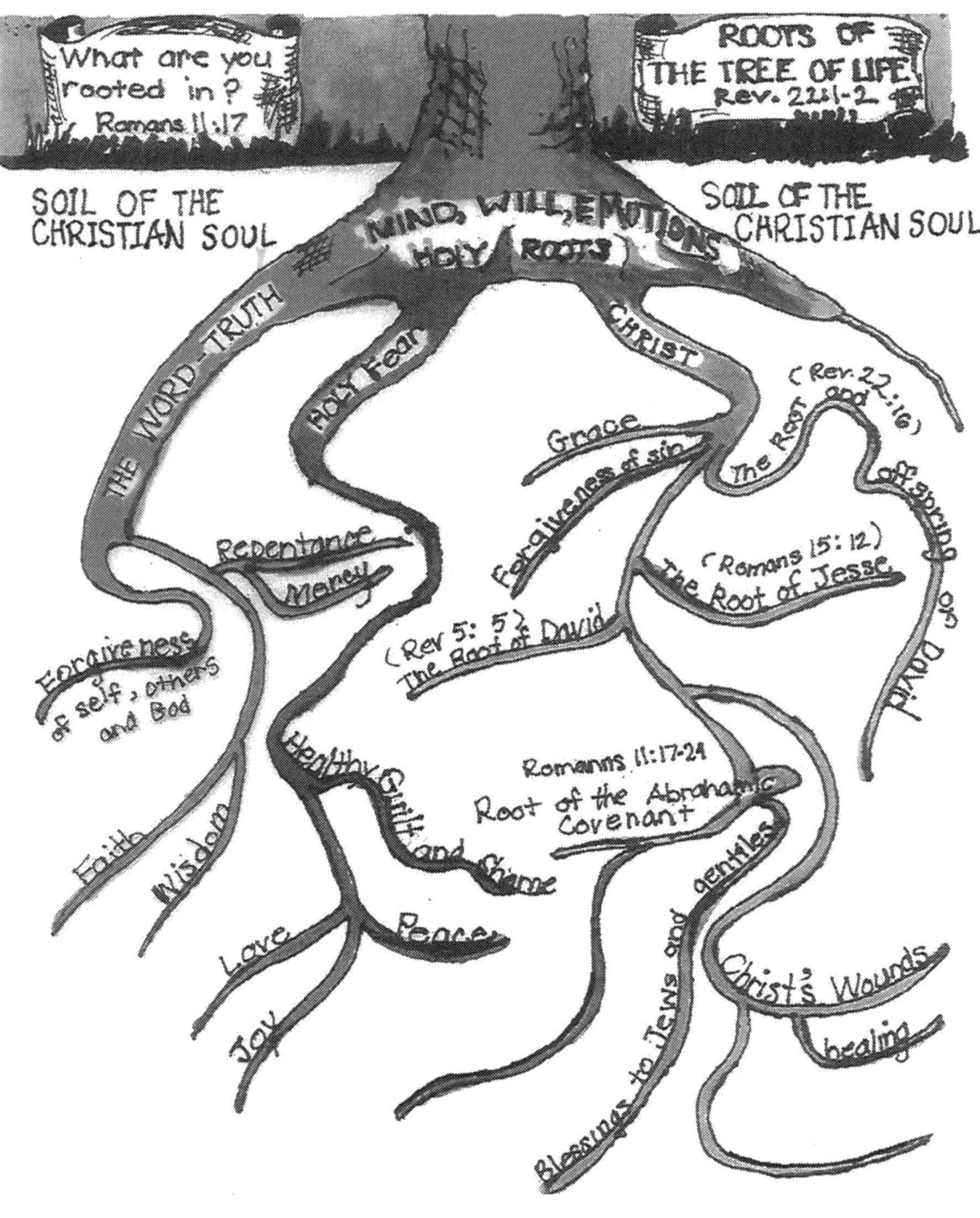

265

By His Wounds You are Healed

Please stop and read Isaiah 53:3-12. Isaiah gives a painful description of the final times of our Lord's life.

The healing referred to in Isaiah 53:5, "By His wounds we are healed." is referring not only to sin and sickness but to spiritual and inner healing: the restoration of the soul and spirit through Christ's wounds. Isaiah is focused on your <u>entire</u> <u>health</u>. By Jesus' death on the cross, you are healed of sin, sickness, and in the "soul man."

I studied every type of woundedness that Jesus suffered that is recorded in the four Gospels. In all the years I've been privileged to hear people's stories as their therapist, nothing compares to the suffering and abuse experienced by our Lord Jesus.

He is referred to as the "Suffering Servant," not only because of the excruciating pain He suffered on the cross, but the day to day ways that people treated Him even as early as His childhood. The types of woundedness that lead to the brokenness of Man are by their very nature caused by rejection. Jesus suffered much rejection.

Jesus' Wounds

As Jesus walked this earth as a man, the Gospels tell that He was rejected in the following ways:

He was:

- ☐ Betrayed.
- ☐ Alienated.
- ☐ Not believed in.
- ☐ Misunderstood.
- ☐ Physically abused .
- ☐ Verbally Abused.
- ☐ Plotted against.
- ☐ Ridiculed.
- ☐ Accused wrongly.
- ☐ Challenged.
- ☐ Abandoned by His loved ones.

At best, He was definitely not appreciated for who He really is.

I believe Jesus has "walked in your shoes." I believe He experienced your human brokenness, (except that He never sinned as the result of any of His wounds). He understands your broken heart, the broken promises, the broken dreams, the broken families and marriages. He understands deeply your brokenness. And His desire is to heal all brokenness.

You may come from or live in a broken home, but there is one home that need never be broken: the home of Jesus in your heart. By His very presence in your heart (your spirit), your heart is healed and all brokenness mended. When your heart is "born again," it is healed.

Your soul on the other hand needs healing, too. That is the work of this chapter.

For this you must venture "underground" into your own soil and your own root system. But first, let us explore the way that sin itself causes wounds and blocks joy.

Day Three

GOOD FRUIT: HEALING FROM SIN

In the Book of Common Prayer, a prayer is found on page 360 called the Confession of Sin. The prayer is read before Holy Communion:

> *Most merciful God,*
> *We confess that we have sinned against You,*
> *In thought, word, and deed,*
> *By what we have done,*
> *And by what we have left undone.*
> *We have not loved you with our whole heart;*
> *We have not loved our neighbors as ourselves.*
> *We are truly sorry and we humbly repent.*
> *For the sake of your Son Jesus Christ,*
> *Have mercy on us and forgive us;*
> *That we may delight in Your will,*
> *And walk in Your ways,*
> *To the glory of Your Name.*
> *Amen.*

I'm borrowing this breakdown of types of sin to keep things simple. Basically, they are:

1. Thought sins
2. Word sins
3. Deed sins
4. Things done
5. Things left undone
6. Not loving God with your whole heart
7. Not loving your neighbor as yourself

Pathways to Healing of the Effects of Sin

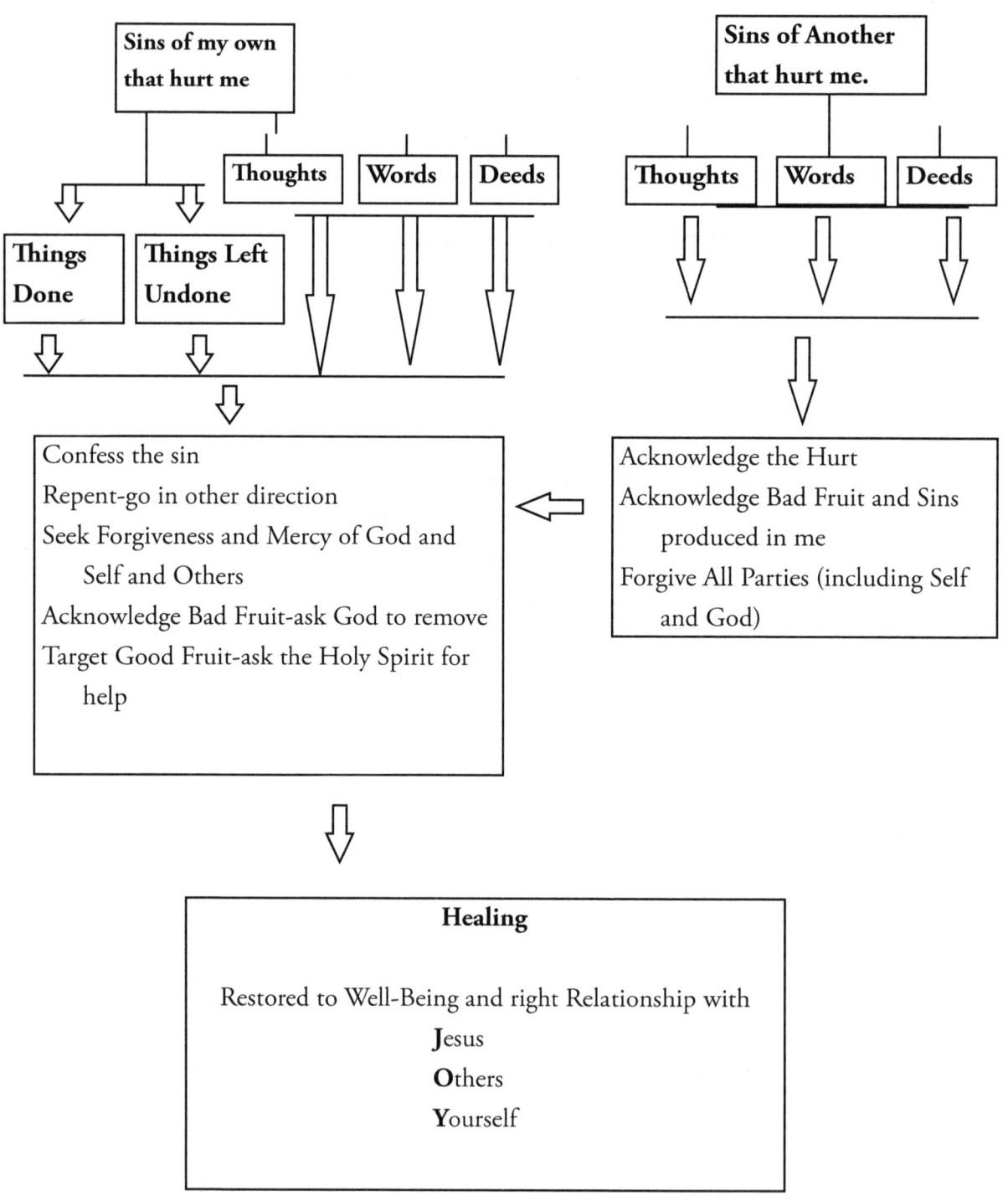

Exercise 4

Record here any sins which come to your mind as you read this chart.

GOOD FRUIT: HEALING OF MEMORIES

Joy Wounds are the often unseen but nevertheless real effects of some experience in your life where your **ability to feel joy** has been damaged. A joy wound can exist in various degrees from permanent and serious (as with most traumas) to mild and temporary. They are stored as memories in your soul.

For example, incest might be permanent and serious in its impact on one person's joy. On the other hand, a job promotion that didn't come through might be a temporary and less destructive blow to one's ability to experience joy. It is all relative. I've seen many incest survivors heal and go on with joyful lives, whereas I have witnessed people suffer setbacks in their careers who never fully recover.

All of us experience joy wounds. There is no escaping them. It is what we do with them that matters.

Take some quiet time now to ask the Holy Spirit which memories He wants to heal. Write about it here:

After you explore if there is any bad fruit blocking your emotional or spiritual health, or even affecting you physically, there will be exercises on the healing of memories in Day Five of this unit.

For I will pour water on the thirsty land, and streams on the dry ground; I will pour out my Spirit on your offspring, and my blessing on your descendants. They will spring up like grass in a meadow, like poplar trees by flowing streams.
Isaiah 44:3-4

These men are blemishes at your love feasts, eating with you without the slightest qualm-shepherds who feed only themselves. They are clouds without rain, blown along by the wind; autumn trees, without fruit and uprooted-twice dead.
Jude 1:12

Day Four

Bad Fruit

Exercise 5

<u>Directions</u>: Read over the list of bad fruits and check any that you need to have pruned in your life in order to grow the joy of eternal health.

- ☐ Anger At God
- ☐ Unhealed Memories
- ☐ Confusion
- ☐ Refusing Healing
- ☐ Torment
- ☐ Chaos

Bad Fruit: Unresolved Anger at God

Healing is the nature of God. He says in Exodus, "I am the Lord, who heals you." Brokenness prevents true joy because often it is your very relationship with the Lord that becomes disconnected or wounded in some way and you feel separated from God. This is Spiritual woundedness. Often you make a choice out of the hurts and pains of life. You pull away from God, the very source of your healing. Sometimes that choice is made in anger - "Why did God let this happen to me? If He is a loving God, He wouldn't have let this happen!"

In your hurt, anger or fear you pull away, you stop praying or going to church. One Christian psychologist says "To act as if another does not exist is a more hostile act than to slap a person's face . . . The only weapon we can use on God as a vehicle for our anger at all the suffering He allows, is our silence." (Fitzsimmons Alison)

Henri Nouwen said, "I would not be surprised if hostility, anger, resentment, and hatred toward God proved to be the greatest stumbling blocks to our spiritual growth." (*The Return of the Prodigal Son*)

As a result of unresolved anger at God, you find yourself feeling alienated, disconnected, abandoned, dry as a desert, angry at churches or their representatives, ending in despair and meaninglessness.

God is big enough to take your biggest anger. If you are to have a healthy, restored relationship with Him, He needs to hear from you. But, then you need to be open to hearing from Him.

Exercise 6

Tell God what you are angry about with Him.

Even in your most desperate moments your Lord can relate. His final moments of agony were moments where He felt forsaken by His Father, his Daddy. In anguish He cries out from the cross, "My God, my God, why have you forsaken me?" (Matthew 27:46)

So why did Jesus have to suffer so much in His short life? Jesus suffered and died to become your PAIN. If you let your pain flow up to Him on the cross and let go, He <u>transforms</u> that pain. Miraculously, peace, love, and joy flow out of Him and His blood back to you standing at His feet. As you choose to come into His Presence, all healing begins. As you are washed in His blood and made clean, you can really know Him as He knows you. This is His gift to you, His lamb.

THE PASSION OF JESUS

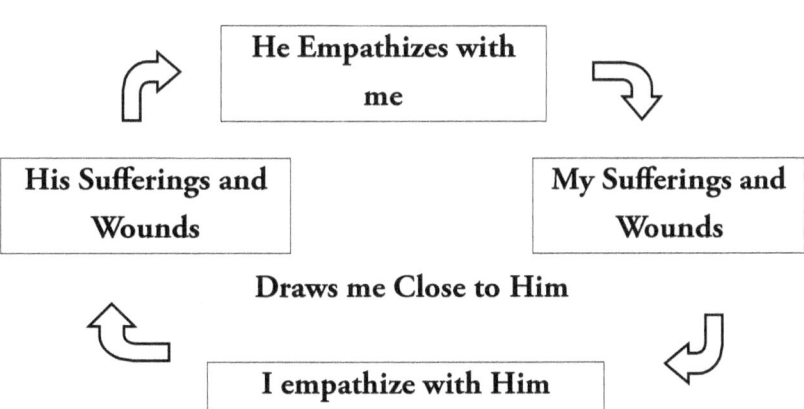

pso Tree of Glory

The word PASSION means pain. The passion of Jesus on the Cross transforms all of your pain (passion) into something new and different. If given to Him, your pain becomes a passionate love of Jesus, a desire to worship and serve your Master.

The Cross of Christ and the blood He shed produce a healing power so effective that it can wipe away all of the following Bad Fruit.

Exercise 7 - THE DANGEROUS D'S

Look over this list and check those areas in your life that need the healing touch of Jesus.

- ☐ Doubt
- ☐ Despair
- ☐ Depression
- ☐ Disappointment
- ☐ Deprivation
- ☐ Distress
- ☐ Disease
- ☐ Defenselessness
- ☐ Disgrace
- ☐ Damage
- ☐ Dread
- ☐ Desertions
- ☐ Degradation
- ☐ And any demonic force that would try to destroy you and your relationship to Jesus.

You Share in His Sufferings

My son James was not yet three when he began to grapple with the biggest question of the universe in the last two thousand years: why did Jesus have to die on the Cross?

His great-grandmother's crucifix hung on the wall. James appeared by my bed with tears in his eyes. "Why is Jesus bleeding, Mommy?"

Stunned, I stumbled for words. "Because some bad guys put Him on that Cross."

He was gone for a few minutes and when he returned he gently held the crucifix. Wrapped around the small body of Jesus graphically painted with red blood, were Band-Aids from the hall closet.

"I fixed Jesus' bo-bos, Mommy!"

How do you explain to a two year old what it says in 1 Peter 2:24 "He himself bore our sins in his body on the tree, so that we might die to sins and live for righteousness; by His wounds you have been healed."

EXPERIENCING JOY

Day Five

Note: The following section is to be done slowly and prayerfully. Put on the full armor of God (page #26) and ask the Holy Spirit to be your Guide (Ephesians 6:10-18).

GROWING GOOD FRUIT

Healing of Joy Wounds: Deep Hurts, Memories, or Traumas From Childhood

Let's look at one of the events in your life that has stolen your joy and possibly wounded your ability to experience the joy Jesus wants you to have.

Exercise 8

Describe one joy wound from <u>childhood</u> (conception to age eighteen) here:

Exercise 9

Use the scales below to indicate the degree to which this experience you just wrote about still affects the joy in your life. Be as honest as you can be. Circle the number which comes closest to your own estimation of this joy wound.

Not Serious											**Serious**
	1	2	3	4	5	6	7	8	9	10	
	1	2	3	4	5	6	7	8	9	10	
No Effect Today											**Still affects me today**

Exercise 10 - JOY CONNECTIONS

Which part of your self was damaged (wounded, blocked, hurt, rejected, etc.) as a result of the joy wound? Please check all that apply.

1. My connection to my True Self:

- ☐ My sexual self
- ☐ My physical self
- ☐ My intellectual self
- ☐ My emotional self
- ☐ Other
- ☐ My social self
- ☐ My playful, child-like self
- ☐ My practical self
- ☐ My learning self

2-A. My connection with other(s):

- ☐ Specifically, my relationship with _____
- ☐ Or my relationship with _____

2-B. Response-ability (My ability to respond to others):

- ☐ My ability to trust
- ☐ My ability to open up
- ☐ My willingness to be vulnerable
- ☐ Other:
- ☐ My ability to share
- ☐ My ability to listen
- ☐ My ability to forgive

3. Creation Connection:

- ☐ My connection to nature, beauty, God's creation, my creative self, music, art, dance.

4. Spiritual Connection:

- ☐ My connection between God and my spiritual self.

Elaborate:

Exercise 11 - CHILDHOOD FORGIVENESS CHECKLIST

Regarding this <u>childhood joy wound,</u>

I have completely forgiven...
- ☐ Myself
- ☐ Others: Who?_____
- ☐ God

I have been forgiven by...
- ☐ Others: Who? _____
- ☐ God
- ☐ Myself

I still need to forgive...
- ☐ Myself-for: _____
- ☐ Others-for: _____
- ☐ God-for: _____

Exercise 12

The Holy Spirit has shown me the following strongholds (lies or bitter root judgments or vows) are infesting this particular joy wound from childhood: (e.g. "All men are bad." "No one can be trusted." "Life's a joke.")

Intergenerational Healing
You've probably seen a picture of a "family tree." You are connected by trunk, limbs, roots, etc., to all the generations before you. The flow through the generations of unrepented sin and curse can affect you today. To find out more on this aspect of healing, please read any of the materials by Father Robert Degrandis or Francis and Judith McNutt.

Seeds of Faith

Matthew 6:14-15

Exercise 13

The Holy Spirit has shown me the following generational issues are connected to this <u>joy wound from childhood</u>: abandonment issues, addictions, infertility, suicide, etc. Please describe:

Note: The exercises you have just completed will indicate the type of healing work you need on this one particular joy wound from childhood.

For example, the incest victim may need to work through the broken connections to herself and to others, learning to trust and to be open in her adult intimate relationships. Some connections can be mended or in some, letting go of the relationship is the only answer. A trained Christian counselor can help with this difficult but necessary healing process, but God will always direct your path.

My father experienced a difficult childhood, being raised in two orphanages and spending little time with his real parents, even though they were alive. Yet, it is unmistakable that the intervention of God in his life and my father's incredible faith have made him a loving, generous man with little evidence of a joy wound

As an infant, my father was placed in an all-girls' home run by an Episcopal order of nuns. His mother was very ill and hospitalized for the remainder of her life. My grandfather may have had no other choice but to put my father in the care of these religious women. Unlike orphanages of Charles Dickens fame, my father has shared fond memories of his early life. These Godly women profoundly affected him, especially spiritually. To this day I have not heard my father say an unkind word to anyone. He's never been drunk or out of control, and never has intentionally harmed anyone. His love of Christ shines through in all he does.

People who have suffered childhood trauma, especially to their spirit and don't have God in their lives, have a much more difficult time getting over the pain or the hurt. The Joy connection to God, is a powerful factor in the healing of joy wounds.

Note: If you included the fourth type of connection, the connection to God, as having been damaged as a result of this wound, please pay attention to Unit 11 when we discuss the healing of a broken connection with God. Spiritual wounds are often the deepest and require God's help if they are to be mended. He wants a vital union with you.

Exercise 14 - FORGIVENESS PRAYER

> *Lord Jesus,*
>
> *My Healer and Beloved Friend, please heal me from this memory. Remove any strongholds, repair any damage and pull out any effect that is not pleasing to you. Purify and cleanse my soul and restore me so that I may be more and more like You.*
>
> *Help me to forgive where needed..._____. Forgive me for my reactions to this joy wound specifically when I have sinned..._____ _____. Help me Lord, to forgive myself especially for _____ _____.*
>
> *Any places in me you have healed now fill with your Holy Spirit and seal my brokenness so that I may be used in your Kingdom.*
>
> *Thank you for the blessing of your healing touch.*
>
> *Amen*

Exercise 15

For the **Joy Wound from Childhood** you just described, what type of help do you need to seek?

- ☐ Individual or group psychotherapy
- ☐ Hospital treatment program
- ☐ Support group
- ☐ 12-step meetings
- ☐ Talking with a friend
- ☐ Writing a prayer journal
- ☐ Pastoral counseling (priest, rabbi, pastor, etc.)
- ☐ Spiritual direction
- ☐ Workshops, seminars, classes on inner healing
- ☐ Other_____
- ☐ None of the above, but I plan to_____

Note: *If there are other painful joy wounds from <u>childhood</u> which are blocking your ability to experience true joy, please use the exercises 8-15 to explore them more fully. Again, you may need the help of a trained professional to fully undo the damage to your ability to receive the joy you richly deserve.*

Day Six

HEALING JOY WOUNDS:
DEEP HURTS, MEMORIES, OR TRAUMAS FROM ADULTHOOD

Exercise 16

Describe one joy wound from adulthood (age eighteen until the present time) in the space provided here:

Exercise 17

Use the scales below to indicate the degree to which this experience still affects the joy in your life. Circle the number which comes closest to your own estimation of the joy wound.

Not Serious   **Serious**

      1   2   3   4   5   6   7   8   9   10

      1   2   3   4   5   6   7   8   9   10

No Effect on my ability to receive joy   **Still affects me (Difficult to stop the effects and experience real joy)**

Exercise 18 - JOY CONNECTIONS

Which part of your self was damaged (blocked, wounded, hurt, rejected, etc.) as a result of this joy wound? Please check all that apply.

1. Connection to my true self:

- ☐ My sexual self
- ☐ My physical self
- ☐ My intellectual self
- ☐ My emotional self
- ☐ My social self
- ☐ My playful, child-like self
- ☐ My practical self
- ☐ My learning self
- ☐ Other:

2-A. My connection with other(s):

- ☐ Specifically, my relationship with
- ☐ Or my relationship with

2-B. Response-ability (my ability to respond in relationship to another):

- ☐ My ability to trust
- ☐ My ability to open up
- ☐ My ability to share
- ☐ My ability to listen
- ☐ My ability to forgive
- ☐ My willingness to be vulnerable
- ☐ Other: _____

3. Creation Connection:

- ☐ My connection to nature, beauty, God's creation, my creative self. Elaborate here.

4. Spiritual Connection:

- ☐ My connection between God and my spiritual self. Elaborate here.

Exercise 19 - FORGIVENESS CHECKLIST

Regarding this adulthood joy wound,
I have completely forgiven...

- ☐ Myself
- ☐ Others: Who?
- ☐ God

I have been forgiven by...

- ☐ Others: Who?
- ☐ God
- ☐ Myself

I still need to forgive...

- ☐ Myself-for:
- ☐ Others-for:
- ☐ God-for: _____

Matthew: 6: 14-15

Exercise 20

The Holy Spirit has shown me the following strongholds (lies, bitter root judgments, vows) are infesting this particular joy wound from adulthood: (e.g. "All men are bad." "No one can be trusted." "Life's a joke.") Please describe:

Exercise 21 - INTERGENERATIONAL HEALING

The Holy Spirit has shown me the following generational issues are connected to this joy wound from adulthood: abandonment issues, addictions, infertility, suicide, etc. Please describe:

The exercise you have just completed will indicate the type of healing work you need on this one particular joy wound from adulthood.

Exercise 22

> *Lord Jesus,*
>
> *My Healer and Beloved Friend, please heal me from this memory. Remove any strongholds, repair any damage and pull out any effect that is not pleasing to you. Purify and cleanse my soul and restore me so that I may be more and more like You.*
>
> *Help me to forgive where needed..._____. Forgive me for my reactions to this joy wound specifically when I have sinned..._____. Help me Lord, to forgive myself especially for _____.*
>
> *Any places in me you have healed now fill with your Holy Spirit and seal my brokenness so that I may be used in your Kingdom.*
>
> *Thank you for the blessing of your healing touch.*
> *Amen*

Exercise 23

For the joy wound you just described, what type of help do you need to seek?

- ☐ Individual or group psychotherapy
- ☐ Hospital treatment program
- ☐ Support group
- ☐ 12-step meetings
- ☐ Talking with a friend
- ☐ Keeping a prayer journal, writing, painting, exercise
- ☐ Pastoral counseling (priest, rabbi, pastor, etc.)
- ☐ Spiritual direction
- ☐ Workshops, seminars, classes on inner healing
- ☐ Other:_____
- ☐ None of the above, but I plan to:_____

Note: *If there are other painful joy wounds from <u>adulthood</u> which are blocking your ability to experience true joy, please use the exercises 16-23 to explore them more fully. Again, you may need the help of a trained professional to fully undo the damage to your ability to receive the joy you richly deserve.*

Exercise 24

Close your eyes and imagine nailing to the Cross anything and everything that blocks your joy. Don't worry about the noise - the hammering is joy to Jesus' ears! It means you are deciding to give Him something in exchange for His peace, love, and joy.

When you are done, stay in the presence of the Cross and hear what Jesus has to say to you.

It is time to let go.

Day Six

PREPARING THE SOIL OF THE SOUL:
UPROOTING UNHOLY ROOTS

Jesus came to make you whole. He wants to restore your soul. His healing touch is all you need.

In order to grow this good fruit, you need to allow Him to pull up your "unholy roots". These roots block your joy at the deepest level. Deep healing to the soul brings true joy.

Exercise 25

"Healing is needed in the following areas in my life....":(check all that apply)

- ☐ Memories
- ☐ Traumas or terror
- ☐ Strongholds
- ☐ Generational Issues
- ☐ Curses
- ☐ Unforgiveness towards God
- ☐ Unforgiveness towards another
- ☐ Unforgiveness towards myself
- ☐ Other:
- ☐ Some combination of the above

Jesus is a healer, and He still heals today. The good fruit of health and wholeness is His gift.

You may have "unholy" roots producing bad fruit. Inner healing of the soul occurs when you partnership with the Holy Spirit to uncover these deep roots and allow Him to pull them out.

Exercise 26

Read aloud the following prayer and ask the Holy Spirit to help you identify your unholy roots.

> **Dear Holy Spirit,**
>
> *Please be my Guide as I enter into my soul with you. Shine your light on any area that needs healing and lead me into health. Place the full armor of God on me and those I love as I do the work in this unit.*
>
> *Amen.*

Day Seven

A CHANGE OF HEART

Healing restoration occurs in the heart as well as the soul. Jesus longs to bring His precious ones to full health in the spirit.

Exercise 27

Look over this list and describe how Jesus is changing your heart so that you can give Him your whole (restored) heart. Check all words that apply to you.

My Old Heart Was:	My New Heart Is:
Afflicted	Softened
Unforgiving	Healed
Hardened	Forgiving
Resentful	Mended
Bitter	Whole
Despairing	Delivered
Divided	Released
Bound	Solid
Calloused	Free
Wounded	Unbound
Broken	Whole
Other	Other
"For I am poor and needy, and my heart is wounded within me." Psalm 109:22	"Trust in the LORD with all your heart and lean not on your own understanding." Proverbs 3:5

Who's Guarding Your Heart?
There are no wounds in your future. I do not say that as a prophet or as some cruel joke. The reality <u>for this moment</u> is that the only woundedness you carry in your soul is from events that have occurred in the past.

Healing therefore, has to do with unloading the wounds in the soul that have <u>already happened</u>. Then, life is a matter of proper maintenance of the heart and soul and body.

Jesus Christ is the same yesterday and today and forever. Hebrews 13:8

And the peace of God, which transcends all understanding, will guard your hearts and your minds in Christ Jesus. Philippians 4:7

Father Joseph Girzione, author of the "Joshua" books, and <u>Never Alone</u> advises that you quickly forgive any offense so that nothing new enters your heart to wound and damage. Let forgiveness and the peace it brings "guard your heart".

After a while, there will be less and less scar tissue and wounded places in the soul to heal, and your focus can be on loving and praising God instead of "licking your wounds." Of course, you can do none of this without the Holy Spirit.

Soul Searching

As a result of the work I've done in this unit:

MIND
What new beliefs or thoughts do I have?

What old beliefs am I ready to put on God's altar?

WILL
What new choices have I made?

What old choices can I give to God?

EMOTIONS
My feelings have changed in the following way:

What feelings or emotions am I giving to the Lord?

Unit Ten

The *Joy* of Creation

  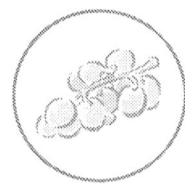   

Joy Choice # 10

Joy is being a creature, created by the Creator in the likeness of His Son, choosing to use the creativity and imagination He gave me to be a co-creator.

For those God foreknew he also predestined to be conformed to the likeness of his Son, that he might be the firstborn among many brothers.
Romans 8:29

"I am my beloved's. I am His by creation. I am made by God for himself. Creation is not a thing of the past. He is always renewing and sustaining me, keeping me alive, giving life, health, consciousness, and awareness."

Gonville ffrench-Beytagh, *Tree of Glory*, p. 36, Morehouse Publishing, 1988

And we, who with unveiled faces all reflect the Lord's glory, are being transformed into his likeness with ever-increasing glory, which comes from the Lord, who is the Spirit.

2 Corinthians 3:18

Day One

This time as you approach the orchard, something is different. The lighting is brighter. The colors more vibrant. Each flower and bird appear to know you. All creation seems to sing as you anticipate the arrival of Jesus.

"Hello my precious one. I'm delighted to see you. Did you know that you are treasured above all creation? I should know.

My Father and I are *the Creators of all things*.	I am *The Builder*.
I am *the Author and Finisher of Faith*.	I am *the Carpenter*.
I am *the Beginning of the Creation of God*.	I am *The Image of the Invisible God*.
I am *the Foundation*.	I am *The Last Adam*.
I am *the Prince of Life*.	I am *The Image of God*.
I am *the Living Stone*.	I am *The Rose of Sharon*.
	I am *The Lord of the Sabbath*.

As you are being created, I know great joy. All creation is just a reflection of the glory of My Father's house. The beauty, splendor and majesty on Earth pale in comparison to the New Jerusalem!"

Jesus reaches down and touches a wilted flower with His finger. Immediately, the flower responds to His touch, lifting its drooping head as if in praise. Somewhere, deep within, <u>you</u> actually feel His touch and something in you is raised up to see His face. For that moment, you and the Lord are completely one. You are sealed in this oneness and will never be the same.

"You are a creature created by the Creator. As a new creation in Me, you are made in the image of Him who made you. If you are in Me, you are a new creation; the old has gone, the new has come.

Shout from the mountain tops,

'I am a Repairer of Broken Walls, a Restorer of Streets with Dwellings.
I am His workmanship, created in Christ Jesus unto good works, which God hath before ordained that I should walk in them.
I am a new creation!'

I call you out by name as I called Lazarus from the tomb. I call you to new life, alive in Me. I empower your gifts and talents. My creative nature I call forth in you. Unleash those visions and dreams. This brings joy to you and joy to me! Rejoice! Become a co-creator with Me."

Enjoy some time with Jesus and let your holy imagination be His possession.

Getting to Know Jesus

Jesus wants you to know all aspects of His revealed nature so that you may integrate these attributes into yourself. He invites you to be a co-creator with Him.

Read over the list of His names and check all aspects of Himself He has revealed to you thus far in your life.

Exercise 1

"I know Jesus is...."

- ☐ the Creator of all things (including me.)
- ☐ the Author and Finisher of My Faith.
- ☐ the Beginning of the Creation of God.
- ☐ my Foundation.
- ☐ my Prince of Life.
- ☐ my Living Stone.
- ☐ my Carpenter.
- ☐ my Builder.
- ☐ the Image of the Invisible God (to me.)
- ☐ my Last Adam.
- ☐ the Image of God (to me.)
- ☐ my Rose of Sharon.
- ☐ my Lord of the Sabbath.

Exercise 2

As you read these names out loud, what is Jesus telling you about Himself?

GETTING TO KNOW GOD

The following names or titles for God reveal how He is seen throughout scripture as producing the good fruit of the Creation of Jesus in your heart.

"My Name Is...."	"I Am...."	"I Create..."
Yahweh-Elohim Maker Lord our Maker Creator of the Ends of the Earth Creator of All Things Creator of Israel Father-Creator	Creativity Gifts Talents Rest Energy Virtue The Perfect Image	A NEW CREATION

He who was seated on the throne said, 'I am making everything new!' Then he said, 'Write this down, for these words are trustworthy and true.
Revelation 21:5

GETTING TO KNOW THE HOLY SPIRIT

The Holy Spirit is "*Ruach Elohim,*" the Spirit of God who is Co-Creator with God Himself. (Genesis 1:2) He makes you a new person in Jesus. He changes your life into the image of Jesus. He is the giver of life and has made you.

In each Unit, you have seen your Creator calling forth something new:

Unit 1: Your new spirit.
Unit 2 Acceptance of yourself.
Unit 3: Truth.
Unit 4: Security.
Unit 5: Well-being

Unit 6: Righteousness.
Unit 7: Fullness and Satisfaction.
Unit 8: Healthy relationships.
Unit 9: Your restored soul.

In Creation is seen God's attribute of renewal. There is nothing more exciting than seeing the arrival of Spring flowers, the face of a newborn baby, or the burst of the sun's rays through the storm clouds. Don't you get excited when something you are creating is almost near completion?

Let's look at the joy unspeakable you are giving the Lord of all Creation as He sees your own creation-story unfolding.

When you send your Spirit, they are created, and you renew the face of the earth.
Psalm 104:30

You have heard these things; look at them all. Will you not admit them? From now on I will tell you of new things, of hidden things unknown to you. They are created now, and not long ago; you have not heard of them before today. So you cannot say, 'Yes, I knew of them.'
Isaiah 48:6-7

Day Two

GOOD FRUIT: THE JOY OF CREATION

Exercise 3

Directions:
Put an X next to the fruit that you still need to grow.

- ☐ Talents
- ☐ Music
- ☐ Writing
- ☐ Art
- ☐ Purpose
- ☐ Likeness of Jesus
- ☐ Gifts
- ☐ Poetry
- ☐ Direction
- ☐ Rest and Recreation
- ☐ Imagination
- ☐ Sabbath Rest
- ☐ Creativity
- ☐ Stewardship
- ☐ A New Creation

Hundreds of years ago a woman named Hildegard de Bingen wrote that we must become co-creators with God. I take this advice to heart.

"How did you think of the words for your book, Mommy?" my daughter asked. Since she was in my womb, being formed by God's hands, I have been working on this book. It is as much her book as it is mine. How could I tell her of the joy this project has brought as I have tried to be God's co-author! It's imperfections are because I am human, but I pray it brings Him joy.

How are you a co-creator with God? Let's have some fun with this fruit from the Creator!

God Is Creator
The creation story in Genesis is so joyful. I see God having a blast using color, shape, sound, and texture to produce His fabulous universe. We are told He thought it was good (beautiful). I think He should have said "Fabulous!"

But the joy of creation did not stop millions of years ago. God has continued to form and shape and mold and bend things, as well as people.

As I watch my children grow, I'm amazed at the changes in their inner and outer beings. It gives me great joy. I imagine it gives God great joy to see you continue this growth. But what is He creating in you? What is His goal and purpose?

The Bible tells me that I am being made into a "new creation". I am being formed into the very image of Christ Himself! How can this be? I sure "feel" like the same old me a lot of the time.

Good Fruit: A New Creation

Did you know you have to <u>exchange</u> to be changed?

In God's economy, if you want to be changed into His image, you must be ready to exchange something. Exchange what? Your whole life? Your whole being? Yourself? Yes! All of it.

Remember Silly Putty? It came in a little plastic egg. You squished it and molded it and flattened it and then pressed it hard onto the nearest funny pages (comics). Incredibly, there was the perfect imprint, the exact image on the face of the reshaped silly putty.

As you allow God to mold and shape your life, He gradually imprints His image onto your very being! You are changed forever, not just on the surface, but deep down, "from glory to glory."

Exercise 4

Have you exchanged your life - given all to Him? What are you holding back?

Seeds of Faith

But be glad and rejoice forever in what I will create, for I will create Jerusalem to be a delight and its people a joy.
Isaiah 65:18

For by him all things were created: things in heaven and on earth, visible and invisible, whether thrones or powers or rulers or authorities; all things were created by him and for him.
Colossians 1:16

You are worthy, our Lord and God, to receive glory and honor and power, for you created all things, and by your will they were created and have their being.
Revelation 4:11

Then God said, 'Let us make man in our image, in our likeness, and let them rule over the fish of the sea and the birds of the air, over the livestock, over all the earth, and over all the creatures that move along the ground.'
Genesis 1:26

God saw all that He had made, and it was very good...
Genesis 1:31

Ephesians 4:24

2 Corinthians 3:18

2 Corinthians 4:16

Colossians 1:15-17

He has made everything <u>beautiful</u> in its time. He has also set eternity in the <u>hearts</u> of men; yet they cannot fathom what God has done from beginning to end.

Ecclesiastes 3:11

Welcome to God's Beauty Parlor
If I offered you an all expense paid visit to an exclusive salon would you take it? Be careful what you say yes to!

Years ago, I briefly dated a man in Los Angeles who owned an exclusive Salon in Beverly Hills. After one dinner date, he decided I needed a few changes. I was invited to spend the day at his salon where I was "made-over" from head to toe! Wonderful, you say. A little jealous are you? Don't be. I walked into the salon with brown hair. I walked out with an orange that only a pumpkin would covet.

When I think of beauty now, I think of going to Walmart for my $5.00 makeup and my $2.00 shampoo. I was never one of those teenagers that would spend hours in front of the mirror. In fact, the less mirror time, the better for me.

Sure, I've tried the diets, the aerobic classes, the new clothing styles, the right lipstick color, but the reality is, I never think I'm beautiful and so I give up trying. I've had some pretty great houses. I've driven everything from Porches to Forerunners. I've run with the jet set in Beverly Hills and I've dined with the Stars.

Still, <u>I didn't feel beautiful</u>.

OK, I thought, if cars, clothes, makeup, hair, jewelry, fake nails, houses on the beach, etc., don't cut it, what will?

Everything is Beautiful
The author of Ecclesiastes says, "He (God) will make <u>everything</u> beautiful." (Ecclesiastes 3:11)

Well, I think, does that include me? Will I get to feel God's hand making me beautiful? Where's God's beauty parlor? I'll call for an appointment right now!

The world defines what is beautiful in one way. Is it true that beauty is "skin deep" and is "in the eye of the beholder?" What is God's definition of BEAUTY?

Who would win the "Miss God" contest? Who is the true Mr. Universe? Does He judge me by the outside? Does He go for the brainy type or the clever or the humorous?

If I can't tell a joke to save my life, would He still choose me?

You know the answer, of course... that in God's eyes everyone is beautiful and again, according to this scripture, He **has made** (past tense) **us beautiful**. It's a done deal!

Images of Beauty
Obviously the story I told you says a lot about my image of myself at that time in my life. Where did I get such a messed up image of what would make me beautiful?

This chart shows some of the places we get our beauty imagery.

Exercise 5

Where do you get your images for yourself? Check all that apply

- ☐ Mother
- ☐ Father
- ☐ Family
- ☐ Friends
- ☐ Teachers
- ☐ Coaches
- ☐ Magazines
- ☐ Movies
- ☐ Stars
- ☐ The Church
- ☐ Husband
- ☐ Children
- ☐ Words
- ☐ Actions
- ☐ Sins of others
- ☐ Expectations
- ☐ Roles
- ☐ Traumas
- ☐ Lies
- ☐ Pain
- ☐ Wounds
- ☐ Mistakes
- ☐ Job/career
- ☐ What you "do"
- ☐ Good works
- ☐ Other:_____

It's important that you answer this question before you move on. Until you let go of the <u>false images</u> you yearn for, the true image that God has in mind for you will be blocked.

Seeds of Faith

Isaiah 65:18

Psalm 51:10

Isaiah 65:17

Amos 4:13

You shall not make for yourself an idol in the form of anything in heaven above or on the earth beneath or in the waters below. Exodus 20:4

Graven Images

The imagination and all the images stored there will block your ability to be remade in the image of Jesus. Your imagination is like a piece of film where images are engraved. Those graven images are now locked in the vault of the mind forever and only the Holy Spirit has the key to get in. Will you allow Him in to gently remove those graven images?

You must ask God to remove the images formed in your imagination, in order for the image of His Son Jesus to be completely formed in you.

Exercise 6

> **Dear God,**
>
> ***Please clean up my imagination and remove all graven images. Replace them with the Image of your Son, Jesus.***
>
> ***Amen.***

The second part of our scripture says something else:

"He has made everything beautiful **in its time**." (Ecclesiastes 3:11)

So, the way God works is in and through time. This implies to me that my beautification project takes time. It is a process with certain steps involved. It may not be instant gratification. I want it now, quick, instantly. God says, "Let Me make you a thing of beauty, but it will be on My time schedule."

The Bible says that there are certain things that are beautiful, <u>FULL OF BEAUTY</u>. Two of those are Heaven and Jesus.

Now right away, that starts to tell me that maybe my idea of beauty and God's idea of beauty are very different. Just like the desire for joy that God placed in your heart, He also placed in your heart the desire to become beautiful. It is not a bad thing.

These deep desires of the heart are only satisfied by God Himself. He alone can satisfy the desire of your heart. The trouble is if you are so consumed with false ideas about beauty, you may miss the mark completely and shoot for the wrong target. Did you know that that is the translation of the word SIN? "To miss the mark."

You can actually be in sin when you're just doing what everyone else is doing-trying to become a more beautiful person in the eyes of the world instead of God's eyes.

The third part of our key scripture is this: "He has also set eternity in the hearts of men..." (Ecclesiastes 3:11)

What does that mean and why did God do that?

The two parts of this verse put together may mean:

"God will make you beautiful in His special timing and will assure you that you have the rest of time to become the beauty He knows you are and will be." (translation mine)

Beautiful Hearts
Could it be that that is what seasons of life are all about? Could it be that the times and circumstances of one's life story are the beautification process that is unique to each person?

And where does God make you beautiful? In the heart.

So let's spend a minute looking at this part of you that Hallmark Cards and Valentine's Day have made such a household word. You must never forget just how important the heart is and what its purpose is in the Beauty Parlor of the Kingdom of God.

In Units Two through Nine, you focused on the soul and the loving way the Lord restores your soul to the condition it was meant to be in the first place. Your soul contains the mind, the will and emotions and carries all of your memories throughout life.

In Unit Ten, you are going to go straight to the heart of the matter. It is time to look into your heart and see what is going on in your <u>human</u> spirit. What is being created?

Your human spirit is the part of you that is capable of responding to God. There is no way to describe in words just exactly what the spirit is simply because it is just that, spirit. You rely so heavily on your five senses, but the spirit can not be seen, touched, x-rayed or photographed. You forget sometimes that you have one. God gives you your spirit.

My spirit is my God-Consciousness and can be said to have such qualities as
the capacity to have faith, to hold on to hope and to love.

My spirit allows me to see myself as God sees me.
It allows me to step into my true self and accept all of Him and all of me.

Now the question any First grader would ask is, "Well, where is my spirit? The best answer I have for that is, 'In my heart!'"

My spirit lives in and around and through what the Bible calls my heart. Just as the physical heart is the center of my physical body, my spiritual heart is the center of my spiritual body.

Just as my physical heart has blood and water that flows in and through it, my spiritual heart has a life source that flows in and through it: the blood of Jesus and the water of His Holy Spirit.

The Hearth of My Heart
I like to think of the heart as a Home, a Temple, a Sanctuary, a Tabernacle, or a Dwelling Place for Jesus, God and the Holy Spirit. As a Christian, you can be assured that the entire Trinity family lives in the home of your heart.

Meditate for a minute on the amazing truth of the statement that you have the Divine Godhead living on the inside of you. The Incarnation is truly Emmanuel, "God within you."

Your spirit is the part of you that receives Jesus as Lord and Savior and then immediately is "Born Again."

Kids will ask, "Where does Jesus live?" The answer often is, "He lives in your heart!"

So the heart is this amazing place where because of God's amazing grace, He has chosen you as His resting place until such time as He comes again.

He's there. You need to go in and meet Him there. He reveals Himself to you in the heart. That is where He talks to you. That is where He hands out His gifts.

The heart is like a home with a hearth, a fireplace, and the fire is lit when the Holy Spirit dwells in the heart of a believer. Like Moses and the burning bush, the fire in the hearth of the heart is where you can hear God calling you, telling you His will for your life and directing your path.

Everyone has a spirit or a heart because God made humans that way. But those that are born again in the spirit by receiving Jesus into their heart home, can begin to do an amazing thing: they can begin to have a change of heart, as the characteristics, values and virtues of our Lord replace those of their own.

This is what you will be doing in this unit-letting Jesus into more of your heart home and taking a closer look at what the Bible calls "the inner self, the unfading beauty of a gentle and quiet spirit." (1 Peter 3:4)

The heart is the command center of your true self in Christ. I say this to remind you that there are two operating centers: the soul and the spirit. The soul gets contaminated (so to speak) in life by false ideas, traumas, hurts, wounds. The spirit, on the other hand, tends to want to seek God and stay true to Him. But, the human spirit is at risk of getting off track too and must remain fit for the task at hand: becoming more like Jesus.

God's Homing Device: Joy
God knows your heart, the Bible says, and He searches it, looking for growth in the seeds He planted. He's looking for good fruit.

> *But the Lord said to Samuel, 'Do not consider his appearance or his height, for I have rejected him. The Lord does not look at the things man looks at. Man looks at the outward appearance, but the Lord looks at the heart.'*
>
> 1 Samuel 16:7

The heart is the place that can experience God's love. Remember that God has set eternity in your heart, like E.T., the little character in the movie that kept saying "E.T. phone home". Your spirit wants not only to phone home, it wants to be back home with God forever. Your spirit is the part of you with a built in homing device called joy which won't be satisfied until it finds its Maker. The heart is the place that wants to be transformed into the likeness and image of Jesus and return home to Him.

Home of Jesus in me

Eternity set in me by God

All of my heart has to be given to Jesus

Rejoicing follows when my heart belongs to Jesus

Turned and transformed into the likeness and image
    of Jesus

The Bible says my heart has all of the capabilities it needs to <u>communicate</u> and to be in a <u>relationship</u>. For example, my heart can think thoughts through meditation and prayer. My heart can feel feelings as in desires and yearnings. My heart can also understand, imagine, remember, speak, sing, plan, and have attitudes.

My heart matures like the rest of me and can learn from mistakes. In short, the heart is the <u>seat</u> of my authentic true self, made whole and complete in Christ.

I the Lord search the heart and examine the mind, to reward a man according to his conduct, according to what his deeds deserve.
Jeremiah 17:10

Homecoming Invitation
Understanding your spirit's dwelling place and its nature is critical for your spiritual journey. Your heart can decide decisions and follow paths and leanings. Your heart is what chooses life or death. Cassie, the young girl killed at Columbine High School in 1999 is famous for saying "YES!" It is reported that when she was asked if she believed in God, she hesitated for just a second. She went into her heart to get the answer and the wisdom that if she said "yes," the result would be certain death. And the answer of her heart was indeed YES. Would your heart be that courageous? Would you find the right answer in your heart? She must have heard God say, "All will be well Cassie, I love you. Come home to Me, now."

Paul writes in Galatians 4:6 -
"Because you are sons, God sent the Spirit of His Son into our hearts, the Spirit who calls out, 'Abba, Father.'

Cassie's heart must have called out to God, "Daddy I love you!" He must have replied, "Come home!"

Cassie had just recently turned her life over to Jesus. She had begun a season that all new Christians enter where they open their hearts to the Lord and discover His love for the first time. She had no idea that her decision to follow Christ would be the decision that would lead to her physical death. But that decision also gave her the key to open the gates of heaven for all eternity, the same eternity that God had placed in her heart as her true home.

It was her Homecoming invitation and she was Homecoming Queen, dressed in the beauty and splendor of her Lord Jesus! Alleluia.

"...Yet they cannot fathom what God has done from beginning to end."
(Ecclesiastes 3:11)

Cassie, like all of us, could not understand what God had in store for her or the way in which He would make her beautiful. Like Cassie, you have to trust that the Lord wants your heart to turn to Him. The making of the beautiful heart is His job. <u>He</u> makes all things beautiful. All you have to do is turn the face of your heart to Him. You would not be reading this workbook if you weren't already doing just that. You are already far along the spiritual journey of your heart and are glowing with His beauty. You are moving from "glory to glory" and the face of your heart is shining with the love of Christ. (2 Corinthians 3:18)

Day Three

Back to the Beauty Parlor

Remember the scene in the Wizard of OZ...where Dorothy goes to a beauty parlor in order to see the Wizard? Of course it is no wizard you are going to live with for all of time, but the creator of the Universe!

Do you know the story of Esther in the Old Testament? She also went to God's Beauty Parlor. Read Esther 2:8-20.

Esther was a beautiful Jewish orphan who lived in Persia. She had to keep her true Jewish identity hidden. The King was looking for a new Queen, and she was one of many girls selected to try out for the job. All of the young girls selected were brought into the King's harem for an entire year to be prepared to go before the King. For a season in her life, Esther was covered in rich oils, soaked in luxurious baths, and dressed in fabulous robes and jewelry. She was already beautiful when she went into the harem...can you imagine what she must have looked like when she came out?

For Such a Time as This

Eventually she was chosen to be Queen, disclosed at a key moment her true identity and ended up saving the Jews in her country from annihilation. Her outer beauty paled in comparison to the inner character that was developed in a time of trial and pain.

Her heart was already strong in faith, but God pressed in and drew out of this woman a heart of courage, a heart of compassion, and a heart of love for God's people that allowed her to do the impossible and risk her life.

God wants to do the same thing in you, doesn't He? He knows what you are going through in your life and the season you are in. He wants to use this time to make you even more beautiful than you already are! (Men, this includes you!)

But like Cassie and Esther and other brave, faithful people, this all starts with a commitment of your heart to Him and a revealing of your true inner beauty and identity in Jesus.

Exercise 7

If you have not already done so, please turn back to Unit One and say the prayer to invite Jesus into your heart and accept Him as Lord and Savior.

The moment this prayer is said in faith, God can begin to make your heart more like Jesus as your spirit is born again. The Holy Trinity, God the Father, God the Son and God the Holy Spirit comes to reside in the home of your heart to prepare you for the trip to your eternal home.

*Be still, and know that I am God;
I will be exalted among the nations,
I will be exalted in the earth.
Psalm 46:10*

God tells us in Jeremiah 29:11-13 "For I know the plans I have for you,... plans to give you hope and a future... when you seek me with all your heart."

At that critical moment when the universe stood still waiting for Cassie's response, she found the only answer her whole heart could give: YES!

Pilgrimage of the Heart
Psalm 84:5 and 7 says that your heart is on a pilgrimage. Where is your heart journeying to? There are two answers to this question.

1. You are on a journey to <u>be-come</u>:

- ♥ to become who you are supposed to be,
- ♥ to become your true self
- ♥ to become more aware that the fullness of the Trinity abides in you.

You have to open wide your heart to see this. In other words, you are on a journey of the spirit to become more like Jesus. At the Fall, Adam and Eve were no longer <u>like</u> Jesus. Now, through Him, God wants to restore your likeness to that of His Son.

2. And, you are on a journey <u>home</u>.

You are a pilgrim on a journey to the throne room of God. This pilgrimage happens in and through time as God plans it. He has the road map and you must develop the eyes of the spirit to read the map.

This means putting aside what comes naturally: seeing your life with the eyes of your emotions, your body or your mind or seeing through the eyes of the world. It means seeing another dimension of your essence which cannot be touched by human hands, but only by God Himself who yearns to lead you out of the darkness into the light.

"Therefore judge nothing before the appointed time; wait till the Lord comes. He will bring to light what is hidden in darkness and will expose the motives of men's hearts. At that time each will receive his praise from God." (1 Corinthians 4:5)

Seasons of Your Heart
So what do we call the pilgrimage of our spirit? The seasons of the heart. No two people are in the same season.

> *Lord Jesus,*
>
> *Thank you for coming into my heart. Thank you Lord for being with me. I open my heart to you Lord, and ask that you touch me in a special way. I want to be more beautiful in your eyes Lord, and without you my best attempts are futile.*
>
> *Come, Lord Jesus. Send your Holy Spirit to the heart of your faithful child and speak the words You want my heart to hear. I love you, Lord Jesus. I praise you Lord. I thank you, Lord. I joyfully anticipate coming like Esther into your courts dressed in beautiful robes of white linen. Come Lord Jesus.*
>
> *Amen.*

The Sacred Heart of Jesus: His "Likeness"
Let's meditate on this concept of the heart of Jesus and the sacredness of His heart. Sacred means holy. It means set apart and clean. It means divine in its nature, in the <u>likeness</u> of God Himself.

Do you remember the story of Moses and the Burning Bush? Moses was tending some sheep on Mt. Sinai when he saw what appeared to be a bush on fire and yet the bush was not consumed. This was the first thing that attracted Moses attention from his busy daily life. "So Moses thought, 'I will go over and see this strange sight-why the bush does not burn up.' When the Lord saw that he had gone over to look, God called to him from within the bush, 'Moses! Moses!' Moses said, 'Here I am.' 'Do not come any closer,' God said. 'Take off your sandals, for the place where you are standing is holy ground.'" (Exodus 3:3-5)

Moses is attracted to the fire and responds to the voice he hears, but then what happens? "Then he said, 'I am the God of your father, the God of Abraham, the God of Isaac and the God of Jacob.' At this, Moses his face, because he was afraid to look at God." (Exodus 3:6)

Moses was afraid to look at God and yet he ultimately did obey and God used him to free his people from the Egyptians, set down His laws, and lead His people to a better place.

The point is that Moses and God first met at the burning bush and God told Moses that he was standing on Holy ground. Later, during the forty years journey to the Promised Land, Moses is again meeting with God. This time however, they are meeting as old friends who have gone through a lot together and trust each other a great deal.

Moses may never have seen God's real face. The two of them were speaking from their hearts. The faces mentioned in this scripture may be the "faces of their hearts." They were speaking in their spirits: the Spirit of God speaking to the spirit of Moses.

Holy Ground

Now this is an amazing thing and it leads me to believe that if God Himself comes into the heart of a person to speak, then the heart must also be Holy Ground. It is the very place where the burning bush burns once you belong to Jesus. In reverence to Him, you take off the shoes of your heart and talk to Him, bow down and worship Him, sit in His presence, wait for His direction and will, etc.

The sacredness of the Heart of God is indisputable. The sacredness of His Son's heart is equally indisputable. But is my heart also sacred? Do I have a place in me that is Holy Ground? Is a burning bush burning within my heart that does not consume or destroy me, but brings the Word of God Himself to my being so that I too, can be transformed?

If so then everything that is within me wants to cry out to Him, "I am unworthy!" "Don't come Yet! Wait until I get my act together. Wait until I am pure and holy and ready to receive you!" But God says "NO" just like He told Moses "NO" to all of his objections. He says, "You are in a season of preparation, but I am willing to travel with you on your journey just as I did with the tribes of Moses. They were not ready either, but I promised to travel to the Promised Land with them. I will do the same for you!"

Heart Receivers: Turn on and Tune In

In ten lifetimes, you can't develop into Christ's image and likeness. Not in your own strength, anyway. But give God one lifetime, and all things are possible in Him! Give Him your lifetime and God can use every circumstance, and experience, and like a wine maker, press and press and prune and pinch until the grapes produce good wine.

Once, Jesus came down in full divinity. He still meets you in this time of life with one purpose: to draw you to Himself and draw out the full image of Himself already in you. You just have to become aware and allow Him to do what He wants.

He uses a still small voice and calls you by name. Keep the "receiver" of your heart open, tuned in and ready to hear Him. God wants to meet you face to face in your heart today - to help you get ready to make it a more beautiful place.

And how does God get you ready? First, He introduces you to His Son. Then Jesus begins to take back the territory of holy ground that is really His to begin with: the ground of your heart. After all, it is His dwelling place or tent and He has a right to make it the way He wants it to be, even if He has to redecorate!

I believe that as He gently and lovingly reveals Himself to your heart, those aspects about Himself that He wants you to have begin to grow. The more time you spend with Him, the more time He will have to reveal Himself to you, and the more like Him you become.

Time Well Spent.
There are dozens of revealed names of our Lord in the scriptures and each of these names have different characteristics. He may start by introducing the soft, gentle side of Himself to you as the Good Shepherd. Or the mighty and strong side of Himself that is your Refuge, your High Tower, your Champion and Shield, your Sure Defense. Then, of course, none of these sides of Jesus make sense unless you know Him as your Savior and He resides in the home of your heart as Lord. As Jesus reveals Himself to your heart, He opens up in you a piece of Himself. It's just like when you hang out with a friend. You may start to sound like her, act like and dress like her, have the same likes and dislikes, think the same way about things, etc.

The more time Moses stayed in the tent of meeting and talked with God, the more he became like God. Moses was truly transformed in God's presence and so are you. The more time you spend in God's presence and in the presence of His Son, the more you will become like Jesus.

In fact, when Moses came down from Mount Sinai with the Ten Commandments, he had been there so long chatting with God that his face was glowing. He had to put on a veil!

I have been told that at some convents, the nuns have to stay behind "bars," because they are so beautiful from being in the presence of God that they have to be protected from outsiders. They are glowing with the intimacy of being with their Lord and others become attracted to the Burning Bush they can literally see on the face of the hearts of these nuns. They actually are appealing because of their incredible "beauty".

Just as with Moses and the tablets of stone, God wants to write on the soft tablets of your heart and engrave His image and the image of His Son. You have to be willing to take off your shoes in reverence and listen with the ears of your heart to what He has to say.

You looked at the image man and the world would project onto the screen of your imagination. Now look at the image God would like you to see on that screen. On the next page are some of the words that describe Jesus' heart.

I will give you a new heart and put a new spirit in you; I will remove from you your heart of stone and give you a heart of flesh.
Ezekiel 36:26

You show that you are a letter from Christ, the result of our ministry, written not with ink but with the Spirit of the living God, not on tablets of stone but on tablets of human hearts.
2 Corinthians 3:3

Exercise 9 – The Sacred Heart of Jesus: "How Beautiful!"

Directions: These are some of the words which would describe the sacred heart of Jesus and His attributes. As you are becoming more like Him in this season of your spiritual life, you will recognize more of these as your own attributes.

Circle 5 hearts that Jesus is growing in you at this time.

- ♥ Rejoicing Heart
- ♥ Serving Heart
- ♥ Cheerful Heart
- ♥ Singleness of Heart
- ♥ Yearning Heart
- ♥ Wise Heart
- ♥ Discerning Heart
- ♥ Steadfast Heart
- ♥ Seeking Heart
- ♥ Devoted Heart
- ♥ Truthful Heart
- ♥ Unafraid Heart
- ♥ Open Heart
- ♥ Contrite Heart
- ♥ Pure Heart
- ♥ Waiting Heart
- ♥ Gentle Heart
- ♥ Kind Heart
- ♥ Joyful Heart
- ♥ Empty Heart
- ♥ Hungry Heart
- ♥ Peaceful Heart
- ♥ Obedient Heart
- ♥ Resilient Heart
- ♥ Teaching Heart
- ♥ Hopeful Heart
- ♥ Courageous Heart
- ♥ Praying Heart
- ♥ Affectionate Heart
- ♥ Faithful Heart
- ♥ Devoting Heart
- ♥ Disciplined Heart
- ♥ Powerful Heart
- ♥ Quiet Heart
- ♥ Honorable Heart
- ♥ Nurturing Heart
- ♥ Ethical Heart
- ♥ Righteous Heart
- ♥ Respectful Heart
- ♥ Moral Heart
- ♥ Objective Heart
- ♥ Receiving Heart
- ♥ Surrendering Heart
- ♥ Secure Heart
- ♥ Sober Heart
- ♥ Accepting Heart
- ♥ Satisfied Heart
- ♥ Content Heart
- ♥ Listening Heart
- ♥ Enduring Heart
- ♥ Dependable Heart
- ♥ Trusting Heart
- ♥ Willing Heart
- ♥ Loyal Heart
- ♥ Giving Heart
- ♥ Unselfish Heart
- ♥ Rejoicing Heart
- ♥ Charitable Heart
- ♥ Purposeful Heart
- ♥ Focused Heart
- ♥ Solid Heart
- ♥ Happy Heart
- ♥ Faithful Heart
- ♥ Loving Heart
- ♥ Compassionate Heart
- ♥ Healing Heart
- ♥ Merciful Heart
- ♥ Laughing Heart
- ♥ Holy Heart
- ♥ Sincere Heart
- ♥ Meek Heart
- ♥ Worshipful Heart
- ♥ Upright Heart
- ♥ Softened Heart
- ♥ Humble Heart
- ♥ Singing Heart
- ♥ Believing Heart
- ♥ God-Fearing Heart
- ♥ Led by the Holy Spirit Heart
- ♥ In Total Love With God Heart
- ♥ Full and Complete Heart
- ♥ Responsive to God Heart
- ♥ Honest Heart
- ♥ Just Heart
- ♥ Forgiving Heart

The Nectar of God

The butterfly is no fool
He goes right to the heart of the matter.
He knows where the sweetest nectar lies.
He hovers above the flower
Until He sees the heart
Where the gifts lie waiting
For Him to receive.
He lingers, drinking in that which
Quenches His thirst.
Then and only then,
He flies away
In search of yet another
Tender heart
Whose sweetness beckons Him
To come and drink again.

Allyson Tomkins 1999

As you spend time in His presence, seeking the face of His heart, He allows these same characteristics to be revealed. There is no striving involved. No trying as hard as you can to reach your goal. Our culture would have you think that by trying really hard, you can achieve almost anything.

But God says, "'Be still (cease striving), and know that I am God.'" (Psalm 46:10) You have to be still in His presence long enough for Him to write something new on your heart. He wants to change you, but if you are moving too fast, or you are too loud with your own thoughts, not even God will strive to catch up with you in your tryings. He will graciously wait and hope and never give up!

The King of Glory, Jesus, wants to bring you from "glory to glory", allowing you in a series of seasons to become more like Him. When He becomes the Lord of your heart, He moves in to plow the ground and plant new seeds. These seeds are words, like, "you are loved" and "you are mine" and "you are beautiful." As He does this plowing of the soil and planting of seeds, something starts to happen. The ground that once was hard, begins to soften and seedlings begin to grow. Where once there was hopelessness, there is now hope. Where once was fear there is now courage and strength. Where there was once bitterness there is now a sweet compassion.

What is being born? The image of Christ Himself, the best fruit of all!

It was there all along, like a seed waiting for the Spring frost to melt. Given time, the temperature will rise and if tended, the flame will grow until the plant itself resembles a tree that is on fire, a burning bush.

Love the Lord with all your heart and with all your soul and with all your strength.
Deuteronomy 6:5

I will give them a heart to know me, that I am the Lord. They will be my people and I will be their God, for they will return to me with all their heart.
Jeremiah 24:7

You will seek me and find me when you seek me with all your heart.
Jeremiah 29:13

Jesus replied, "Love the Lord your God with all your heart and with all your soul and with all your mind.
Matthew 22:37

And God said, 'Let there be light,' and there was light.'
Genesis 1:3

Son-flowers

The seeds of the sunflower each have the capacity to grow into a full sunflower. Each sunflower contains many seeds. It is a perfect symbol of the way in which God has built into each of us the capacity to become just like His Son. And then as others come like birds and pluck our seeds, they too can grow into sturdy "Son-flowers".

The heart of the sunflower starts out small and grows and grows until the seeds are mature and ready to become sunflowers themselves. Our spirits must go through seasons of maturing, seasons of waiting, seasons of preparation until finally they too shine with glory as they look into the face of the glorious heart of Jesus.

So let the glory begin to fall into your hearts. Let the face of your heart begin to seek the face of its Lord, until the day comes when you will no longer see Jesus in the mirror dimly but truly see Him face to face.
(1 Corinthians 13:12)

GOOD FRUIT: CO-CREATION

To be a co-creator with God in His created Universe! What a joy!

Art, music, dance, acting, teaching, healing, preaching, writing, poetry, etc.! These are not only good fruits in themselves, but the very act of co-creating brings a fruit of joy unlike most others. This fruit is certainly not limited to the Monets and Beethovens of the world. You were meant to be a creator in God's likeness and great joy awaits you for this cooperative process. Are you a scientist, an inventor, an engineer, a mechanic, a baker, a homemaker, a gardener? Can you see God's creative hand in your work? Do you give Him the Glory?

The true joy, however, comes with the passing of a great test to all humans. When we step back and say "aha, it is finished," do we then say, "Thank you Lord, it is yours." or do we say, "Thank you" to the self and go forward to receive the glory?

And so, to be a co-creator with God is to bring order out of chaos, harmony out of disharmony, unity out of disunity. And then to give credit where credit is due, remaining humble in it all.

When you "speak" life into your creations, you join with the Creator as He spoke and all came into existence. What are you speaking "life" into today?

Exercise 10

I am creating:

GOOD FRUIT: DIRECTION AND PURPOSE

All creation requires a plan. It is a formation process. The forming of something (or someone) has direction and purpose even if you don't see it.

Scripture says God knew you before you were born. He then "knit me together." (Psalm 139:13) He shapes, molds, fashions. He is the potter, you are the clay. (Isaiah 64:8)

That is how He knows you so deeply. He has a calling on your life which is uniquely yours. Can you hear it? It is His will for you. Your job is to be obedient as the clay is obedient to the Master's hand.

Exercise 11

What direction, purpose or calling is on your life? Pray before you answer this one.

GOOD FRUIT: STEWARDSHIP

The creative process requires an inventory of materials and supplies. The good fruit of stewardship grows when the supply God gives is well-used and not wasted.

God's providence is abundant, but He does want you to take care of what He gives you. This notion is most often tied into the tithing of your resources to the work of the Church. The seeds stored in the storehouse for next year's harvest creates the food for next year's hungry bellies.

On a global scale, the care of the environment focuses on God's creation and its natural resources. On a personal scale, are you being a good steward of the gifts and talents God has given you? Are they being used for His Kingdom?

Seeds of Faith

May God Himself, the God of peace, sanctify you through and through. May your whole spirit, soul and body be kept blameless at the coming of our Lord Jesus Christ.
1 Thessalonians 5:23

Seeds of Faith

"Then he said to them, 'The Sabbath was made for man, not man for the Sabbath. So the Son of Man is Lord even of the Sabbath.'" Mark 2:27-28

This only have I found: God made mankind upright, but men have gone in search of many schemes. Ecclesiastes 7:29

But I am afraid that just as Eve was deceived by the serpent's cunning, your minds may somehow be led astray from your sincere and pure devotion to Christ. 2 Corinthians 11:3

Good Fruit:
Sabbath Rest and Recreation

When God created the world, Genesis 2:1-3 says that He rested when He was done. He stopped when He was finished. How simple yet so difficult for the modern world. Some of us do not give ourselves permission to rest. Others go overboard.

God never grows weary, but you do, and so you need to stop at times.

In Exodus 20:8, God commands you to keep a sabbath day and keep it holy (set apart). Why? To worship Him.

The paradox of creation is that there are moments of stopping and finishing (Jesus said "It is finished." John 19:30). Yet creation is an on-going, never-ending (eternal) process.

Sabbath rest is related to our term recreation: "Re-creation." What is being re-created? You! Into the image of Jesus.

So you must have Sabbath rest for Jesus to create Himself in you and to allow your creative juices to flow. Remember, Jesus often withdrew from the crowds to rest and pray. He teaches that it is imperative to be alone and stop <u>all</u> that you are doing so you can just be with God.

Exercise 12

Read the list below and check the ways you need to use your creative power to grow the good fruit of Sabbath rest in your life.

"I need to..."

- ☐ <u>Create</u> a quiet space inside my heart for communion with God.
- ☐ <u>Create</u> a place to be with Him.
- ☐ <u>Create</u> a place to enjoy His creation.
- ☐ <u>Create</u> a non-busy life.
- ☐ <u>Create</u> a time to read His Word.
- ☐ <u>Create</u> a desire to draw closer to Him.
- ☐ <u>Create</u> a discipline (meditation, prayer, worship, fasting, celebration, etc.).
- ☐ <u>Create</u> silence.

Good Fruit–Seeking Him in Creation: The Fruit of Wonder

My favorite creations in God's Kingdom (excluding my family) are whales and dolphins. I have never felt such pure excitement as when I saw a whale breach in the Pacific Ocean. I could see her from my bedroom window! What joy!

Do you have your favorite natural creatures that bring this type of joy? Or maybe it is someone else's creation that does this: music, art, drama. Or maybe it is a type of sport such as skydiving, scuba diving, mountain climbing, wind surfing, etc. God created the capacity for us to be thrilled and excited. (Again, anything taken to excess can become addictive.)

Exercise 13

Write below the ways you personally enjoy God's creation and all His glory in it:

Growing Good Fruit: Creation

Exercise 14

What did you learn about creativity as a child? Please describe:

Seeds of Faith

The apostles gathered around Jesus and reported to him all they had done and taught. Then, because so many people were coming and going that they did not even have a chance to eat, he said to them, 'Come with me by yourselves to a quiet place and get some rest.' So they went away by themselves in a boat to a solitary place...
Mark 6:30-32

Exercise 15

Were you given support or discouragement for your own creativity?

Exercise 16

What are your creative "gifts"?

Exercise 17

Ask Jesus to help you grow this fruit in your own prayer below:

Dear Jesus,

Amen

Day Four

BAD FRUIT

The ax is already at the root of the trees, and every tree that does not produce good fruit will be cut down and thrown into the fire. (Matthew 3:10)

Exercise 18

Every tree that does not bear good fruit is cut down and thrown into the fire.
Matthew 7:19

Yet I hold this against you: You have forsaken your first love.
Revelation 2:4

Directions: Read over the list of bad fruits and check any that you need to have pruned in your life in order to grow the joy of creation:

- ☐ Apathy
- ☐ Lethargy
- ☐ Spiritual sickness
- ☐ Procrastination
- ☐ Laziness
- ☐ Doubt
- ☐ Busyness
- ☐ Divided Heart
- ☐ Heart of Stone
- ☐ Unproductive
- ☐ Corrupting your planet, your uerse, your body
- ☐ Life without shape, form or vision

BAD FRUIT: BUSYNESS

"Are you busy?" If you always say "Yes," to this question, something is wrong.

Another paradox in the Bible is the call to get busy because the fields are white and ready for harvest, but then the tension to keep the sabbath rest.

Busyness on the other hand is the "dog chasing its tail" syndrome. It is the "hurry-up" in life. It is the filling of the moments so you don't have to feel your feelings or face your emptiness.

God is both busy and yet always available. Are you following His lead?

Jesus didn't have a Day-Timer, but He seemed to always have time. He was busy with His Father's business (Luke 2:49) and yet it was never a bad fruit.

Wake up, O sleeper, rise from the dead, and Christ will shine on you.
Ephesians 5:14

By these waters also the world of that time was deluged and destroyed. By the same word the present heavens and earth are reserved for fire, being kept for the day of judgment and destruction of ungodly men.
2 Peter 3:6-7

Exercise 19

Listed below are a few common ways life can be filled with busyness. Check all that are creating bad fruit in your life that the Lord needs to prune.

- ☐ Hectic life
- ☐ Schedules
- ☐ Plans
- ☐ Commitments
- ☐ Good Works
- ☐ Good intentions
- ☐ Noise
- ☐ Other distractions:_____
_____
_____

BAD FRUIT: DOUBT, APATHY, LETHARGY

You have seen that the process of co-creation can in and of itself bring healing, wholeness and joy. It is born in a place where the fire is stoked and begins to burn brightly.

But what is the opposite of this fiery energy? The apathy and boredom, the lethargy and doubt that fills the soul with all of the "I can't" excuses.

"I can't paint, play music, write books or songs or poetry. I can't invent or produce something new and unique. I can't even reproduce that which someone else has designed. I'm not good enough, talented enough, smart enough, trained enough, etc."

Therefore, operating from this voice of doubt eventually lulls you to sleep, to semi-consciousness, or to a place of complacency. In this inactive zone, nothing reaches you. The eyes and ears of the heart grow blind and deaf.

God calls you to wake up like Jesus called Lazarus to wake up from his "sleep". (John 11:43) The Holy Spirit breathes life into your being and the bad fruit of doubt, lethargy and apathy must be thrown into the fire. Arise, be resurrected with and by your Lord.

BAD FRUIT: CORRUPTION

The opposite of creation is destruction. God certainly made this creature as well (remember The Flood). But corruption of that which He creates is not His design. God hates the corruption of anything designed to be holy, including our bodies, our language, our homes, our behavior, etc.

"Uh-oh!" you say. "Don't start on me about my diet, my dirty house and my occasional curse word." No. But you get the point. Corruption of the planet or your body or anything else are all the same to God. He ain't happy!

Psalm 16:10 reminds us that God did not want His son to "undergo" or "see" corruption or decay. This means the final corruption from death. He is risen and so has never tasted this final bad fruit. In Him, you have freedom from this corruption as well. Alleluia!

Exercise 20

Are there ways that you are involved in the corruption of anything God has created?

BAD FRUIT: SPIRITUAL SICKNESS

John Wimber says, "...sickness of the spirit is caused by what we do, sickness of the soul is generally caused by what is done to us."

The danger is that out of a broken heart or divided heart, you turn further and further from God, separating yourself from Him with a heart of stone like a big brick wall.

David said in the 51st Psalm, "...My sin is always before me." (Psalm 51:3) He is describing the very thing that was blocking his relationship with the One true God. Are you any different? Are you any less capable of being like Hitler, or the two Columbine boys or King David?

If something is before me, it blocks my way between me and the Cross of Jesus. It must be acknowledged and then removed. Who removes it? Jesus Himself takes my sins once and for all on His Cross and lovingly creates in me a clean, whole heart, a heart ready to love Him.

Seeds of Faith

The Lord is not slow in keeping his promise, as some understand slowness. He is patient with you, not wanting anyone to perish, but everyone to come to repentance.
2 Peter 3:9

The Lord was grieved that he had made man on the earth, and his heart was filled with pain.
Genesis 6:6

Psalm 38:8

The sacrifices of God are a broken spirit; a broken and contrite heart, O God, you will not despise.
Psalm 51:17

So my spirit grows faint within me; my heart within me is dismayed.
Psalm 143:4

Proverbs 15:13

A cheerful heart is good medicine, but a crushed spirit dries up the bones.
Proverbs 17:22

The Spirit of the Sovereign Lord is on me, because the Lord has anointed me to preach good news to the poor. He has sent me to bind up the brokenhearted, to proclaim freedom for the captives and release from darkness for the prisoners...
Isaiah 61:1

When I am spiritually sick, I try to cover up the condition of my heart from the One True God. The only way to be spiritually healthy is to be honest with myself and God about the condition of my heart. "Open heart surgery" is needed, but Jesus always provides His Holy Spirit as anesthesia. As you open your heart in prayer, God can come and do laser surgery with the light of the truth. If you trust in the Great Physician to restore your heart to health, He will be faithful.

The curse of sin is spiritual death. Sin corrupts the human nature and turns thoughts to evil acts, arouses wrong desire, and so weakens the will that you choose wrong even when you know what is good.

Jesus does not want a single person to be destroyed, but wants all to turn away from sin. Spiritual health depends on this.

The Holy Spirit is the director of your life and convicts you of your sins. You must be docile, meek, yielded to His guidance, open and attentive with the eyes, ears and senses of your heart.

Your heart cannot rest until it is completed in Christ. It cannot be completed in Christ if there is the presence of sin. You are eternally growing and transforming and becoming.

Ask God to come into the place where you are and touch your heart in such a way that your sins and the sins of others are removed forever and all of the effects of those sins. This fabulous reconciliation allows you to steer your spirit away from hate and bitterness and eternal death. God in His grace allowed His Son to suffer a humiliating death so that you would never have to be separated from Him. His blood washes you white as snow!

Bad Fruit: A Broken Heart

Perhaps nothing "hurts" worse than a broken heart or a crushed spirit. But Charles Spurgeon said, "Jesus is born in a broken heart." (Morning and Evening)

The danger lies in allowing in your brokenness, your spirit to become so crushed, so wounded, that you become disconnected from God, others, and yourself. Rather than avoiding your broken heart and crushed spirit, you need to bring it to Jesus. You see, the best news is that Jesus said He came to heal the broken hearts of the world. (Isaiah 61:1) He was bruised, broken and crushed for you and me. He became broken bread and crushed grapes. He suffered in His spirit just like you do.

The enemy of your soul and spirit calculates his blow to maim and crush, causing you to turn your heart from God. Jesus Christ is stronger than the enemy and is more powerful. He came to crush Satan and He is victorious. Your heart can become the battlefield but the war is won. You need to bring the Lord your broken heart to be fixed and He will gladly do it.

Bad Fruit: Divided Heart

The Bible says, "See to it, brothers, that none of you has a sinful, unbelieving heart that turns away from the living God." (Hebrews 3:12)

Exercise 21

What divides the heart?
- ☐ Sin
- ☐ Temptation
- ☐ Lies
- ☐ Confusion

Go back over this list and ask yourself if anything has caused your heart (spirit) to be divided. Division can lead to conflict and conflict to war. Unfortunately, when it comes to your spirit, the enemy is then seen as God Himself. So, you pull away.

It is not the heart of God that turns away. When you turn away from the living God, your heart rips and tears. Scripture says nothing can separate you from the love of God in Christ Jesus (Romans 8:38), but your heart can become divided in what love you give back to Him, and your allegiance to the King.

Exercise 22

Offer to the Lord the things which have divided your heart and ask Him to perform open heart surgery.

Seeds of Faith

You, dear children, are from God and have overcome them, because the one who is in you is greater than the one who is in the world.
1 John 4:4

Teach me your way, O Lord, and I will walk in your truth; give me an undivided heart, that I may fear your name. Psalm 86:11

Do not let your heart turn to her ways or stray into her paths. Proverbs 7:25

He did evil because he had not set his heart on seeking the Lord. 2 Chronicles 12:14

...he is a double-minded man, unstable in all he does. James 1:8

As water reflects a face, so a man's heart reflects the man. Proverbs 27:19

But you have behaved more wickedly than your fathers. See how each of you is following the stubbornness of his evil heart instead of obeying me. Jeremiah 16:12

BAD FRUIT: A HEART OF STONE

The more hardened your heart becomes, the closer you are to real danger. Take warning. If your heart has become like stone, you are in desperate need of Jesus. A heart of stone is unavailable to hear from God.

The Danger of Association

If you meditate day and night on hate and anger, it will turn your heart toward evil. You will be associating with Satan! Remember, you be-come most like that upon which you dwell.

If you are not associated with the Christ in you, you become the unauthentic person you never were created to be in the first place. The danger exists that then you will be aligned with evil, even when you call yourself a Christian!

It comes down to the will: what choices am I making in the matters of the heart? The bottom line is in the word surrender. Have I surrendered everything to Jesus? If not, then the little I surrender to the Self opens the door to a complete surrender to my separation from God, and then spiritual death. God wants you to choose LIFE.

Exercise 23

Directions: Where are you on the line? Are you surrendered to God or to self? Mark with your pen where you were 5-10 years ago and where you are now.

Choices of the Heart

Life

Right Actions, Beliefs, Truths

Surrender to Self — Surrender to God

♥ Slave to Satan
♥ Hardened Heart
♥ Evil

♥ Slave to Christ
♥ Good
♥ Softened Heart

Mistakes, Sins, Lies, Separation

Death

Exercise 24 - Doorways of the Human Spirit

Let's look more closely at these "doorways of the human spirit". Imagine your heart is a temple with many doors. Some doors lead you into a deeper likeness of Jesus.

Here are just a few. Check all that you are now using and those you need to learn more about.

	Use Now	Need to Learn About
Confession		
Repentance		
Praise		
Prayer		
Fasting		
Belief		
Blessing		
Meditation		
Sacrifice		
Obedience		
Service		
Worship		
Works		
Fellowship with other Christians		
Miracles		
Intercession		
Gifts of the Holy Spirit		
Forgiveness		
Can you think of others? _____		

Seeds of Faith

As a result, he does not live the rest of his earthly life for evil human desires, but rather for the will of God. 1 Peter 4:2

Exercise 25

Other doors, however, lead you away from the Lord. What Bad Fruit is produced by using these doors? Check all that apply and then explain below. Examples might be:

- ☐ Resentment
- ☐ Lying
- ☐ Blame
- ☐ Guilt
- ☐ Complaining
- ☐ Violence
- ☐ Trauma
- ☐ Loss
- ☐ Rejection
- ☐ Cursing
- ☐ Sin
- ☐ Hate
- ☐ Temptation
- ☐ Gossip
- ☐ Disobedience
- ☐ Aggression
- ☐ Vengeance
- ☐ Self-pity
- ☐ Anxiety
- ☐ Unforgiveness
- ☐ Jealousy
- ☐ Rage
- ☐ Falsely Accuse
- ☐ Idolatry
- ☐ Strife
- ☐ Envy
- ☐ Selfishness
- ☐ Other

A Beautiful Crown

A spirit of:

1. Love
2. Joy
3. Peace
4. Comfort
5. Acceptance
6. Mercy
7. Righteousness
8. Grace
9. Glory
10. Faith
11. Life

As you read through this list, can you see them as jewels in a crown sparkling and beautiful?

Exercise 26

Read the description of the throne room in Revelation 4:2-3.

Exercise 27

Read also the description of the new Jerusalem, Revelation 21:9-27. We ain't seen nothing yet!

Some of the following human behaviors and attitudes may be defiling the temple, robbing you of a peaceful house of prayer, and robbing you of the precious crown jewels. When you walk through the door, away from Jesus, you develop a different spirit characterized by the list below.

Exercise 28

Directions: Go over this list now and check the words that describe the danger your spirit is in at this time.

- ☐ Hopelessness
- ☐ Hatred
- ☐ Suicide
- ☐ Illness
- ☐ Confusion
- ☐ Brutality
- ☐ Cruelty
- ☐ Evil
- ☐ Condemnation
- ☐ Despair
- ☐ Bitterness
- ☐ Alienation
- ☐ Fear
- ☐ Helplessness
- ☐ Depression
- ☐ Murder
- ☐ Pride
- ☐ Terror
- ☐ Deception
- ☐ Anger
- ☐ Arrogance

Exercise 29

Close your eyes and see our Lord Jesus walking through the door of your heart, turning over the tables, knocking down the chairs, releasing the things which have been brought into your heart that are displeasing to Him. Don't be afraid of His strength, or His anger. He is not angry at <u>you</u> but at the things which get in the way of your relationship to Him.

Jesus wants a clean, holy temple in your heart. Are you opening the doors and allowing Him in? If not, what stops you?

The heart is deceitful above all things and beyond cure. Who can understand it?
Jeremiah 17:9

Cleaning House

When Jesus cleared the temple as recorded in Mark, chapter eleven, He said "... Is it not written: 'My house will be called a house of prayer for all nations? But you have made it a den of robbers.'" (Mark 11:17)

1 Kings 9:3

In his righteous anger, He cleared the physical temple of unholiness. In His spiritual temple, your heart, He warns of the same danger-that you may entertain robbers.

What are the robbers and what do they rob? The most valuable possessions in the throne room of your heart are the crown jewels, the love of God, the joy of a relationship with His Son, the peace that guards your heart, the assurance of your salvation, etc. These precious jewels are just that: precious and not to be taken for granted.

Jesus was furious that the Temple had become a virtual circus and its very purpose as a house of prayer was being defiled. There was too much worldly activity, too much commerce between man and man, therefore the transactions between man and God were being dishonored. Jesus wants to evict the robbers out of your temple, too.

Exercise 30

Dear Jesus,

I ask you now to enter the temple of my heart and in your might please remove anything which would be unpleasant in your sight. If you see any malice, jealousy, complaint, bitterness, disobedience, greed, false accusations, lies, or anything else, please remove it now.

Lord, I ask you now to restore my heart in the beauty of your holiness.

Amen.

Day Five

GROWING GOOD FRUIT

Broken or Crushed Spirit can go either way

Divided Heart ———————————— **Clean and Renewed Heart**

Divided Heart	Clean and Renewed Heart
Lying	Truthful
Closed	Open
Afraid	Secure
Hateful	Loving
Unwilling	Willing
Disobedient	Obedient
Wilfull	Surrendering
Unaccepting	Accepting
Dissatisfied	Forgiving
Critical	Receiving
Unbelieving	Satisfied
	Content
	Believing
	Humble

Therefore, as God's chosen people, holy and dearly loved, clothe yourselves with compassion, kindness, humility, gentleness and patience.
Colossians 3:12

Exercise 31 - PULLING UP WEEDS

How would you honestly describe yourself?

Often I am.....

- ☐ Uncreative
- ☐ Blocked in my talents
- ☐ Wasteful
- ☐ Underachieving
- ☐ Destructive to nature, environment, resources
- ☐ Shut down to my gifts
- ☐ Unable to make anything
- ☐ Uninterested in the outdoors, nature, etc.
- ☐ Uninterested in the creative endeavors of others (art, music, poetry, etc.)
- ☐ Unmoved by sunsets, a soaring eagle, a rainbow and other natural events
- ☐ Unable to have a hobby (gardening, sports, crafts, etc.)
- ☐ Bored
- ☐ Uninspired

Exercise 32

Which of these personal characteristics in Exercise 31 have blocked you from being a co-creator and experiencing the joy of God's creation?

_____
_____
_____

How? Please explain.

Day Six

PREPARING THE SOIL OF THE SOUL: UPROOTING UNHOLY ROOTS

Jesus wants us to be co-creators, freeing our creativity for the glory of His kingdom. As you have worked in this unit, you may have uncovered deep roots in your soul which produce bad fruit.

Exercise 33

Write a prayer letter to Jesus asking His help in this uprooting process.

> **Dear Jesus,**
>
>
>
>
>
>
> **Amen.**

The River of Life, the Holy Spirit, allows your co-creative spirit to stay fully alive, "moist and green" as Hildegard of Bingen would say. You can't create if you are all dried up, just as a vine bears no good fruit if it is not watered from the roots.

Our baptism, submersion in water, assures our wetness and therefore the production of good fruit. You need both the water and the fire (the life giving energy) to produce the finest fruit on the tree of life in God's garden.

A Heart to Heart Chat With God (adapted from Ecclesiastes 3: 1-8)

THERE IS A TIME…(appointed by God) FOR EVERYTHING …(in my life) AND A SEASON (for taking action to allow God to change my heart) UNDER HEAVEN (while I am still on earth).

A TIME TO BE BORN…(born again in my spirit, aligning my heart with His)
AND A TIME TO DIE…(putting off my old self and becoming a new creation in the image of Jesus).

A TIME TO PLANT…(the seeds of the Word of God in myself and others)
AND A TIME TO UPROOT…(all that blocks God's Word from growing good fruit in my life).

A TIME TO KILL…(the ways of my soul that miss the mark and pull me away from God: my sins, my fears, my bad habits, my guilt, etc.).
AND A TIME TO HEAL…(my soul by bringing it to Jesus, my Healer).

A TIME TO TEAR DOWN…(the walls that divide my heart from God).
AND A TIME TO BUILD…(new habits, new disciplines and new attitudes in Christ).

A TIME TO WEEP…(as I let go, yield my life to Jesus and receive the love of God into my heart).
AND A TIME TO LAUGH…(as I accept joy and freedom from Jesus).

A TIME TO MOURN…(over losses, heartbreaks, old mistakes, regrets, lost blessings, lost time, etc.).
AND A TIME TO DANCE…(in celebration of the victory in my life over sin and death, a gift from my Lord Jesus.)

A TIME TO SCATTER STONES…(away from the tomb of my heart and like Lazarus, arise to a new day when called out by Jesus.)
AND A TIME TO GATHER THEM…(to build an altar in my heart and bring Him sacrifices of praise and thanksgiving.)

A TIME TO EMBRACE…(all that Jesus is and who He knows me to be, my _true_ self)
AND A TIME TO REFRAIN…(and turn away from my old self before I knew Him as Lord and Savior.)

A TIME TO SEARCH…(my heart and yield my spirit more and more to the One who made me).
AND A TIME TO GIVE UP…(my bitterness, my anger, my woundedness, my unforgiveness, etc. to Him.)

A TIME TO KEEP… (the peace that guards my heart when I choose to forgive myself, others, and God).
AND A TIME TO THROW AWAY…(the hurts and wrongs of my life in to the waiting hands of Jesus.)

A TIME TO TEAR…(the garment of my heart in sorrow for my sins and the sins of the world).
AND A TIME TO MEND…(hearts back together with the needle and thread of the love of God).

A TIME TO BE SILENT…(bow before the Holy One of Israel and listen with my heart).
AND A TIME TO SPEAK…(as I say, "Yes, Lord!").

A TIME TO LOVE…(God with all my heart, mind, and strength).
AND A TIME TO HATE…(the enemy of my soul who tries to stop me).

A TIME FOR WAR…(spiritual warfare with the enemy, Satan).
AND A TIME FOR PEACE…(that comes from God, a peace in my heart I do not always understand).

HE (God) HAS MADE (created already) EVERYTHING (in my spirit) BEAUTIFUL (well and good, in the likeness and image of Jesus) IN ITS TIME (appointed by God Himself).

HE (God) HAS ALSO SET ETERNITY (the joy of spending the rest of time with God) IN THE HEARTS (the home of Jesus) OF MEN (and women!).

YET THEY CANNOT FATHOM (ever truly understand or appreciate) WHAT GOD HAS DONE FROM BEGINNING TO END (of all the seasons of my life because it is too wonderful, awesome, miraculous, and loving!). (Ecclesiastes 3:1-8)

Christian Formation

God performed a miracle by sending His Son so that you wouldn't be…
Conformed to this world but be…
Transformed in His likeness and therefore be…
In-Formed in your inner being and…
Re-Formed into His image instead of being…
Deformed by the Evil One! Alleluia!

The New Covenant

The great High Priest
Meets me in the Holy of Holies,
Draws out His knife to perform the
Circumcision of my Heart.

My heart pounds
I tremble with fear,
Expecting tremendous pain, even instant death.

Suddenly, He cuts His own heart
And His Blood stains the floor.

My own wounds are healed -
My heart is clean, my robes white as snow!

My Great High Priest
Announces to the world
That my name is written on
His Breastplate

My joy knows no bounds
As my newly changed heart
Cries out the name of
Jesus for all to hear.

I look down with spirit eyes.
There like tablets of flesh, His Name
Is engraved on my heart.
My spirit rejoices for His Homecoming
And I am no longer afraid.

Allyson Tomkins 1999

Seeds of Faith

Isaiah 49:16

Day Seven

A Change of Heart

Exercise 34

As you become a new creation, it is in your heart more than any other part of us that the "newness" is seen and felt.

My Old Heart Was	My New Heart Is
Undisciplined	Disciplined
Powerless	Powerful
Unfocused	Focused
Without Purpose	Purposeful
Other:	Other:
"Come near to God and he will come near to you. Wash your hands, you sinners, and purify your hearts, you double-minded." James 4:8	"Since, then, you have been raised with Christ, set your hearts on things above, where Christ is seated at the right hand of God." Colossians 3:1

Soul Searching

As a result of the work I've done in this unit:

MIND

What new beliefs or thoughts do I have?

What old beliefs am I ready to put on God's altar?

WILL

What new choices have I made?

What old choices can I give to God?

EMOTIONS

My feelings have changed in the following way:

What feelings or emotions am I giving to the Lord?

Soul Searching

The *Joy* of Eternal Union with God: Freedom from Alienation

  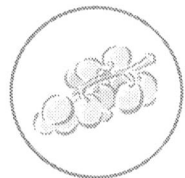 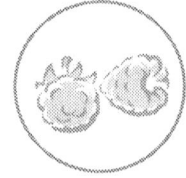 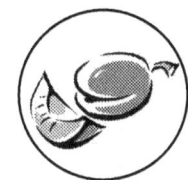 

Joy Choice # 11

**Joy is choosing to accept that because God loves me,
He wants me in His presence for all eternity. He wants me to know Him.
Jesus brings me into the presence of God where I remain and rest.
Joy is being a true worshiper of the Most High God.**

*You have made known to me the path of life;
you will fill me with joy in your presence, with eternal pleasures at your right hand.*
Psalm 16:11

The ascension is the complete fulfillment of the transfiguration. Our Lord returned to His original glory, but not simply as the Son of God-He returned to His father as the Son of Man as well. There is now freedom of access for anyone straight to the very throne of God because of the ascension of the Son of Man. As the Son of Man, Jesus Christ deliberately limited His omnipotence, omnipresence, and omniscience. But now they are His in absolute, full power. As the Son of Man, Jesus Christ now has all the power at the throne of God. From His ascension forward He is the King of kings and Lord of lords.

My Utmost for His Highest, Oswald Chambers, May 17

"To Him who is able to keep you from falling and to present you before his glorious presence without fault and with great joy - to the only God our Savior be glory, majesty, power and authority, through Jesus Christ our Lord, before all ages, now and forevermore! Amen"

Jude 24 -25

Day One

Today you decide to come to your meeting place early in the morning. There's a soft glow in the air as the morning sun begins to rise. A gentle mist floats over the river waters.

All else is still. All is quiet. You have come to the quiet this day, and Jesus joins you as He promised.

"Good morning My child. I too loved to be in my Father's presence early in the day when I walked this earth. He joyfully anticipates this time alone with you.

Here you can get to know more about Him and His love for you. Sing out your praises to the Most High God. Glorify His Holy Name. Bring Him your thanksgivings. Honor Him with your requests. And as you bring into His presence those you've allowed into your heart, know that for that time, they too are basking in His love.

You are created as a spiritual being. Your spirit and Mine will be together throughout eternity. To be separated from Me and My Father is to die. God is Spirit. You are becoming a true worshiper, worshiping Him in spirit and in truth.

To be with Me is to live forever. Did you know that I and the Father are one?

I am *the Image of the Invisible God.*
I am *the Angel of His Presence.*
I am *the Everlasting Father Immanuel.*
I am *the Lord of Glory.*
I am *the Branch of Jehovah.*
I am *a minister of the Sanctuary and of the True Tabernacle.*

I am *the Brightness of His Glory.*
I am *the Express Image of His Person.*
I am *a High Priest over the House of God.*
I am *the Son of the Father.*
I am *the Temple.*
I am *Emmanuel, God with us.*

As you eat of this fruit and are in perfect union with my Father, my Holy Spirit and Me, you can forever say:

'I am a temple of God. His Spirit dwells in me.
I am one with the Lord in spirit.
I am God's chosen person, holy and dearly loved.'

Let's sit for awhile with Our Father. Come into the Holy of Holies. In His presence is fullness of joy!"

Take Jesus up on His offer. Hang out for as long as you like. Abide with Him.

Getting to Know Jesus

Thus far you have been shown the various aspects of Jesus as:

Jesus our Savior: The Saving One
Jesus as Affirmer: The Accepting One
Jesus as Truth: The Truthful One
Jesus as Assurance: The Assuring One
Jesus as Comforter: The Comforting One
Jesus as Righteousness: The Convicting One
Jesus as Finisher: The Finishing One
Jesus as Uniter: The Relating One
Jesus as Healer: The Healing One
Jesus as Creator: The Creating One

Now, you meet another revelation of the Lord.

Exercise 1

Read over the list again, checking the names you are familiar with and noting the new ones.

"I know that Jesus is…:

- *the Image of the Invisible God.*
- *the Angel of His Presence.*
- *the Everlasting Father Immanuel.*
- *the Lord of Glory.*
- *the Branch of Jehovah.*
- *a minister of the Sanctuary and of the True Tabernacle.*
- *the Brightness of His Glory.*
- *the Express Image of His Person.*
- *a High Priest over the House of God.*
- *the Son of the Father.*
- *the Temple.*
- *Emmanuel, God with me."*

Exercise 2

What is Jesus revealing about Himself to you?

Getting to Know God

The following names or titles for God reveal how He is seen throughout scripture as producing the good fruit of Eternal union with Himself.

"My Name Is..."	"I Am..."	"I Create..."
Yahweh-Shammal.	Union	U
the Lord is there.	The desire to	N
the Ancient of Days.	know Me	I
the Living God.	Presence	O
the Lord Changing Not.	Oneness	N
Father.		
God the Father.		
Father of Mercies.		

Seeds of Faith

...And surely I am with you always, to the very end of the age.
Matthew 28:20

But may the righteous be glad and rejoice before God; may they be happy and joyful.
Psalm 68:3

Yet you have a few people in Sardis who have not soiled their clothes. They will walk with me, dressed in white, for they are worthy. He who overcomes will, like them, be dressed in white. I will never blot out his name from the book of life, but will acknowledge his name before my Father and his angels.
Revelation 3:4-5

Getting to Know the Holy Spirit

The Holy Spirit is the Spirit of knowledge and fear of the Lord. He is the Spirit of God Himself. He is the Spirit of the living God. He dwells in you forever. He helps you in prayer. He is everywhere. He gives the character of God. The Holy Spirit gives you access to God when you abide in Him.

Now you will see how joyful it can be to just sit in wonder and listen to the One who loves you. For it is in His presence that you have "fullness of joy" (Psalm 16). And yet the habit of walking with Him in the Garden of Eden, talking face to face, can seem very foreign to a modern, busy world. But, when you practice the presence of God, you can return to Eden!

When Jesus walked the Earth, He truly desired that people would come to know and understand His Father. That is precisely why He saved you...so that you will <u>know</u> and worship the Father. He was profoundly interested in sharing how to be intimate with God and this legacy continues today.

But as discussed, in Unit 8, it is in your Godly nature to be intimate but in your brokenness to pull away and hide or to control and dominate. This is true of the relationship with God as well.

So, let's take a deeper look at your own relationship with God and release the joy that comes with a oneness with the One who made you: the joy of abiding!

At least there is hope for a tree: If it is cut down, it will sprout again, and its new shoots will not fail. Its roots may grow old in the ground and its stump die in the soil, yet at the scent of water it will bud and put forth shoots like a plant.
Job 14:7-9

Day Two

GOOD FRUIT: ETERNAL UNION WITH GOD

Exercise 3

Directions:
Put a check next to the good fruit you have already received from Jesus
Put an X next to the fruit that you still need to grow

- ☐ Practicing the Presence
- ☐ Consolation
- ☐ A True Image of God
- ☐ Restored Image of myself
- ☐ Receiving God's Touch
- ☐ Abiding with God
- ☐ Becoming a Temple
- ☐ True Worship
- ☐ A God Story

The Mountain Top of your Heart
During my late twenties I lived in a place known for its mud slides and movie stars, for its fires and its fancies with the New Age Movement. Supposedly only 1% of the population worshipped in a church or temple, as most were lured to the beautiful sandy beaches on Sunday mornings. The little town was Malibu, and I belonged to a small church perched on top of a hill overlooking the Pacific Ocean.

We had a few of the rich and the famous, but for the most part these were all ordinary people. We did a good job of "doing church" on Sundays, but the rest of the week the church stood empty, the doors closed. We were all much too busy making money or learning to wind surf, and a Sunday service was all we needed.

My small group of friends became affectionately known as "Club Med Malibu." Fifty-two weeks a year we had something planned: a scuba trip to hunt for lobster, a ski trip to Utah, a sailing trip to the nearby Channel Islands. The greater the risk, the greater the adventure. My life was full, and I had all I wanted.

Or, so I thought. Little did any of my friends know, but I had begun sneaking down Pacific Coast Highway on Tuesday nights to a small Home Bible Study in Pacific Palisades. Something was happening to me as I met for a year and a half with Christians who did strange things, like study their Bibles and pray out loud to a God they seemed to know personally. I was drawn to the intimacy of this gathering, and the way they lived their lives.

As my Malibu group approached our summer trip to the High Sierras, I privately tucked a desire of my heart into my heavy backpack.

You see, I had met someone I was interested in, but who did <u>not</u> fit my image of the perfect husband. I yearned for a happy marriage and to start a family, as I was now thirty-three. Where had the years gone?

So, as my athletic friends sought to hike to the highest peak they could find, I announced I was staying behind at our campsite, alone.

Have you ever stood alone at 13,000 feet? Before me was Moon Lake, a perfectly round body of water surrounded by boulders. I probably spent the better part of an hour or two getting settled, and then I began to "talk with God." It was stiff, and I felt like I was talking to a stranger. I pressed into my discomfort.

After a little while of laying before Him what <u>I</u> thought was a pretty important issue, something began to happen. I looked up over the end of the lake and couldn't believe my eyes. There from one end to the other was a perfect rainbow stretched across the lake. I was in awe of the colors and of its sheer and delicate beauty. As I stood there, the rainbow began to move across the lake towards me! And as sweetly as if I were being tucked in at night by my Daddy, the rainbow came over me. I was standing inside the band of colors, and then it was gone.

In a moment of pure ecstasy, God had revealed His glory and given me as a gift, His perfect peace. In that precious time with Him, I "walked" with Him as Eve had done in her garden home and all my fears had been allayed. Lucky for Eve, she didn't have to try to meet the Lord. She walked in His Presence daily.

Our "mountain top" experiences have to come in the form of yearly pilgrimages or weekend conferences. Or, do they? No, we don't have to climb to 13,000 feet to have fellowship with the Lord. Whether you are at sea level or 13,000 feet, you can be in God's presence on the mountain top of your heart.

Good Fruit: Practicing the Presence

The notion of "Practicing the Presence of God" is not new by any means but is most recently a buzz-word in Christian circles. Hundreds of years ago, a humble monk named Brother Lawrence taught wonderful ways to commune with the Most High God.

Don't let the term "Practicing the Presence" throw you. You have to literally "practice" talking to God as you go through your day. He enjoys a chat when you wash the dishes as much as He does when you worship Him Sunday mornings. He loves your praises from the shower stall and the choir stall!

Exodus 33 says that Moses set up a "tent of meeting," and that everyone who sought the Lord would go out to this tent. The scripture says "The Lord would speak to Moses face to face, as a man speaks with his friend." (Exodus 33:11) Jesus and His Father long to chat with you. Your spirit home of the heart is a "tent of meeting" as well.

Good Fruit: Consolation

In the Gospel of John, (John 20:6) Jesus says Mary's name. A name is a way we acknowledge someone personally, a friend that we know intimately. She was weeping at the tomb over the loss of her friend, and it wasn't until Jesus said, "Mary," that she recognized Him as Jesus. Mary Magdalene and Jesus were friends, and she had lost Him, or so she thought. In the moment of her desolation, He brought consolation - the consoling of her soul.

Jesus came to her in her worst hour and called her by name. He had promised, as we read in John 16:20, "I tell you the truth, you will weep and mourn while the world rejoices. You will grieve, but your grief will turn to joy." He knew the moment of His resurrection would come, and He promised that His presence would bring us all great joy!

Matthew's Gospel says that Mary and the other women at the tomb, "...hurried away from the tomb afraid yet filled with joy, and ran to tell his disciples." (Matthew 28:8)

Mary was <u>moved</u> to action <u>only</u> after Her Lord had called her by name. She moved from sorrow to joy only after being in His presence. She was freed from her pain only after the resurrected Lord appeared to her, spoke tender words of comfort and then commissioned her to act. Jesus knew that this woman that he had healed from so much misery would give her <u>all</u> back to Him in honor and worship. Are you doing the same?

"Holy-gram" from God
Let me tell you one experience of consolation when I was in a deep valley. The man I had talked to God about by the lake in the mountains became my husband. A few years into our marriage, we were in a tough situation. He lived in California while I was setting up our new home in Louisiana. For seven long months he commuted across the country, and the strain on our marriage was almost unbearable.

Late one night, we came very close to ending the pain by ending the relationship. As I hung up the phone, I stumbled back to bed in the dark, sobbing from the sadness. I sat on the edge of the bed. I believe now that the Holy Spirit must have been praying for me in my grief. I had no words for God. My pain was too deep.

I looked up, eyes opened, and I saw, I **really** saw in front of me, a baby, like a beautiful cherub, arms outstretched, floating like a hologram (or holy-gram) before me. He was smiling, and He had a beautiful glow all around Him. As this baby turned, He turned into an adult man, also smiling. For a brief second He looked into my eyes, and then the vision was gone. I fell into a deep, peaceful sleep. It was as if he said, "All will be well," and it was.

Psychiatrists would say I was hallucinating in my hysteria. But you know who I saw, don't you? Jesus <u>really</u> knows what you go through. He <u>really</u> loves you and wants you to know Him.

Throughout the Bible you hear stories of people playing cat and mouse with the Lord. The Bible says your very sinful nature drives you into darkness to shade your shameful face from Him. "This is the verdict: Light has come into the world, but men loved darkness instead of light because their deeds were evil." (John 3:19)

You somehow "know that you know that you know" that God is displeased when you turn from Him. He calls to you from your hiding place, and as He asked Eve, "…Where are you?" (Genesis 3:9). He calls to you as well. In His passionate love for you, He will meet you in the midst of your passion (pain.) Open your heart to Him.

The Path of Life
He <u>delights</u> in your company, your praises, your worship and He turns His face towards you when you are suffering. All you need to do is come out from your secret places and come to Him who made you. Psalm 16 says,

> *I have set the Lord always before me. Because he is at my right hand, I will not be shaken. Therefore my heart is glad and my tongue rejoices; My body also will rest secure, because you will not abandon me to the grave, nor will you let your Holy One (Jesus) see decay. (He will be resurrected.) You have made known to me <u>the path of life</u>; You will fill me <u>with joy in your presence</u>, with eternal pleasures at your right hand.*

Psalm 16:8-11

Exercise 4

Spend some time now in conversation with the Lord. Offer Him those secret places where you sometimes hide yourself from Him. Listen. He is inviting you to join Him on the Path, into His presence where there is fullness of joy.

Use this space if you wish to write to Him.

Getting to Know You, Getting to Know All About You

Each of us has a "God-Story." This includes what you learned about God as a child, your family's beliefs about God, your personal experiences with growing up, your church's beliefs about God, etc. This God-Story grows with you in life and affects the way you relate to God now.

Everything you've read in this book reflects my own God-Story. I refer to God in the masculine. I assume I can have a personal relationship with Him. I feel loved and accepted by Him.

When I talk to people who have little or no relationship with God, I usually find that their image of God is based on a God-Story that includes <u>spiritual</u> woundedness somewhere in the generations. Along the way, their human spirit has been crushed or damaged. This has transformed their image of God or blocked them from knowing the truth about Him.

For some, their God-Story includes years of simply not seeking a personal relationship with God at all. He is far away, distant, uncaring or simply too busy to bother.

So, wherever you are in your knowledge and relationship, let's do a quick inventory on your own image of God.

Later in this unit will be discussed the Good Fruit of "true worship." You can't talk about worship until you figure out who you are worshiping.

GOOD FRUIT: YOUR GOD - STORY

You are told not to bow down before any "graven images" (Leviticus 26:1, Acts 17:29) - idols formed by human hands or minds. And yet sometimes the image of God has been graven in some other image than the true image of God Himself (based on revelation in scripture).

Exercise 5

What is your image (picture or idea that has form) of God? Describe God.

Where did your image come from?

How has your image changed over the years?

What have been your key faith-building moments in your life that framed your image of God?

Negative Attributes

What I notice most when I do marriage counseling are the ways husbands and wives automatically attribute to one another the worst or the negative characteristic. These usually come with the words "He always ...." or "She never.........." This can be true in your God-Story as well.

Exercise 6

What are the negative attributes you give to God?

"He is..."

- ☐ Critical
- ☐ Harsh
- ☐ Cruel
- ☐ Unloving
- ☐ Unforgiving
- ☐ Distant
- ☐ Blaming
- ☐ Cold
- ☐ Mean
- ☐ Uncaring
- ☐ Fearsome
- ☐ Unmerciful
- ☐ Angry with me
- ☐ Non-existent
- ☐ Hateful
- ☐ Threatening
- ☐ Tricky
- ☐ Other_____
- ☐ None of the Above

Exercise 7

Now, read aloud your chosen words which describe God saying, "the God I worship is ...."

Where or when did these words become part of your God-Story?

Exercise 8 - God's Attributes

These are some commonly held beliefs about God's attributes. Check all those that you include in your personal image of God, your God-Story.

"God is..."

- ☐ Simplicity (indivisible)
- ☐ Unity (God is one)
- ☐ Eternity (free from time/everlasting/eternal)
- ☐ Unchanging
- ☐ Unchangeable
- ☐ Everywhere (omnipresent)
- ☐ Supreme ruler
- ☐ Knows all-all knowing (omniscient)
- ☐ All powerful (Elohim)
- ☐ Love
- ☐ Freedom
- ☐ Righteousness (holy, hates sin)
- ☐ Truth
- ☐ Self-existent
- ☐ Merciful
- ☐ Lord-master
- ☐ A Shepherd
- ☐ A Sanctifier
- ☐ Just
- ☐ A present
- ☐ The Father
- ☐ The Son
- ☐ The Holy Spirit
- ☐ The Holy Trinity
- ☐ Disciplinarian
- ☐ Alive
- ☐ Male
- ☐ Female
- ☐ Provider
- ☐ Mother
- ☐ Father
- ☐ Other:_____

Exercise 9

If you do <u>not</u> include some of the words listed above, explain why.

Exercise 10

Now, read the words aloud you picked in the list above, saying, "The God I worship is......."

Healing and Our God-Story
Whenever there is healing, there is a piece of the God-Story healed too. Your image of God is restored each time He gives healing to your body, soul or spirit.

Healing brings you to a right relationship with God. You can't have a right relationship without wanting to worship. So once again let's look at what may have knocked the image of God off track in your life by looking at the two most important relationships: father and mother.

Father's Day: Adoption

Perhaps more than any other relationship, your relationship to your earthly father(s) impacts your image and relationship to God.

When you accept Jesus, you come into His inheritance. This includes being able to call God your Father! Even the Hebrews did not dare to come so close, to become so intimate, to count themselves equal.

The first two words alone of the Lord's Prayer were revolutionary. Don't take them for granted. Or maybe you should. Maybe that's the way God intended for you to know Him and to come to Him-as a child goes to a loving Father, taking him for granted.

Exercise 11 - THE IMAGE OF GOD AS THE "GOOD" FATHER

Some words that describe a "good" father are listed below and on the next page. As you read them, see if they could be added to your image of God.

Which of the following words describes :
A. Your father?
B. God?
C. (Note: if you have had more than one father, please customize this exercise.)

Attribute	Father	God
Loving		
Playful		
Caring		
Trustworthy		
Respectful		
Good Authority		
Strong		
Provider		
Protector		

Attribute	Father	God
Understanding		
Giving		
Blesses		
Disciplinarian		
Assuring		
Guiding/ Leading/ Directing		
Praying		

Seeds of Faith

This, then, is how you should pray: 'Our Father in heaven, hallowed be your name...'
Matthew 6:9

One God and Father of all, who is over all and through all and in all.
Ephesians 4:6

Then say to Pharaoh, "This is what the LORD says: Israel is my first born son..."
Exodus 4:22

And a voice from heaven said, "This is my Son, whom I love; with him I am well pleased."
Matthew 3:17

You are sons of God through faith in Christ Jesus
Galatians 3:26

Exercise 11 - The Image of God as the "Good" Father

Continued...

Attribute	Father	God
Involved		
Active		
Ruling		
Naming		
Persevering		
Sharing		
Spiritual		
Bonding		
Confidant		
Grounded		
Honest		
Oversees		
Dependable		
Relational		
Admits Mistakes		

Attribute	Father	God
Patient		
Humble		
Supportive		
Enthusiastic		
Interested		
Personal		
Contains		
Affectionate		
Inspiring		
Faithful		
Encouraging		
Ethical		
Assertive		
Truthful		
Teaching/ Instructing		

Attribute	Father	God
Empathetic		
Loyal		
Initiates		
Manages		
Creative		
Defines		
Excludes		
Intimate		
Empathetic		
Loyal		
Wise		
Experienced		
Sets Goals		
Completes/ Finishes (brings to form)		

Exercise 12

How alike or different from your own father(s) (biological, step-father, adoptive father, etc.) is your image of God? Does your image of God include Him as God the Father or with other aspects of masculinity? Discuss...

Exercise 13

How would you describe your relationship with your father(s)?

Is there any similarity between your relationship with your earthly father and your relationship with your Heavenly Father?

Exercise 14

If you've been wounded by your earthly father(s) please describe how this has affected your relationship with God as Father.

Exercise 15

Have you forgiven your father? If not, write here what you need to forgive:

The Forgiving Father
Stop now and read Luke 15:11-32. This is called the "Prodigal Son" or the story of the forgiving father.

One key to this powerful lesson by Jesus is that when the young man (or it could just as easily have been a girl) became "in need," had a "longing to fill his stomach" and finally "came to his senses," then and only then did he say, "I will get up and go to my father..." How true this has been in my own life.

The following verse is to me one of the most powerful images of God that Jesus revealed. "But while he was still a long way off, his father saw him, and was filled with compassion for him; he ran to his son, threw his arms around him, and kissed him." (Luke 15:20)

What a joyful picture! Can you see God, your Father, running to embrace you and kissing you? Even when you've abandoned Him? But-you cry-what about all I've done? "So what, I forgive you," says God, "I'm just so happy you came back! Now give me a hug." Now, that is an image of a good father!

Though my father and mother forsake me, the Lord will receive me. Psalm 27:10

I worked with a teen who had been incested by her father. Her image of "father" became twisted. Looking at young kids with their dads on the playground made her think that lurking in each man's heart was a molester. What she needed was for her image of "father" to be restored so that her relationship with God the Father could remain open, clear, free and trusting.

Note: *If there are any "father wounds" in your life, I encourage you to seek Christian counseling and inner healing prayer. This will put your image of God the Father in right order. (See Unit Nine.)*

IMAGE OF GOD: AS THE GOOD MOTHER

You can't look at the father image without seeing if there is a "mother" image as well. For some, the idea of God having any feminine or motherly qualities is unthinkable. For others, this aspect of the Godhead is more comfortably attributed to Mary, Jesus' Mother or to the Holy Spirit. Your quest here is to determine your own God-story. Some part of it may be tied into your experiences with being mothered.

Exercise 16 – THE IMAGE OF GOD AS THE "GOOD" MOTHER

Mother's Day
Some words that describe a good mother are listed below. As you read them, see if they are included in your image of God.

Which of the following words describes:

A. Your mother?
B. God?
C. (Note: if you have had more than one mother, please customize this exercise.)

Attributes	Mother	God
Nurturing		
Loving		
Caring		
Forgiving		
Gentle		
Kind		
Receiving		
Listening		
Calling		
Holding		
Accepting		
Protecting		
Open		
Expressing		
Connecting		

Attributes	Mother	God
Including		
Touching		
Bonding		
Relating		
Feeling		
Ethical		
Understanding		
Sacrificing		
Merciful		
Sensitive		
Giving		
Seeking		
Gathering		
Other: _____		

Exercise 17

Using some of the words you just checked, tell how alike and how different from your own mother(s) (biological, step-mother, adoptive mother, etc) is your image of God. Does your image of God include feminine or motherly attributes?

Explain:

Seeds of Faith

Can a mother forget the baby at her breast and have no compassion on the child she has borne? Though she may forget, I will not forget you! See, I have engraved you on the palms of my hands; your walls are ever before me.
Isaiah 49:15-16

I give them eternal life, and they shall never perish; no one can snatch them out of my hand.
John 10:28

O Jerusalem, Jerusalem, you who kill the prophets and stone those sent to you, how often I have longed to gather your children together, as a hen gathers her chicks under her wings, but you were not willing.
Matthew 23:37

Exercise 18

How would you describe your relationship with your own mother(s)?

Is there any similarity in your relationship with your mother and in your relationship to God in His more motherly or feminine attributes?

Exercise 19

If you have been wounded in some way by your earthly mother(s), please describe how this has affected your relationship with God.

Exercise 20

Have you forgiven her? If not, write here what you need to forgive:

Day Three

GOOD FRUIT: A RESTORED IMAGE OF MYSELF

Adam and Eve were made in God's image. We know that God must have both "male" and "female," because He made the first man and woman in His image. Each of us is unique which implies the limitless ways in which God reveals Himself in us.

No matter what your gender, you can share in the masculine and feminine aspects of the divine nature of God. God is whole, perfect and united. The facets of His being are like the sides of a flawless diamond. The sum of the whole is greater than His parts.

Repeated here are the lists of words describing the good father (or the true masculine) and then the good mother (or the true feminine). This time check those characteristics which make up your own image, the image you have of yourself.

Again, many people need healing in this area of the masculine and feminine in order to put their own image of God in order. Ask the Holy Spirit to guide you with this next exercise.

Exercise 21 - THE TRUE MASCULINE

Directions: Check all that apply to you.

Attribute	This Describes Me	This Needs Healing
Loving		
Playful		
Caring		
Trustworthy		
Respectful		
Good Authority		
Strong		
Provider		
Protector		
Understanding		
Giving		
Blesses		
A Disciplinarian		

Then God said, "Let us make man in our image, in our likeness, and let them rule over the fish of the sea and the birds of the air, over the livestock, over all the earth, and over all the creatures that move along the ground." So God created man in his own image, in the image of God he created him; male and female he created them.
Genesis 1:26-27

...and have put on the new self, which is being renewed in knowledge in the image of its Creator.
Colossians 3:10

Exercise 21 - The True Masculine (Continued)

Directions: Check all that apply to you.

Attribute	This Describes Me	This Needs Healing
Assuring		
Encouraging		
Praying		
Inspiring		
Truthful		
Patient		
Humble		
Supportive		
Enthusiastic		
Interested		
Personal		
Contains		
Affectionate		
Loyal		
Initiates		
Manages		
Creative		
Defines		
Excludes		
Intimate		

Attribute	This Describes Me	This Needs Healing
Ethical		
Assertive		
Involved		
Active		
Ruling		
Naming		
Persevering		
Sharing		
Spiritual		
Bonding		
Confidant		
Grounded		
Honest		
Oversees		
Empathetic		
Teaching/Instructing		
Guiding/Leading/Directing		
Connected to God		

Exercise 22 - The True Feminine

Directions: Check all that apply to you.

Attribute	This Describes Me	This Needs Healing
Nurturing		
Loving		
Caring		
Forgiving		
Gentle		
Kind		
Receiving		
Listening		
Calling		
Holding		
Accepting		
Protecting		
Open		
Expressing		
Gathering		
Relational		
Wise		
Admits Mistakes		

Attribute	This Describes Me	This Needs Healing
Connecting		
Including		
Touching		
Bonding		
Relating		
Feeling		
Understanding		
Sacrificing		
Merciful		
Sensitive		
Giving		
Seeking		
Dependable		
Sets Goals		
Loyal		
Experienced		
Faithful		
Completes/Finishes (brings to form)		

Exercise 23

Now, write a letter to Jesus asking Him to heal and restore those places in yourself that are broken or undeveloped in the areas you checked.

> *Dear Jesus,*
>
> *I know it is your desire that I come into a closer relationship with God. As you heal my life and especially my own areas of brokenness, the eyes of my heart will more accurately see my God.*
>
> *I pray Lord that you will put in me now the true, divine nature you desire in me. In particular I need to be more:*
>
> *Thank you Jesus for your healing touch which is even now able to form in me the person you intended that I be.*
>
> *Amen.*

GOOD FRUIT: RECEIVING GOD'S TOUCH

When a baby is received into the family, everyone wants to hold her, touch her, talk to her, play with her, and simply be in her presence.

In the same way, as the Lover of your Soul, God wants to hold you, touch you, talk to you, play with you and have you in His presence.

As we learn to practice His presence on a daily basis, (as we do the dishes, drive to work, or bathe the dog) the words of the loving Father can "touch" our hearts. Our heart has spiritual ears to hear Him speak. Remember the word HEART has both words in it, "HEAR" and "EAR." But your heart must be open to hear God speak. And then of course what follows must be obedience to what He tells you.

Parents touch their children with their words: words that bless or words that curse. God <u>touches</u> you with His words. Receiving His touch is part of a deep intimacy. If you have any woundedness about touch or about intimacy, this aspect of your relationship with God will be stilted.

Exercise 24

In this next healing prayer, invite the Holy Spirit to heal any memories or woundedness regarding being touched (physically, emotionally, or spiritually.)

> ***Dear Holy Spirit,***
>
> ***I want to be able to touch the Father's heart in worship. I want to receive His touch as He speaks to my heart. But touch is uncomfortable because:***
>
>
>
>
>
>
>
>
>
> ***As you heal my ability to be touched Lord, I receive your touch and the intimacy it brings with joy instead of fear.***
>
> ***Amen***

Seeds of Faith

We have not received the spirit of the world but the Spirit who is from God, that we may understand what God has freely given us. This is what we speak, not in words taught us by human wisdom but in words taught by the Spirit, expressing spiritual truths in spiritual words. 1 Corinthians 2:12-13

Jesus replied, 'If anyone loves me, he will obey my teaching. My Father will love him, and we will come to him and make our home with him.'
John 14:23

However, the Most High does not live in houses made by men. As the prophet says: 'Heaven is my throne, and the earth is my footstool. What kind of house will you build for me? Says the Lord. Or where will my resting place be?'
Acts 7:48-49

Do you not know that your body is a temple of the Holy Spirit, who is in you, whom you have received from God? You are not your own; you were bought at a price. Therefore honor God with your body.
1 Corinthians 6:19

Good Fruit: Abide with God

Do you prepare for special guests? Clean up, vacuum, scrub the counters, turn on the lights? Do you have special places in your house for entertaining? Special china, silver, crystal? Do you put on special music, or wear special clothes? The key word here is <u>special</u> and it implies honor.

In my home, when we are entertaining at a meal, my husband sits at one end of the dining room table. I always ask a guest to sit at the other end in what would be "my" seat. If it is my father, he gets that seat no matter who else is present. My father is special, and I honor him in that way.

Does God get that place of honor as a special invited guest in your home (the home of the heart)? Do you prepare for His arrival? Is the welcome mat out?

At both entrances to our home we have small plaques nailed to the doorways. One reads, "As for me and my house, we will serve the Lord." The other reads, "May the spirit of the Lord rest on this house." I want all who enter to know that our home is sacred ground because God is welcome. He abides or dwells with us.

Would God feel welcomed into your dwelling place? God chose to dwell among His people back in the days of Moses (Genesis 33), and of course even in the Garden of Eden (Genesis 3:8). Why wouldn't He be looking for a dwelling place now?

Good Fruit: Becoming a Temple

Do you know that as a believer you are the dwelling place of the King of Glory?

God sent Jesus as Emmanuel, "God with us." Then, Jesus sent the Holy Spirit as a deposit or guarantee that He would one day return. The Holy Spirit needs a home. Is He at home with you?

God's people were told to build a large dwelling tent or tabernacle as they journeyed through the desert to the Promised Land. This tabernacle was a sacred place of worship and was indeed very special. The most sacred area in the tabernacle was called the Holy of Holies where God's presence was held in reverential awe and wonder. Later the tabernacle (or tent) was made of stone and called the Temple in Jerusalem, the House of God.

A veil separated the people from God's presence. When Jesus died on the Cross, the veil was torn in two! The separation no longer prevented man from coming into God's holy presence. Alleleuia! Jesus' death opened the only way into God's presence for all believers. Do you take advantage of this gift of Jesus? Do you go to the Holy of Holies daily to bring Him sacrifices of praise and thanksgiving?

If your answer is, "Yes, I go to church every week and we sing a few songs," you are just barely accepting the precious gift that our Lord died to give you. You are able to "enter his gates with thanksgiving and his courts with praise;" (Psalm 100:4) twenty-four hours a day as the angels do who cry "Holy, holy, holy is the Lord Almighty; the whole earth is full of his glory." (Isaiah 6:3) Jesus is the High Priest, and He welcomes His believers and worshipers into His Father's House.

The writer of Hebrews tells us that you too are a royal priest. Royal priests know their king intimately and serve him in the inner courts. They are welcome in his presence and can stand, kneel or bow down in worship. This freedom with God as King was granted to you by the blood sacrifice of the Lamb of God, Jesus. His entry into God's throne room is paved by His sacrificial death on the cross. You walk in behind Him with full rights and privileges granted to a royal priesthood. Your robes are washed white as snow so that you can stand in God's presence for all eternity, as no sin or darkness can enter that most sacred place.

"Wait!" you say, "I am not worthy!"

No. But "Worthy is the Lamb, that was slain," (Revelation 5:12), and now you have His worthiness. You are that important to God.

Exercise 24

As a priest you bring Him a sacrifice, not of a cow or lamb, but praise and thanksgiving and a contrite heart. Take a moment now, and in prayer offer your King a thanksgiving. (You may want to record your prayer here.)

> **Dear Jesus,**
>
> **I'm thankful for...**
>
>
>
>
>
> **Amen.**

Seeds of Faith

Matthew 27:51

For Christ did not enter a man-made sanctuary that was only a copy of the true one; he entered heaven itself, now to appear for us in God's presence. Nor did he enter heaven to offer himself again and again, the way the high priest enters the Most Holy Place every year with blood that is not his own.
Hebrews 9:24-25

Blessed are those who wash their robes, that they may have the right to the tree of life and may go through the gates into the city.
Revelation 22:14

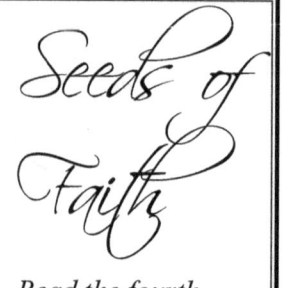

Read the fourth chapter of John.

GOOD FRUIT: TRUE WORSHIP

Worship includes both <u>praise</u> and <u>service</u>. It involves bowing down to show respect, honor, reverence and humility. It is to do as the angels do and sing praises to the Living God as well as to be obedient to do His bidding. It also involves lifting up your body, soul and spirit. In short, worship is all of you.

Worship implies worth and it is a statement that what or who you worship is worthy to you. In the scripture in John 4:23, Jesus says, "Yet a time is coming and has now come when the true worshipers will worship the Father in spirit and truth; for they are the kind of worshipers the Father seeks." Jesus continues by saying, "God is spirit, and his worshipers must worship in spirit and in truth." (John 4:24)

True worship is a way of life. But again, be very clear just Who it is you worship.

God has revealed Himself as a Trinity, a Godhead of three persons, Father, Son and Holy Spirit.

God is Spirit, and He has sent us His Holy Spirit. You too, are spirit. God created in you a human spirit that knows Him and yearns to be united with Him always. Your spirit craves to be filled up with Him. You have seen that you are a creature who shares an image with God and are increasing in his Son's likeness. You share, in a small version, a trinity of body, soul and spirit. Yours is not a divine threesome, but is divinely created and divinely intended to know the One who created it.

You are not god, but have the capacity to have God inhabit you.

This is a huge difference and the Christian faith embraces this difference wholeheartedly.

False religions would have you worship the god-ness in yourself as proof that you yourself are a god.

Why Were You Saved?
God saved you so that you could worship Him. Worship means putting your whole heart in the light of God's presence. When your heart and the heart of Jesus are connected in worship, you can be no closer. That is the definition of <u>true</u> joy. In worship, you bring your false, graven images of yourself and others to be broken on the altar of God. Worship is a time for the image of God and His Son Jesus to be made even clearer.

Come to worship God, willing and hungry. He never sends anyone away empty-handed. When you come to worship Him (which means to bow your heart down to Him), you receive ministry to the heart. Reading God's word softens the heart and is like a warm-up exercise for the spirit. (More in Unit 12.)

Worship allows you to see God with the magnifying glass of your heart. You can for a while see an enlarged (magnified) vision of Him. Your perception of Him changes - not His perception of you.

True Worship Action Plan
God saved you so you could become a "true worshiper." Written below are a few actions involved in worship.

1. Adoration
2. Praise
3. Thanksgiving
4. Penitence
5. Intercession
6. Petition
7. Corporate worship
8. Praying out loud
9. Service
10. Offerings
11. Sacrifices and gift giving
12. Sacred Movement
13. Contemplation/Meditation
14. Singing
15. Other: _____

Exercise 25

Write an action plan to bring your current style of worship to a new level, that of a true worshiper. It is an action plan which promises to increase your joy.

Exercise 26 - JOY MEDITATION

The following meditation is an example of how to come to God with a searching heart.

Get Quiet. *Come, Holy Spirit* "Be still, and know that I am God" (Psalm 46:10)

When I:
Am **lost,** be my Guide.
Am **lonely,** be my Friend.
Am **in trouble,** be my Helper.
Am **weak,** be my Power.
Slip, be my Conviction.

Am **empty,** be my Source
Am **confused,** be my Teacher
Am **in pain,** be my Counselor.
Am **in doubt,** be my Assurance.
Have no words, be my Intercessor.

Am **in conflict,** be my Fruit.
Am **in sorrow,** be my Comforter.
Am **in despair,** be my Inspiration.
Can be used, be my Commission

I receive your anointing, Oh Lord with joy!

2. Enter in and praise God's Attributes. "Enter his gates with thanksgiving and his courts with praise..." (Psalm 100:4)

3. Focus on God's gift of Joy:

JESUS "You have made known to me the path of life; you will fill me with joy in Your presence..." (Psalm 16:11) Lord, I come into Your presence... I offer whatever is blocking my connection to You, Jesus... "...Now is your time of grief, but I will see you again and you will rejoice, and no one will take away your joy." (John 16:22)

OTHERS "Go into all the world and preach the good news to all creation." (Mark 16:15)
I have shared my joy with _____. I give thanks for the joy in my relation to others. I offer You whatever is blocking this joy...(I forgive...) I am exhibiting the fruit of Your Spirit (joy) in my relationship(s). "...the fruit of the Spirit is love, joy, peace, patience, kindness, goodness, faithfulness, gentleness and self-control..." (Galatians 5:22-23)

YOURSELF "...the joy of the Lord is your strength." (Nehemiah 8:10 .)
I accept myself in You, Jesus. "Therefore, if anyone is in Christ, he is a new creation..." (2 Corinthians 5:17) I offer whatever is blocking my acceptance of myself... (I forgive myself for...)

CREATION "Let the heavens rejoice, let the earth be glad; let the sea resound, and all that is in it; let the fields be jubilant, and everything in them. Then all the trees of the forest will sing for joy..." (Psalm .96:11, 12) I experienced our Father's joy in His creation (nature, beauty, song, dance, art, etc.)...
I offer whatever blocks my joy in this area...

Jesus said, "I have told you this so that my joy may be in you and that your joy may be complete." (John 15:11)

4. Let Him speak to you. Stay in His Presence and respond to what He says. "...so that my joy may be in you and that your joy may be complete." (John 15:11)

I am Joy:
seek Me, My Friendship, Lordship, and My saving health.
share Me with others: love and forgive.
receive Me - My acceptance of you is my gift.
wonder at My Father's creation and know He is ever near you.

5. Praise Him again! "...may the righteous be glad and rejoice before God; may they be happy and joyful." (Psalm 68:3)

Day Four

BAD FRUIT

Exercise 27

Directions: Read over the list of bad fruits and check any that you need to have pruned in your life in order to grow the joy of eternal union with God:

- ☐ Alienation From God
- ☐ Idol Worship
- ☐ Despair
- ☐ Self-Reliance

BAD FRUIT: ALIENATION FROM GOD

If you put all of the other "bad fruit" described thus far into one basket it would not come close to the horror of being alienated from God. Some choose to remove themselves from His presence. This may be the person who never prays, never reaches out to God, does not fellowship with Him and definitely does not worship Him. Some feel as if they have been "cast away" from His presence by some grave, unpardonable sin. Others just simply don't care.

Debra is a young woman in her thirties. She was having a hard time sleeping and had all the classic symptoms of depression. She was dissatisfied with her marriage and her kids could do nothing right. In our first session, she happened to mention a miscarriage ten years prior that she still felt guilty about. The fact that this event seemed unhealed led me to say, "Your response to the miscarriage reminds me a lot of how women who have had an abortion respond." The look on her face was telling. "Yes, she said quietly. I had one of those, too. I live with the fact every day that I'll never see my babies in Heaven because I know I'm going to Hell."

Debra believed her abortion at sixteen was later punished by her miscarriage at twenty-three. God had kept a grade book, and she had received an "F." No one with "F's" can come to God, she believed.

Debra's image of God was formed in these life experiences and even caused her to misunderstand scripture. It wasn't until the two (her image of God and her memories of the past) were healed that Debra could experience the joy of a close relationship with God. Her ability and desire to worship came alive.

Seeds of Faith

Therefore I tell you that the kingdom of God will be taken away from you and given to a people who will produce its fruit.
Matthew 21:43

He cuts off every branch in me that bears no fruit, while every branch that does bear fruit he prunes so that it will be even more fruitful.
John 15:2

Ephesians 4:18

Romans 8:1

Consequently, you are no longer foreigners and aliens, but fellow citizens with God's people and members of God's household, built on the foundation of the apostles and prophets, with Christ Jesus himself as the chief cornerstone. In him the whole building is joined together and rises to become a holy temple in the Lord. And in him you too are being built together to become a dwelling in which God lives by his Spirit. Ephesians 2:19-22

Isaiah 45:22-23

Isaiah 41:29

Isaiah 61:3

2 Corinthians 4:7-8

She needed to hear that

 **TRUTH** — **Our God is a forgiving God, truly merciful, slow to anger, and eager to have us in His presence. (Psalm 103:8)**

She couldn't receive that truth as long as she believed the lie:

 **LIE** — **"What I've done is unforgivable and God is a punishing God."**

Her self-imposed alienation from God ended, and her joy blossomed.

Alienation from God began with Adam and Eve. But God wants you to be an "alien nation," a nation of people who live in this world but are not of this world. You are to be holy, set-apart, and different so that you can worship the one, true God.

BAD FRUIT: IDOLATRY OR IDOL WORSHIP

Idolatry is the worship of anything other than God. In the days of Isaiah, idol worship was a big problem. Over and over the Prophets warned the people of Israel not to bow down to anything but the One True God. "From the rest he makes a god, his idol; he bows down to it and worships. He prays to it and says, "Save me; you are my god." Isaiah 44:17. God's answer to this foolishness of Man is, "I am the Lord, and there is no other, apart from Me there is no God." Isaiah 45:5.

Examine your ways carefully. Are there any idols in your own life? Write them here:

BAD FRUIT: DESPAIR

It says in Isaiah, chapter 61:3, Jesus has been anointed to give us " a garment of praise instead of a spirit of despair." I always think of despair as meaning "without spirit." It is impossible for a Christian to be completely without spirit even if it feels like it. Despair is an emotional sand trap that should be avoided at all costs. If you detect despair, get help immediately.

BAD FRUIT: SELF-RELIANCE

Jesus died and as your self dies with Him, you no longer live, but Christ lives in you, Galatians 2:20. Any bad fruit of self-reliance, leaning on your own strength and understanding, is often the last fruit left on the tree that needs pruning. In this world, you learn from an early age the "virtue" of self-reliance. Then, when you are born again, all those skills and attitudes must "die."

Ask the Holy Spirit to shine His light on those areas where you are still self-reliant. He will gladly support you as you begin to lean on Jesus more and more each day.

Day Five

GROWING GOOD FRUIT: UNION WITH GOD

Since this is perhaps God's favorite fruit, I believe He provides all you need to till your soil, pull out weeds and grow good seed. When this fruit begins to grow it must bring Him great joy! The whole purpose of saving you was so you could become a true worshiper and "come before him with joyful songs." (Psalm 100:2)

This is really where He partners with us to help up grow good fruit. As the Gardener, He prunes away at anything that will block your union to Him. All eleven Units provide the tools to help your tree of life grow the good fruit of a close relationship to the Trinity, the juiciest fruit of all.

Exercise 28

"I would like to become more..."

- ☐ Worshipful
- ☐ Reverent
- ☐ Able to praise
- ☐ Still and quiet
- ☐ Faithful
- ☐ Able to listen
- ☐ Grateful
- ☐ Open to God's wisdom and guidance
- ☐ Of a seeker
- ☐ Flexible to hear God and change my plans
- ☐ Able to pray (prayerful)
- ☐ Comfortable with being alone with God
- ☐ Disciplined in my time with God
- ☐ Humble
- ☐ Inner centered
- ☐ Other:_____

Seeds of Faith

."... Yet when you relied on the Lord, he delivered them into your hand. For the eyes of the Lord range throughout the earth to strengthen those whose hearts are fully committed to him...2 Chronicles 16:7

Humble yourselves before the Lord, and he will lift you up.
James 4:10

Exercise 28 - Pulling the Weeds

How would you honestly describe yourself?

"I often am..."

- ☐ Ungrateful
- ☐ Disrespectful of God
- ☐ Presumptuous
- ☐ Resistant
- ☐ Worshipful of other "Gods" in my life (money, work, etc.)
- ☐ More likely to follow my own inclinations
- ☐ Alienated from God
- ☐ Unable to be quiet
- ☐ Too much in charge
- ☐ Afraid of God
- ☐ Irreverent
- ☐ Angry with God
- ☐ Unknowing about God
- ☐ Afraid of what God will tell me
- ☐ Competitive
- ☐ Controlling
- ☐ Dominating
- ☐ Confused
- ☐ Passive
- ☐ Easily dominated fearful
- ☐ Jealous
- ☐ Rigid
- ☐ Without boundaries
- ☐ Unethical
- ☐ Overwhelmed
- ☐ Legalistic
- ☐ Overly-religious
- ☐ Unloving
- ☐ Hating of the feminine or toward women
- ☐ Hating of the masculine or toward men
- ☐ Other:_____

Exercise 29

Which of these characteristics are causing the most difficulty in your relationship with God?

_____
_____
_____

How?

EXPERIENCING JOY

Day Six

PREPARING THE SOIL OF THE SOUL: UPROOTING UNHOLY ROOTS

Jesus leads us to a union with His Father and a deepening intimacy with God Himself. No unholy root can exist if you are to share in this holy <u>communion</u> with the Almighty.

His Holy Spirit gladly removes all that is impure so that you may be closer to the One who made you.

All idols, all sin, and all bad fruit hinder this joy connection of being in the Father's presence.

Examples of this might be:
An imagination that has been corrupted so you can not properly image God
Worship of other gods in other temples, shrines, or unholy places
Sin that is still un-repented
Hatred (including self-hatred)

Exercise 30

Ask Jesus to remove anything unholy which blocks an intimate relationship for you with God.

Exercise 31

Put your name in the following scripture where it says "you" and read it out loud.

> *"The Lord your God is with you (_____),*
> *He is mighty to save (you _____).*
> *He will take great delight in you (_____),*
> *He will quiet you (_____) with His love, he will rejoice over you (_____) with singing."*
>
> Zephaniah 3:17

Seeds of Faith

Romans 11:16-24

Day Seven

A Change of Heart

Exercise 32

Directions: Check all that apply to the transformation happening in your heart.

My Old Heart Was:	My New Heart Is:
Foolish	Seeking, Disciplined
Stubborn	Waiting, yearning
Idolatrous	Quiet, respectful
Proud	Listening, devoted
Not loyal	Holy
Unhearing	Worshipful, Faithful
Hostile	Humble, responsive, contrite
Disrespectful	Reverential (God-fearing)
Unfaithful	Attentive
Other:	Loyal
Other:	Other:
"The fool says in his heart, "There is no God." They are corrupt, and their ways are vile; there is no one who does good." Psalm 53:1	"Come near to God and he will come near to you. Wash your hands, you sinners, and purify your hearts, you double-minded." James 4:8

The fullness of joy comes in the presence of God. This good fruit is freely accessible to you at any time. But a heart that does not respond to its own yearnings to worship (and commune with the Most High God) will never have this joy. Jesus turns your heart, to "see" the heart of God. How is He turning your heart?

It's time to write a prayer asking Jesus to help remove all stumbling blocks to the joy of being in God's presence.

Exercise 33 - Conversion through Conversation

It is in and through conversations with God and Jesus and by the Holy Spirit that you are converted. Remember, you are His beloved.

You have to "walk the walk" (with God) and "talk the talk" (with Him.) Why not right now?

> *Dear Jesus,*
>
> *You are the image of the Invisible God for me and I want to know Him as You know Him. You are the Son of the Father and have opened the way into the Holy of Holies so I may commune with the Most High God.*
>
> *Please help me: (fill in you own words here)*
>
>
>
>
> *Thank you Jesus for renewing my mind and changing my heart. I long to be with you. You are my joy.*
>
> *Amen.*

Spiritual Growth

Have you ever sat and watched a tree grow? There's not much to see, right? Don't be too harsh on yourself, expecting a fast growth in your spiritual life. Like the tree, if your spirit gets proper care and nourishment, it will steadily grow.

Seeds of Faith

He is like a tree planted by streams of water, which yields its fruit in season and whose leaf does not wither. Whatever he does prospers. Psalm 1:3

Soul Searching

As a result of the work I've done in this unit:

MIND
What new beliefs or thoughts do I have?

What old beliefs am I ready to put on God's altar?

WILL
What new choices have I made?

What old choices can I give to God?

EMOTIONS
My feelings have changed in the following way:

What feelings or emotions am I giving to the Lord?

The *Joy* of Eternal Victory:
The Celebration of a Life with Christ

  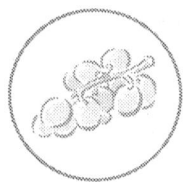   

Joy Choice #12:

Joy is choosing to live a victorious life and sharing the victory with others. Joy is the victory I have in Christ Jesus over sin and death.

We are victorious because He is victorious.
Revelation 6:2

He who has an ear, let him hear what the Spirit says to the churches. To him who overcomes, I will give the right to eat from the tree of life, which is in the paradise of God.
Revelation 2:7

"Those of us who do a good are like an orchard full of the fruit of good works. Such persons are like the Earth, which is strengthened and adorned by rocks and trees. But if we do evil works in the stubbornness of sin, we shall remain sterile in God's eyes, like the stubborn Earth that bears no fruit."

Hildegard de Bingen Fox, *Book of Divine Works* p. 117

"A river reaches places which its source never knows. And Jesus said that, if we have received His fullness, 'rivers of living water' will flow out of us, reaching in blessing even 'to the end of the earth' (Acts 1:8) regardless of how small the visible effects of our lives may appear to be. 'This is the work of God, that you believe (italics)...' (John 6:29). God rarely allows a person to see how great a blessing he is to others."

"A river is victoriously persistent, overcoming all barriers...Do you see God using the lives of others, but an obstacle has come into your life and you do not seem to be of any use to God? Then keep paying attention to the source, and God will take you around the obstacle or remove it. The river of the Spirit of God overcomes all obstacles. Never focus your eyes on the obstacle or the difficulty...Never allow anything to come between you and Jesus Christ-not emotion nor experience-nothing must keep you from the one great sovereign Source."

"Think of the healing and far-reaching rivers developing and nourishing themselves in our souls! God has been opening up wonderful truths to our minds, and every point He has opened up is another indication of the wider power of the river that He will flow through us. If you believe in Jesus, you will find that God has developed and nourished in you mighty, rushing rivers of blessing for others."

My Utmost for His Highest, Oswald Chambers, September 6

Day One

This time, you joyfully anticipate meeting Jesus in the orchard. He approaches but the glory that shines around Him almost blinds you. He is wearing radiant golden crowns. Jesus smiles at you in a welcome embrace of love. He meets you under the Tree of Life and says, "Come, follow me. I want to show you My Father's house, the City of God. I have prepared a place for you." You walk with Him on the Path of Life where the River of Life is flowing nearby. The colors and light are breathtaking.

All around you see people wearing dazzling crowns and you hear beautiful voices singing anthems of praise to the King. They lay their crowns at His feet with absolute joy on their faces.

Jesus says, "Your name is written in My Book of Life and I have a special crown just for you. My final fruit for your tree is the fruit of a Victorious Life. It would give me great joy if you would accept this fruit. Taste and see how good it is!

You know who I am...

"I am *the King of Glory*.
I am *the Resurrection and the Life*.
I am *Lord of All the Earth*.
I am *He who will baptize with the Holy Spirit*.
I am *the Head of the Church*.
I am *the Faithful and True Witness*.
I am *the Forerunner*.
I am *the Desire of All Nations*.
I am *the One Whom God Raised from the Dead*.
I am *A High Priest of Good Things to Come*.
I am *the King of kings and Lord of lords*.
I am *the Prince of the kings of the earth*.
I am *the Lord of the Harvest*.
I am *the Lord Our Banner*.

I am *the One who holds the seven stars in the right hand*.
I am *the One who walks among the seven golden lampstands*.
I am *the Lord of the Dead and Living*.
I am *the Great Shepherd*.
I am *the Teacher*.
I am *the Amen*.
I am *the King of the Jews*.
I am *The Root of David*.
I am *the Branch of David*.
I am *the True Vine*.
I am *the Tree of Life*!"

We are victorious together because I have overcome the world. Together you and I can conquer anything. In great joy you can now say...

'I am a citizen of Heaven and seated in Heaven right now.
I am a chosen people, a royal priesthood, a holy nation, a people belonging to God that I might declare the praises of Him who called me out of darkness into His wonderful light.
I am God's field.
I am God's building.
I am not ashamed of the gospel.
I am a kingdom and priest to serve our God.
I am a witness unto Jesus.
I am Christ's ambassador.
I am the salt of the Earth.'

And you can say...

'I am the aroma of Christ among those who are being saved and those who are perishing.
I will be a crown of splendor in the Lord's hand, a royal diadem in the hand of your God.
I am a branch on the True Vine.
I am a fellow worker with God.
I am chosen and appointed to go and bear fruit-fruit that will last.
I am an overcomer.'

And now my child, I send you into the world. I give you the fruit of a victorious life for one purpose: so you will go into the world telling others about Me. Be faithful, even to the point of death, and I will give you the crown of life. I am coming soon. Hold on to what you have. No one can take your crown. To him who overcomes, I will grant to eat of the Tree of Life, which is in the Paradise of God."

Jesus dips a goblet into the River of Life and hands it to you. As you lift the cup to your lips, you notice the water has turned to wine! And as you drink in this new wine, you know true joy.

Bask for a time in the divine presence of the Beautiful Savior Jesus.
Christ is risen. Christ is risen indeed. Alleluia!

GETTING TO KNOW JESUS

Throughout this book Jesus has revealed the splendor and brilliance of the multi-faceted diamond of His character. In this final unit, He shows you His most glorious dimension . This is only a taste of His glory revealed in the Bible. When you see Him face to face, His full glory will be revealed. I'm anxious for that moment. Are you?

Exercise 1

Let's go back over this list of the names of Jesus and see with the eyes of the spirit what new revelation He has for you.

"I know Jesus as…"

- ☐ *my King of Glory.*
- ☐ *the Resurrection and the Life.*
- ☐ *my Lord of All the Earth.*
- ☐ *my Head of the Church.*
- ☐ *my True Vine.*
- ☐ *the Lord my Banner.*
- ☐ *the Desire of All Nations.*
- ☐ *my Lord of the Harvest.*
- ☐ *my Faithful and True Witness.*
- ☐ *the Amen.*
- ☐ *the Forerunner.*
- ☐ *the King of the Jews.*
- ☐ *the Lord of the Dead and Living.*
- ☐ *the One who holds the seven stars in the right hand.*
- ☐ *the One who walks among the seven golden lampstands.*
- ☐ *my King of kings and Lord of lords.*
- ☐ *my Great Shepherd.*
- ☐ *my Teacher.*
- ☐ *the One Whom God Raised from the Dead.*
- ☐ *my Tree of Life.*
- ☐ *the Root of David.*
- ☐ *the Branch of David.*
- ☐ *He who will baptize me with the Holy Spirit.*
- ☐ *Prince of the kings of the earth.*
- ☐ *my High Priest of Good Things to Come.*

Exercise 2

As you read over this list, what <u>new</u> aspects of Himself is Jesus revealing to you?

GETTING TO KNOW GOD

The following names or titles for God reveal how He is seen throughout Scripture as producing the good fruit of the Joy of Victory.

"My Name Is…"		"I Am…"		"I Create…"
Yayweh Nissi Battle Lord of all the Earth The Lord my Banner The Almighty Crown and Diadem Sun The High God God of Heaven The Most High God Everlasting God The King of Heaven The Great God God of Gods King Great King High and Lofty One Lord of lords The Great The Almighty The Awesome God	therefore	Honor Glory Majesty The Standard Triumph Leadership Command Love Sovereign Excellence Beauty Radiance Dominion	therefore	V I C T O R Y

Exercise 3

Read the lists above out loud and meditate on the revealed nature of God who provides the fruit of Victory.

GETTING TO KNOW THE HOLY SPIRIT

The Holy Spirit gives spiritual gifts to you when and how He decides. He uses believers to work miracles. He directs all the work of the Gospel. He gives you the power (anointing) you need. Remember, He is received by faith and not by your works. He is the source of the harvest for God. Rely on Him. He is <u>POWER</u>! He gives you the victory.

The Holy Spirit is the River of Life.
As Jesus lets you drink deeply from the Spirit,
receive the powerful presence of God all the way down to your toes!

Day Two

GOOD FRUIT:
THE JOY OF ETERNAL VICTORY

Directions:
Put an X next to the fruit that you still need to grow.

- ☐ Gifts of the Spirit
- ☐ Servanthood
- ☐ Optimism
- ☐ Spirit Filled Life
- ☐ Being an Overcomer
- ☐ Spiritual Fitness
- ☐ Praise
- ☐ Prayer

Abundant Fruit
Jesus has given you many good fruits and has helped you remove some of the bad fruit growing in your life.

He has given you...

- ♥ The joy of Salvation
- ♥ Acceptance of yourself in Him
- ♥ The Truth
- ♥ Well-Being
- ♥ Completion
- ♥ Creation and the Fullness of joy of being in His Presence.
- ♥ Righteousness
- ♥ Security
- ♥ Healing

Now let's look at the joy He bestows on those believers who walk awhile with Him on the path of life and continue to learn from Him as Raboni (Teacher or Rabbi). (John 3:2)

Blessed are those who wash their robes, that they may have the right to the tree of life and may go through the gates into the city. Revelation 22:14

Even now the reaper draws his wages, even now he harvests the crop for eternal life, so that the sower and the reaper may be glad together. John 4:36

You did not choose me, but I chose you and appointed you to go and bear fruit-fruit that will last. Then the Father will give you whatever you ask in my name. John 15:16

Jesus went throughout Galilee, teaching in their synagogues, preaching the good news for the kingdom, and healing every disease and sickness among the people. Matthew 4:23

There the angel of the Lord appeared to him in flames of fire from within a bush. Moses saw that though the bush was on fire it did not burn up. So Moses thought, "I will go over and see this strange sight-why the bush does not burn up." Exodus 3:2-3

...his word is in my heart like a fire, a fire shut up in my bones. I am weary of holding it in; indeed, I cannot. Jeremiah 20:9b

Fruit Pie

If I take a blueberry pie, cut it into 12 pieces and examine each piece as separate from the whole, each piece is distinct, and yet carries characteristics of the whole.

It will be true to say as well that each piece is a vision from the maker, but it is not the maker of the pie. It is a created thing. It is true that each individual piece will be good and delicious, but that it will not be enough to satisfy my desire for more of the whole.

Jesus said God wants you to bear much fruit and that you only grow good luscious fruit by living with Him. He wants to give you the whole pie and to desire to give others what you yourself have tasted.

The Tree of Life - A Burning Bush

I have a small, glass votive candle holder with a fruit tree etched into the glass. When a candle burns behind the image of the tree it looks just like a burning bush!

With the Burning Bush, the glory of the Lord was as brilliant and radiant as fire and yet the bush was not consumed. This mystery was what drew Moses closer and closer to this marvelous sight. It was irresistible. His curiosity outweighed his fear. As he drew near and gazed on this glory, God called him by name and the rest is history (His-story).

If you are a fruit tree, on "fire" for the Lord, He can speak to others through you. You become the "light of the world." When you have the Holy Spirit dwelling within, you become a burning bush! Imagine that.

Are others seeing the fire in you? Are others able to see the fruit on your tree and the glory of the Lord ablaze in your heart? Here is victory. Here is the overcomer: the dear one who can shine like a candle in the darkness of the world. You are the one who can, despite all, share the joy of the Lord with others, as a light on a hill.

Who is seeing the "burning bush" in you? Who is a "burning bush" in your life? The tree and the fruit are not consumed by the fire. The tree is alive and growing, branches reaching far and wide. God's call from the bush is still to "COME."

Moses could have stopped after the experience on Mt. Sinai and no good fruit would have come forth. But he didn't. He continued to seek God and to meet Him "face to face." (Exodus 33:11) And, he did his best to obey God.

What makes a victorious Christian different from other Christians? This final unit will identify the areas of your life that can produce luscious fruit that brings glory to God and great joy to those whose lives you touch.

You had a complete heart transplant when Jesus put a new heart in you and your spirit was born again. You may have had a crushed heart that was handed to Jesus for repair and healing. You might have needed open heart surgery where the Holy Spirit lovingly restored your heart bound by sin and darkness. Your prisoner heart was freed, and a captive heart was released. Your divided heart was made whole. Your broken heart was bound up and mended by the loving hands of God.

The next step is to hear the Lord say to "GO." You are to go and be the heart beat for others. You are to be a warm heart home for others who seek God and who need a refuge. You are to continue to have "heart to heart" talks with God as you meet Him like Moses did, "face to face".

Good Fruit: Being an Overcomer

The Book of Revelation tells of many different blessings for the Overcomers including:

1. Access to the Tree of Life
2. Receiving the Crown of Life
3. Abiding with God forever
4. All needs will be met.
5. Your name written in the Lamb's Book of Life
6. Walking with Jesus, dressed in white.

When Adam and Eve were driven out of the Garden, God placed a flaming sword to guard their way to the Tree of Life. It became forbidden fruit. When Jesus shed His blood for you, and sent you His Holy Spirit, the Tree of Life was once again made available to the children of God who believe in His Son. Now that is Joy!

He who has an ear, let him hear what the Spirit says to the churches.
To him who overcomes, I will give the right to eat from the tree of life,
which is in the paradise of God.

Revelation 2:7

Seeds of Faith

From the rising of the sun to the place where it sets, the name of the LORD is to be praised.
Psalm 113:3

Yet you are enthroned as the Holy One; you are the praise of Israel.
Psalm 22:3

He who overcomes will inherit all this, and I will be his God and he will be my son.
Revelation 21:7

Genesis 3:24

1 John 5:4-5

Revelation 2:26-28

Revelation 3:5

Revelation 3:12

Revelation 3:21

Whoever eats my flesh and drinks my blood remains in me, and I in him. Just as the living Father sent me and I live because of the Father, so the one who feeds on me will live because of me.
John 6:56-57

Day Three

Good Fruit: Praise

Praise is an excellent way to stay spiritually conditioned as it exercises your heart and opens it to hear God in a new fresh way. If you're not having joy in your life, look at how much time you spend in praising the One who made you.

Good Fruit: Passionate Prayer

Spiritual health requires focus: keeping your heart set on just <u>one</u> thing, Jesus. You need to want Jesus more than anything or anyone else. It is a quest and you need to settle for nothing less than Jesus Himself. After all, He settles for nothing less than all of you. Like Jesus, you must stay diligent, sincere, searching, risk-taking, and do whatever it takes to seek God and worship Him.

Just like the physical body needs aerobic exercise to get the blood pumping, your spiritual exercise is <u>prayer</u> which keeps the blood of Christ, your life blood, flowing in your veins. His blood gives you that new life which is eternal. It is a supernatural and mysterious thing, and yet you can count on the blood of Jesus to cleanse and cover you, seal and heal you.

To walk the walk, you must talk the talk: you walk and talk to Jesus as He walks and talks with you! Let your life become a prayer.

Good Fruit: Holy Hunger

You come with a hungry heart when you enter God's Presence. You come expecting God to speak His words to your heart and fill your emptiness with a fullness that is completely satisfying. You need Holy Hunger.

Come to the Lord's supper for spiritual food and drink. It is a celebration feast because you are taking His Body and Blood into your heart, nourishing you and making you strong in Him. No athlete can run a race if he is malnourished. The scripture says Blessed are those who hunger and thirst for righteousness, for they will be filled. (Matthew 5:6)

God loves to feed His children. He has prepared a table before you, a wedding feast for the Bride which is His church. He gives you the Bread of Heaven, Jesus, who is enough to feed five thousand questions in my heart and yours. He wants to be the companion in all of the seasons of your life, (companion meaning someone to share bread on the journey). Your job is to stand in reverent stillness before God, with an open, prepared heart, a heart of worship. Jesus had a heart hungry to worship His Father, too.

The more spiritually fit you are, the stronger and more enduring your heart will be to finish the race. You are not a member anymore of the Human Race as a Christian. You're running an Eternal Race and the prize is heaven. The overcomer gets the victory crown. But again, this isn't about striving. Jesus endured the Cross so that you wouldn't have to strive.

As a member of a sacramental church, I will add here that the Eucharist (Mass, Lord's Supper, or Communion) is the place where you are united with Jesus in a powerful way. *The Book of Common Prayer* says, "The Church's sacrifice of praise and thanksgiving, is the way by which the sacrifice of Christ is made present, and in which He unites us to His one offering of Himself."

This is the mission of the church: to provide a place for the union with Jesus the Son of God to occur. Again, the *Book of Common Prayer* states, "The mission of the Church is to restore all people to unity with God and each other in Christ."

We are the Church! We are the Bride.

GOOD FRUIT: SPIRITUAL FITNESS

So, why do you have to be spiritually fit? Why do you need to do anything at all with your heart? Well, in case you've never heard, Jesus <u>is</u> coming back! You have to get ready and stay ready. It says in 2 Peter 3:10 that He is coming, and no one knows exactly when. God has set Eternity into your heart, so you know that you have an eternal home waiting for you. Spiritual fitness keeps you ready until Jesus comes again. In the first coming of our Lord, Jesus the Messiah suffered and died and rose from the grave to redeem those who believe in Him. In His second coming, He will appear as a warrior and put an end to all of God's enemies. The battle is waging. War requires a fit soldier.

His Second Coming will occur in a season of time just as His first did. You don't know the season but are told in 2 Timothy 4:2 to be "prepared in season and out of season." You need to be ready to say "Here I am, Lord," whether you <u>feel</u> ready or not.

Seeds of Faith

Revelation 19:9

My soul thirsts for God, for the living God. When can I go and meet with God?
Psalm 42:2

1 Samuel 13:14

Revelation 21:20

Your heart needs to be spiritually aware, alert, awake and discerning. You need to be able to "know" in the spirit, truth from lie. If your heart really recognizes Him now, how much more prepared you will be if you continue to stay spiritually fit for His return.

When you keep your heart in good spiritual condition, whole and not divided, soft and not hardened, then you, like Jesus, can hear God tell you when to come and go in furthering His kingdom. You can stay in the Father's will as Jesus did and know the when, where, how and what that your Father wants you to be and do.

GOOD FRUIT: A CO-MISSION

This personal readiness for His Second Coming as well as helping prepare the world for His coming again has far-reaching ramifications. Jesus is counting on you! He has a plan for your life: a commission, a divine purpose. Your spirit simply must be ready to receive the message to "come and go." Alert Christians will observe the signs, live expectantly and with complete assurance. Be ever vigilant for the day. The Lord looks at the heart. He searches and knows your heart.

God chose David as a "man after his own heart" to be a leader. God is still looking for leaders with the right kind of heart. What kind of heart will he find in you today? You, like Esther, are in a season of beautification to become a Bride, the glorious Bride of Christ. You are in a season of getting ready for the return of the Bridegroom. Jesus has been faithful to the words of the prophet Isaiah. He has given each of us "…a crown of beauty instead of ashes, the oil of gladness instead of mourning, and a garment of praise instead of a spirit of despair. (Isaiah 61:3)

You are dressed and ready for the coming of King Jesus. So let us all with joyful hearts echo the cry in the last verses in the Bible, "Come, Lord Jesus!"

GOOD FRUIT: OPTIMISM

As your faith becomes unshakable, strong, determined on God alone, your mood becomes purely optimistic - <u>no matter what</u>. Jesus and Paul had this kind of optimism - a seeing with the eyes of the heart what God can do. James 5:13 asks if anyone is in "good heart." The mood of your human spirit can and must reflect this spirit of optimism. The bad fruit of pessimism only produces more bad fruit: discouragement, apathy, and a flatness of your faith.

Exercise 5

Is anything trying to push your optimism down or out altogether? Please describe.

Exercise 6

What do you know about God that can increase your heart's optimism and strengthen your faith?

GOOD FRUIT: SERVANTHOOD

> *Deacons, likewise, are to be men worthy of respect, sincere, not indulging in much wine, and not pursuing dishonest gain. They must first be tested; and then if there is nothing against them, let them serve as deacons. In the same way, their wives are to be women worthy of respect, not malicious talkers but temperate and trustworthy in everything. A deacon must be the husband of but one wife and must manage his children and his household well. Those who have served well gain an excellent standing and great assurance in their faith in Christ Jesus.*
>
> 1 Timothy 3:8-13

The Holy Spirit equips you to be a servant in the world today. Putting on the "seven fold gifts" of the Holy Spirit are like pulling on a beautiful coat with seven buttons. You must put on the garment of the Holy Spirit to enter into the world and serve God. You are all called to service. You are all called to be a servant. This is the next good fruit on the Tree of Life: the joy of servanthood.

Jesus shows you how to be a servant to others. Servanthood helps open hearts to receive Jesus. It is hard to be a true servant until many seasons of testing, pruning, and planting have passed.

Just as our Lord washed the feet of the disciples (even Judas' feet) (John 13:14) you are called to get down on your knees, not just for prayer but in humility! Jesus' act of great humility shows that you must serve not only those you dearly love, but also sometimes there is a call to be a servant to someone you fear, you despise or you know is wicked. Why? Because if it is God's will, you must be obedient, even if your very life is at risk. His washing Judas' feet did not stop the evil that was about to happen. It showed that our Lord's character even to the end was that of a true (pure, divine, obedient, authentic) servant.

Seeds of Faith

"And the disciples were filled with joy and with the Holy Spirit." Acts 13:52

Philippians 2:7

Isaiah 11:2-3

Seeds of Faith

John 16:20

Exercise 7

Are you ready to do that? Are you in a position right now where you are torn between service to God and something holding you back? Describe below.

The good fruit in this unit promises a profound joy, but it also requires a deeper level of faith and obedience. You can't have one without the other. Obedience produces more fruit. The fruit increases your faith which increases the tendency to obey and so forth.

<u>Caution</u>: Don't grow so fond of your service or your place of servanthood that you don't obey God when He says to stop or move on. The very joy that comes with servanthood can be diminished with the sorrow of having to let go or walk away from the object of your service. The deeper the joy, the deeper the sorrow. But Jesus promises all your sorrow will be turned to joy. Once you jump <u>into</u> the River of Life, these seasons of joy and sorrow will become as natural as the changes in a tree through the seasons of its life. A healthy fruit tree must lose all of its leaves and fruit to grow new ones!

Day Four

BAD FRUIT

Exercise 8

Directions: Meditate on the bad fruits that you need to have pruned in your life in order to grow the joy of eternal victory. Elaborate:

BAD FRUIT: NO FRUIT AT ALL

> *Early in the morning, as he was on his way back to the city, he was hungry. Seeing a fig tree by the road, he went up to it but found nothing on it except leaves. Then he said to it, "May you never bear fruit again!" Immediately the tree withered. When the disciples saw this, they were amazed.*
>
> Matthew 21:18-20

The fig tree produces leaves and fruit at the same time. This fig tree only had leaves-no fruit for Jesus. He was hungry and wanted the fruit. When He sees that there are leaves but no fruit, He curses the tree that it will never bear fruit. At the moment in time He came, this tree was not ready for Him. The tree withers in response to the words of Jesus. I would not like to be this tree, would you?

Two thousand years ago, the nation of Israel rejected Him. They were unfruitful when He came to them and wanted their fruit. They were not ready or willing. They looked like a "fig tree" with leaves as did this tree, but in close inspection there was nothing good to be taken from the tree. It was a fruit tree in name only.

Are you like this tree? Perhaps a Christian but in name only? Are you producing fruit? If Jesus came today to your home, (your work, your relationships, your quiet time) would you have figs to give Him?

Seeds of Faith

And if anyone takes words away from this book of prophecy, God will take away from him his share in the tree of life and in the holy city, which are described in this book.
Revelation 22:19

...The shouts of joy over your ripened fruit and over your harvests have been stilled. Joy and gladness are taken away from the orchards; no one sings or shouts in the vineyards: no one treads out wine at the presses, for I have put an end to the shouting.
Isaiah 16:9-10

If anyone does not remain in me, he is like a branch that is thrown away and withers; such branches are picked up, thrown into the fire and burned. John 15:6

Isaiah 25:8

1 Corinthians 15:54-55

1 John 4:4

I will increase the fruit of the trees and the crops of the field, so that you will no longer suffer disgrace among the nations because of famine. Ezekiel 36:30

BAD FRUIT: DEFEAT

For the believer, there is no eternal defeat. Death is swallowed up in the victory of the Cross. Death and sin are left behind. All believers will be resurrected. Praise God!

But for the un-believer, the report is not so encouraging. There is <u>certain</u> defeat.

Remember, as a believer, you can walk in victory, or you can be held captive by the "feelings" associated with defeat (despair, enslavement to idols, fear of perishing, unworthiness, etc.).

Actually, if you take all of the bad fruit identified in this book and put it on one tree, you might come close to this bad fruit. As I said at the beginning, no believer has a tree of death, with no life at all.

Based on "feelings" alone, it can sometimes <u>appear</u> that you have been conquered by the enemy and have become enslaved to sin.

Exercise 9

If there is a part of your life (probably somewhere kept very hidden) in which you "feel" defeated, write about it here and ask the Holy Spirit to illuminate your steps into God's Promised Land where there is eternal victory.

Day Five

GROWING GOOD FRUIT

Exercise 10: LIFESKILLS: VICTORIOUS CHRISTIAN LIFE

"I would like to become more..."

- ☐ Spirit-filled
- ☐ Of an overcomer in my life
- ☐ Open to celebration in my worship
- ☐ Able to share my joy with others
- ☐ Joyful <u>through</u> all circumstances
- ☐ Enthusiastic (experiencing God within me.)
- ☐ Comfortable sharing my faith
- ☐ Aware of my spiritual gifts
- ☐ Of a conqueror
- ☐ Receptive to an anointing in God's work in this Kingdom
- ☐ Of a servant
- ☐ Of a faithful steward of the resources God has given me.
- ☐ Other: _____

Exercise 11

The three which would help me most to develop this fruit of Victory in my life are: (from the list above)

1. _____

2. _____

3. _____

Exercise 12

How would you or your life be different if you had these lifeskills? (the three chosen above)

Bring the best of the firstfruits of your soil to the house of the Lord your God. Do not cook a young goat in its mother's milk.
Exodus 34:26

1 John 5:4-5

Seeds of Faith

Luke 12:16-21

Exercise 12

PULLING UP WEEDS-COMPENSATION: BLOCKS TO VICTORY

You may have been compensating (making do or covering up) for not having these skills. Check all that apply.

How would you honestly describe yourself?

"I am often..."

- ☐ Seeking a spiritual high
- ☐ Living in my own strength
- ☐ Church hopping
- ☐ Too afraid to share my faith or testimony.
- ☐ Too controlled to show my joy
- ☐ Enslaved by rules about religion
- ☐ Apathetic or "on the fence"
- ☐ Proud of my good works and "resting" on them
- ☐ Overly concerned with everyone else's spiritual life
- ☐ Seeking the manifestation (signs and wonders) of the Holy Spirit (e.g. tongues, miracles, etc.)
- ☐ Too afraid of what others will think
- ☐ Afraid of going "overboard" with my faith
- ☐ Others:_____

Exercise 13

Which three of these personal characteristics (on the list you just checked) are blocking your joy of being victorious in your Christian walk and being an overcomer the most? Choose three.

1._____
2._____
3._____

Exercise 14

Describe <u>how</u> these are blocking the victory in your Christian life.

Exercise 15

Which one of the list above gives you the most trouble, the most pain in your life?

Why?

Exercise 16
Daily Action Steps for Walking Out your Victory

In order to grow this fruit, I must take action. To walk in my victory, I will use the following disciplines: (Check all that apply)

- ☐ Prayer
- ☐ Read the Bible
- ☐ Quiet time
- ☐ Praise (sing, dance, shout, etc.)
- ☐ Commit daily to please God by confessing my faith in Jesus.
- ☐ Dedicate my home (job, family, music) to Jesus
- ☐ Lead a balanced life
- ☐ Put on the whole armor of God - Resist Satan
- ☐ Fellowship with believers
- ☐ Pray with a prayer partner
- ☐ Talk to a spiritual director regularly
- ☐ Talk to a Christian Counselor
- ☐ Openly accept all He's done to heal me
- ☐ Forgive - seek reconciliation, restoration
- ☐ Receive Communion (Eucharist)
- ☐ Bless others - give
- ☐ Belong to a church (A body of believers who are guided by the Holy Spirit, who pray, worship the Lord in praise and thanksgiving, where there is joy, where there is evangelism, where people are discipled, where you hear the Good News of God's Bible about the redemption of the world through Jesus Christ.)
- ☐ Other:_____

He replied, "Every plant that my heavenly Father has not planted will be pulled up by the roots."
Matthew 15:13

Hebrews 6:7-8

Day Six

Preparing the Soil of the Soul: Uprooting Unholy Roots

Victory is yours in the Lord. You are an overcomer in and through Him. Jesus equips you to share His joy with others, to praise Him, to worship Him, and to overcome the obstacles in life.

Take this time to pray first and then release to the Lord in prayer, anything else which may be blocking the joy of victory in your life.

Exercise 17

Write a prayer letter to Jesus and confess this blockage to Him. He will hear you and will help you if you let Him. Remember He is your Friend and wants this for you more than you do for yourself.

Dear Jesus,

Amen

EXPERIENCING JOY

Day Seven

A Change of Heart

Mark how your heart is changing:

My Old Heart Was...	My New Heart Is...
Cold	Rejoicing
Uninspired	Serving
Apathetic	Joyful
Stone	Giving
Dead	Charitable
Other:	Compassionate
Other:	Healing
Other:	Merciful
Other:	Singing
Other:	Grateful
Other:	Praising
Other:	Other
"I will give you a new heart and put a new spirit in you; I will remove from you your heart of stone and give you a heart of flesh." Ezekiel 36:26	"Let the peace of Christ rule in your hearts, since as members of one body you were called to peace. And be thankful." Colossians 3:15

Revelation 14:3

I have been crucified with Christ...
Galatians 2:20

Now if we are children, then we are heirs-heirs of God and co-heirs with Christ, if indeed we share in his sufferings in order that we may also share in his glory.
Romans 8:17

Exercise 19 - Sing a New Song

Your heart has a new song to sing to God. As He changes your heart to be able to release this song to the heavens, you experience true joy. Has your heart sung its song? Have you heard it? Is there something still stopping the ears of your heart to hear the tune or the words? Have fun and write a "new song" to God giving Him praise and thanksgiving:

THE TREE OF GLORY: YOUR TREE OF LIFE

The Christian life is often likened to the life of a soldier in a battle. The war is already won and yet you are "stuck" in a time and place where your conquering King is not yet on the horizon on His white horse. You know He is coming in glory, majesty and power. You know He will return waving a Victor's banner over His head.

Until then, what do you do? You become broken bread and poured out wine.

Victorious in Christ, you are <u>not</u> focused on your self, but your life becomes a living prayer for others. Your healing is a gift to others as much as it is for yourself. It is how you show the evidence of Jesus in your life.

Your restoration becomes the blueprint for another soul's repair work. You carry hope to others by telling them of what great things the Lord has done for you. That makes it possible for someone else who thought it impossible. Don't withhold from others what Christ has done for you. Pour out the sweet wine-share the broken bread of your life in a precious communion feast with another hurting or lost soul.

Then the glory of Jesus revealed in you can light the path for someone else and the message can go on and on. So your final step circles you back to your beginning. You may never have stood before a crowd and given your "testimony," but you do have one. If someone were to "see" your Tree of Life today, they would see <u>who</u> the Lord has been to you so far and what He is growing <u>in</u> you. Your tree is a direct reflection of the glory of Jesus Christ in you. His glory shines with beams of joy and peace and love. His glory is revealed in you. Don't ever forget it!

Your Glory Story
I call the personal story of your Tree of Life growing in you, your "Glory Story." Corny, I know, but we're almost through!

Your Glory Story will never be finished. Your life today and the story of how you got here is just a snapshot. How are all of the names and aspects of our Lord Jesus revealed in the face of your life? Feel free to go back over the work you have done in this workbook, especially the change of heart exercises. Your Glory Story need not be long. But it needs to be centered on Jesus, because it is His glory, never yours, that is revealed in a true worshiper.

Glory Is:	Scripture
A gift to those who believe	John 11:40, Romans 2:10
A future reward	Romans 8:18, 1 Corinthians 2:7
Something to seek	John 8:50
To be given to God	Luke 17:18, 1 Corinthians 10:31
Something to hope for	Romans 4:20, 5:20, Colossians 1:27
The atmosphere of heaven	John 3:13
An attribute of Jesus	James 2:1
The true Shekinah	Jude 24

<u>Glory is NOT</u> to be given to ourselves
This is the Bad Fruit of Pride!

Seeds of Faith

I consider that our present sufferings are not worth comparing with the glory that will be revealed in us.
Romans 8:18

Exercise 20
GIVE GOD THE GLORY: GIVE HIM YOUR CROWN (REVELATION 4:10)

In the space below, write your own testimony, giving God the glory.

MY GLORY STORY

Date:_____

Summary:

You have made the choice: to seek the Creator and walk with Him. He calls to you and as He asked Adam and Eve, He says, "Where are you?"

He delights in your company, your praises, your worship. He compassionately turns His face toward you when you are suffering. All you need to do is come out from your secret places and come to Him who made you.

The Good News

> *We are witnesses of everything he did in the country of the Jews and in Jerusalem. They killed him by hanging him on a tree, but God raised him from the dead on the third day and caused him to be seen.*
>
> Acts 10:39

To fully understand joy is to fully understand that you need not fear death. Death for believers does not mean the end. <u>Physical</u> death means the separation of our bodies, from our spirit and the soul. <u>Spiritual</u> death means eternal separation from God. As born again Christians, sealed as Christ's own forever, you will face the first death but never the second. Alleluia!

Your joy then comes ultimately from this final truth - you will never be separated from God, even though you may "feel" separated from Him from time to time on this earth. He needed to separate Himself from your sin, but in the new Jerusalem, in the City of God, He welcomes you back into His presence. You will overcome and therefore wear the white linen robes of Christ's righteousness. Your own robes are washed clean in His blood. You are to be given the Victor's Crown of Life along with all other believers!

> *Then the angel showed me the river of the water of life, as clear as crystal, flowing from the throne of God and of the Lamb down the middle of the great street of the city. On each side of the river stood the tree of life, bearing twelve crops of fruit, yielding its fruit every month. And the leaves of the tree are for the healing of the nations.*
>
> Revelation 22:1-2

At this one special place, all the pieces of God's plan come together. In God's paradise you will be fed from the Tree of Life, by the Bread of Life (Jesus). You'll drink from the River of the Water of Life, receive the Victor's Crown of Life and having followed the Way of Life, live with Father, Son and Holy Spirit forever!

Seeds of Faith

Do not be afraid of what you are about to suffer. I tell you, the devil will put some of you in prison to test you, and you will suffer persecution for ten days. Be faithful, even to the point of death, and I will give you the crown of life. He who has an ear, let him hear what the Spirit says to the churches. He who overcomes will not be hurt at all by the second death.
Revelation 2:10-11

There is a river whose streams make glad the city of God.
Psalm 46:4

Christ redeemed us from the curse of the law by becoming a curse for us, for it is written: "Cursed is everyone who is hung on a tree." Galatians 3:13

Acts 10:39

1 Peter 2:24

He who overcomes will inherit all this, and I will be his God and he will be my son. Revelation 21:7

Jesus is the Living Door
Eternity is now. Eternal life is the life of the believer. The guard once posted in Eden lets you in and you can enjoy the fruits on the Tree of Life <u>now</u>. All you need is belief that Jesus did all that He did so that you could have this Victory, so that you could be an overcomer, "in this world and the next."

You meet Jesus under the life-giving tree described in Revelation. In one heavenly place not bound by time, all that God wants for you comes together.

As you come to the Communion table and receive the Body and Blood of Jesus Christ, let His Real Presence flow through you and see if you can't taste the fruit on that awesome tree. It's yours for the taking. Why? Because Jesus died on a tree and because His Cross became your Tree of Life!

Jesus is God's Healing Joy. I find no better way to explain joy or to encourage you to seek this union with the Lord, than to say, that I look forward to spending life with you, eating fruit with Jesus under that great tree. See you there!

The Tree of Life is the Cross!
The Tree of Life is Jesus! Now go, and share the Good News.

JESUS IS ALIVE!

Dear Jesus,

I thank You for who You are in all Your revealed names. I thank You for all of the fruit You are growing in my life. I thank You for the fruit You are pruning in me and the way You are uprooting unholy roots. I thank You for tilling the soil of my soul so that new healthy roots can tap into the River of Your Holy Spirit.

I pray Lord, that You will continue to be my Gardener until that day when my tree of life will look like a jeweled crown, sparkling with Your Glory. I thank You for going to prepare a place for me in the New Jerusalem where the Tree of Life grows by the River of Life. You and You alone lead me on the Path of Life. I yearn to be with You forever, wearing a Crown of Life and seeing my own name in the Lamb's Book of Life. What joy that will be!

I give You all the glory as You are the Lord of Life and You are my Tree of Life.

Alleluia and Amen!

Seeds of Faith

...he will receive the crown of life that God has promised to those who love him.
James 1:12

REFERENCES

Chambers, Oswald, *My Utmost for His Highest*. Grand Rapids, Michigan, Discovery House Publishers. 1992.

Ffrench-Beytagh, Gonville. *Tree of Glory*. Wilton, CT: Morehouse Publishing. 1988.

Girzone, Joseph F. *Never Alone: A Personal Way To God*. New York, New York. Doubleday Publishers. 1994.

Lewis, C. S., *Surprised by Joy*. New York: Inspirational Press, 1994.

Lockyer, Herbert, *All the Divine Names and Titles in the Bible*. Grand Rapids, Michigan: Zondervan Publishing House. 1975.

MacNutt, Ph.D. Francis, *Healing*. Notre Dame: Ave Maria Press, 1974, 1999.

May, Gerald G., *Addictions & Grace*. New York, New York: Harper Collins Publishers. 1988, 1991.

Egan, Eileen, and Egan, Kathleen, *Suffering Into Joy: What Mother Theresa Teaches About True Joy*. Servant Publications. 1994.

Nouwen, Henri, J. M., *The Return of the Prodigal Son*. New York, New York: Doubleday Publishers. 1992.

Payne, Leanne, *Restoring the Christian Soul*. Grand Rapids, Michigan: Hamewith Books, Baker Book House. 1991.

Peck, M. Scott, M.D. *People of the Lie: The Hope for Healing Human Evil*. New York, New York: Simon & Schuster. 1983.

Revell, Fleming H. *The Practice of the Presence of God*. Grand Rapids, Michigan: Spire Books, 1958, 1967.

Richards, Lawrence O. *The Bible Reader's Companion*. Wheaton, Illinois: Chariot Victor Publishing. 1991.

Spurgeon, Charles H., *Morning and Evening: Daily Readings*. Hendrickson Publishers, Inc., 1995.

Strong, James, L.L.D., S.T.D. *The New Strong's Complete Dictionary of Bible Words*. Nashville, Tennessee: Thomas Nelson Publishers. 1996.

The Book of Common Prayer. New York, New York: Oxford University Press. 1990.

The author also wishes to recommend to the reader the following for further study and healing:

The Rev. Mike Flynn: www.freshwindministries.org

Father Robert DeGrandis, S.S.J.: all of his books

Leanne Payne: Pastoral Care Ministry School, www.pcmschool.com

Wheaton, Illinois, www.LeannePayne.org

Dr. Francis and Judith McNutt: www.christianhealingmin.org

Christian Jew Foundation Ministries. www.CJF.org

And finally, thank you to Barbara Leahy Schlemon who so many years ago asked me one simple question,

"What do you want to say to Jesus?"

TO CONTACT ALLYSON TOMKINS:

atomkins6802@bellsouth.net
(985) 893-7569 extension 3

To order *Experiencing Joy,* visit www.advantagebookstore.com

www.ingramcontent.com/pod-product-compliance
Lightning Source LLC
Chambersburg PA
CBHW081913170426
43200CB00014B/2718